Critical issues in
social research
Power and prejudice

Edited by
**Suzanne Hood, Berry Mayall and
Sandy Oliver**

Open University Press
Buckingham · Philadelphia

Open University Press
Celtic Court
22 Ballmoor
Buckingham
MK18 1XW

email: enquiries@openup.co.uk
world wide web: http://www.openup.co.uk

and
325 Chestnut Street
Philadelphia, PA 19106, USA

First Published 1999

A catalogue record of this book is available from the British Library

ISBN 0 335 20141 5 (hbk) 0 335 20140 7 (pbk)

Library of Congress Cataloging-in-Publication Data
Critical issues in social research : power and prejudice / edited by
  Suzanne Hood, Berry Mayall, Sandy Oliver.
    p. cm.
  Includes bibliographical references and index.
  ISBN 0-335-20141-5 (hb)   ISBN 0-335-20140-7 (pbk)
  1. Socially handicapped–Research. 2. Action research.
3. Marginality, Social. I. Hood, Suzanne, 1957– . II. Mayall,
Berry. III. Oliver, Sandy, 1955– .
HN29.C69 1998
300′.72—dc21   98–25147
                                                    CIP

Typeset by Graphicraft Limited, Hong Kong
Printed in Great Britain by Biddles Limited, Guildford and Kings Lynn

▷ Contents

▷ Notes on contributors

All the contributors and editors worked at the Social Science Research Unit (SSRU), Institute of Education, University of London over the period when this book was designed and written. Valerie Hey and Susan Williams have since moved to other academic groups at the Institute.

Priscilla Alderson's main work is about children's and teenagers' views and experiences of education and health services, and their share in making personal decisions. She is currently researching school students' views about their civil rights and the United Nations Convention on the Rights of the Child, and the views of young adults with serious congenital conditions about prenatal screening. Books include *Children's Consent to Surgery* (Open University Press 1993), *Listening to Children: Ethics and Social Research* (Barnardo's 1995) and, with J. Montgomery, *Health Care Choices: Making Decisions with Children* (Institute for Public Policy Research 1996).

Chris Bonell is undertaking doctoral research on the politics of evidence based decision making in human immunodeficiency virus (HIV) services, funded by a fellowship from the British National Health Service (NHS) Research and Development Programme. His research interests include health policy, HIV prevention, evaluation methodology and the sociology of knowledge. He has previously worked in the HIV voluntary sector and for a South London Health Authority.

Christopher Goodey previously held teaching posts at Ruskin College and at the Open University. He has published on various aspects of learning disability: its early conceptual history; the views of learning disabled children and their families; and the politics of genetic research and inclusive education. He is the author, with Priscilla Alderson, of *Enabling Education: Experiences in Special and Ordinary Schools* (the Tufnell Press 1998).

Valerie Hey is a research lecturer with the academic group Culture, Communication and Societies at the Institute of Education. While at the Social Science Research Unit (SSRU) she undertook a variety of qualitative studies. She is currently directing an Economic and Social Research Council (ESRC) funded project looking at the relations between schooling cultures, classroom pedagogies and cultures of masculinity. She has recently published *The Company She Keeps: An Ethnography of Girls' Friendship* (Open University Press 1997).

Suzanne Hood's research interests include children's daily lives, children's services and service development. She combines research experience in these areas with a background in social work management and practice. She is currently working on a process evaluation of a new and innovative multi-agency after-school centre.

Berry Mayall has worked on many research projects concerned with health and education issues in the lives of children and parents. She is currently exploring children's understandings of childhood. Her most recent book, *Children, Health and the Social Order*, is also published by Open University Press (1996).

Ann Oakley has been working in social science research for over 30 years. Her early work was on the concept of gender, the sociology of housework, and women's experience of the transition to motherhood and of medical maternity care. In 1984 she completed a sociological history of medical care for pregnant women, *The Captured Womb* (Basil Blackwell 1984), and in 1992 she published *Social Support and Motherhood* (Blackwell 1992), an account of a randomized controlled trial and qualitative research on the role of supportive social science interviewing in promoting the health of mothers. Other recent books are *Essays on Women, Medicine and Health* (Edinburgh University Press 1993) and *Man and Wife* (HarperCollins 1997).

Sandy Oliver's research interests focus on the contributions of lay people to health services research, whether they work independently or in partnerships with health professionals or professional researchers. Having learnt many of the principles of health services research as a volunteer in the voluntary sector she is now developing ways of training and supporting lay people who are planning, conducting or using research.

Greet Peersman has been involved in the establishment and running of a training, information and resource centre on evidence based health promotion at the SSRU since 1995. She is particularly interested in HIV prevention and sexual health promotion. One of her concerns is the lack of information exchange within and between countries worldwide, resulting in duplication of effort and limiting the potential to learn from others. She is therefore actively involved in a number of international collaborative programmes to make the findings from health promotion research more accessible. Before joining SSRU, she worked as a researcher at the University of Antwerp and as a volunteer for a non-governmental organization in Zimbabwe.

Helen Penn has had a career as a senior administrator in education, but since 1990 has been university-based. She undertakes a wide range of research and consultancy work on early years issues, in the UK and abroad. She is a consultant to Save the Children Fund UK and has recently completed a review for the Department of International Development on Early Childhood Services in Developing and Transitional Countries. Her most recent book is *Comparing Nurseries* (Paul Chapman 1997).

Penelope Scott is a Jamaican social researcher who joined the SSRU in September 1992. She has carried out research funded by the ESRC and the British Diabetic Association (BDA) into the factors affecting the management of diabetes among the Caribbean community in the UK.

A. Susan Williams is an historian who has written on a wide range of issues, especially women's lives and work. Her authored books include *Women and Childbirth in the Twentieth Century* (Sutton 1997) and *The Rich Man and the Diseased Poor in Early Victorian Literature* (Macmillan 1987); her many edited and jointly edited books include *The Politics of the Welfare State* with Ann Oakley (UCL Press 1994), *Mother Courage: Letters from Mothers in Poverty at the End of the Century* (with C. Gowdridge and M. Wynn, Penguin 1997), and several Penguin anthologies of women's writing. She is currently writing a book on the politics of sex and class in interwar Britain.

▷ Acknowledgements

The editors gratefully acknowledge the hard work of those who contributed through discussion at our seminars and through their papers for this book. We are very much beholden to Jackie Lee who has efficiently put together the papers and turned them into a book.

▷ Introduction

▷ **Berry Mayall, Suzanne Hood, Sandy Oliver**

The book

This book addresses critical issues for people carrying out social research studies. In particular, it takes as a central focus the point that people who are the objects of research interest – by funders, policy makers and researchers – are predominantly members of socially disadvantaged groups. Advantaged groups, by their nature, are not commonly available for critical scrutiny; they are protected from research by powerful majority interests. But other groups of people come in for designation as problems, as threats to the social order, so warranting intervention to restore harmony; or they are variously identified as socially, economically or politically disadvantaged and in need of help or redress. Chapter headings in this book reflect this situation. They point to particular groups such as children, disturbed people and the frail elderly. More broadly, huge sections of the population may be designated as problematic by those powerful enough to effect such designation. In recent years, governments have supported the view that ordinary people are a problem for the nation's economy; through their behaviour, they risk poor health and therefore cost the country dear.

We argue in this book that the research process in all its stages is constructed and reconstructed through the intersections of three sets of interests: those of the researchers; those of disadvantaged groups and of the individuals within them; and those of socially dominant political structures, organizations, social groups and individuals. Thus researchers are faced with the demands, priorities and time-scales of funding bodies, and, often, with those of the organizations where they work. These demands may or may not tie in with their own agendas, priorities and time constraints. In addition, in designing, carrying out and developing output from the research, the researcher is commonly working with, on or for disadvantaged people who themselves have complex interactive relationships with powerful sectors of society. The disadvantaged may be working within, and possibly against, the political and social structures that condition their daily lives, careers and understandings. In their encounters with powerful individuals and institutions, disadvantaged individuals and groups face negotiation about the status of their knowledge, their rights as citizens and their entitlements to material and cultural resources. The researched are also disadvantaged by the act of being researched, since the balance of power lies with the researcher. Their own agendas commonly remain unheard. So while researchers may be working to a particular agenda, at the interface those researched may work to alter that agenda and to try to interpose their own.

Within the research process, encounters between all three sets of interests can be seen, intrinsically, as mediated by social positioning within power structures and as characterized by negotiations, trade-offs and compromises. Running through these negotiations, whatever the precise topic and whoever the individuals concerned, are issues to do with the factors that structure membership of a disadvantaged group: gender, age, ethnicity, socioeconomic status.

Traditionally, theory development has been the central activity of social research; and here the researched's values and goals have lesser status than the researcher's, although the notion of grounding theory in empirical investigation seeks, perhaps over optimistically, to counterbalance this disparity.[1] In recent years, researchers in academic institutions have been asked to move away from a principal interest in the development of theory towards policy- and practice-oriented research. For instance, the Economic and Social Research Council (ESRC), which dispenses government funds to researchers, not only stresses the importance of theory development, but also requires researchers to indicate how they will collaborate with 'users' during the research process. 'Users' include at least three sets of interest groups: the people researched, policy makers, and providers of services – whether statutory, voluntary or private. Many funders, such as the Department of Health, the Department for Education and Employment and the Health Education Authority, as well as some voluntary bodies, seek practice-oriented answers immediately relevant to their own questions.

The genesis of this book is the challenges faced in their daily work by a group of researchers at the Social Science Research Unit (SSRU), Institute of Education, London University. Many of us had already worked together, engaging with research issues collectively. We held a set of seminars to address issues of power in research, the linkages of research paradigms to methods, and the social and political positioning of the researcher *vis-à-vis* those researched. The seminars were held in the summer of 1997 and were advertised within the university. In each seminar a researcher focused on a particular minority group or topic, and discussed research traditions, issues and methods. In a final seminar we reviewed and discussed the main themes of the series. This introduction was discussed with the contributors to the book and revised to take account of their views.

Research is a complex business, carried out on shifting ground. Changing fashions in research methods reflect changing understandings of the purposes of research. Within particular areas or topics of research, research goals and methods become lodged as traditions – even regarded as self-evidently the most appropriate goals and methods – but also face challenges from those who address other questions. Some contributors to this book have worked in areas where the entrenchment of goals and methods, supported by professional opinion, has made it especially difficult to carry out research with other goals, using other methods. These difficulties run all the way through the research process, from attracting funding to discussing findings. So the chapters draw on personal, varied experiences in a range of fields, and the standpoint and values of each author vary accordingly. In this book, we have not sought to iron out or disguise differences of opinion between contributors, but offer these chapters as their explorations of the complexities they face in carrying out their work.

Between them, the chapters consider the research process in all its stages: from the initial set of questions, through design, funding, access, fieldwork, analysis and output. For some of the topics addressed, some parts of the research process are more challenging than others. For instance, Valerie Hey, commissioned to discuss their community care 'needs' with people defined as 'frail elderly', found that the crucial element in the process was the discussion itself: what it *revealed* of their agendas, and the mismatch with providers' agendas. Helen Penn, commissioned to provide advice to early years services providers in the Majority World, emphasizes (among other points) the difficult relationship of the researcher with those providers.

Themes and issues

Social disadvantage

Within the book's diversity are some common themes. Social disadvantage is one. The population, or group, or individuals in question can variously be described as, for instance, 'successfully labelled',[2] members of a political minority group,[3] socially marginalized or excluded.[4] It has become a recognized feature of research with the disadvantaged to stress the importance of making their voices heard. But while one route towards that goal includes recording actual voices, these voices can be made audible in other ways too. For instance, it is through the evidence of large-scale data that we know about the inequalities in access to health services and in health status suffered by ethnic minority groups. One of the issues in research, therefore, is to choose appropriate methods for the precise question posed.

Thus, for instance, Penelope Scott built on the existing clinical and epidemiological data about increased risk of death from diabetes among Caribbeans in Britain compared to white British people. Diet is a key factor; so may be access to services. She used qualitative, as well as quantitative, methods to elucidate and explore these two factors.

Methodology: the quantitative/qualitative debate

An issue discussed in several chapters is the competition, even antagonism, between advocates of quantitative and qualitative methods. As Ann Oakley says, feminist research has been notable for its espousal of qualitative methods as *the* means of tapping into women's knowledge. Feminism carries considerable responsibility for the argument that quantitative methods are imbued with male assumptions: that researchers should decide what is investigated, should set the parameters and need not listen to alternative views. Such research keeps all the power to itself, and is unresponsive to the complexity of the social world. It would seem that, by contrast, feminists have appropriated for themselves the sensitivity and reflexivity appropriate to revolutionary aims. So we are asked to think of quantitative as bad and qualitative as good, because they are used by those with, respectively, bad and good understandings of the social order and of social research.[5] In the field of HIV/AIDS research, Chris Bonell points to good and bad studies of each kind. As our contributors note, work for the disadvantaged can usefully use many methods. In the field of childhood studies, Berry Mayall discusses how political sympathy with the condition of childhood has led to re-analysis of existing large-scale data, and further large-scale data collection in order to describe the social, political and economic circumstances of children worldwide.[6] These data provide a useful interactive context for considering smaller scale data collected with children.

Research as a political activity

One line of argument in this book is that some groups are disadvantaged partly because they have been so defined within the context of medico-psychological paradigms; 'diagnosis' of emotional disturbance or learning difficulties leads to proposals about care and especially 'cure', which oversimplify the task, isolate the people concerned and reinforce their proposed difference from other people. Priscilla Alderson and Chris Goodey were faced with the social separation, in special institutions, of school-age young people. Using ethnographic observation and informal discussion, they show how the difficulties that attended the young people's progress were compounded and reified by the system of diagnosis, and how its complement

– the 'special' services – turned out to be damaging to those assigned to them.

Research is undoubtedly a political activity. And the researcher may argue that there are some features of the social order where description is all that is needed to point up an unacceptable situation; that is, that no one should be the object of such policies. Research in this case is akin to journalism, as when Dickens describes the filthy conditions in which the people lived in the London slums. For some of the contributors, the inequalities suffered by individuals and groups in the UK indicate an urgent need to try to show how they experience the world. Research has a directly political function; to describe and so expose the unacceptable with the aim of shifting policy and practice.

The goal of describing the world as experienced by over half its population, in order to shift knowledge of the world, policy and practice towards its inhabitants, has, of course, been a major goal of feminist research, which has sought to challenge male understandings and knowledge by describing how the world is experienced and understood by women. It is argued that data collected from women needs to be worked on and worked up into a feminist theory of social relations.[7] As Ann Oakley argues, the research task of contributing to the enterprise of shifting understandings about how society works and should work demands that research be not only valid and reliable but also trustworthy. This requires that methods and sampling be both transparent and appropriate to the research questions. Transparency – often tedious in the telling – is easier than appropriateness, since the researcher, however well intentioned, may face such barriers as resource shortages, time constraints, access problems and the like.

Research as politics comprises tensions between the triangle of interests alluded to above. However noble the researcher's goals, she or he may be constrained by the funder's agenda, and restricted in presenting the data, or in interpreting them. And the researcher has limited power to influence the policy-making process. Yet, compared to the researched, the researcher has greater control over the character and use of data. The researcher–researched relationship can be understood in the light of Lukes's identification of three kinds of power: overt tyrannical power exercised without the consent of the oppressed; 'democratic' power, where the ruled are consulted but do not rule; and power exercised through a range of social institutions, customs and discourses so pervasive that the ruled are not aware of their subordination.[8] Researchers may ignore the interests of the researched. Or they may consult the researched but finally say what they choose, or what the funder chooses. Both the researched and the researcher may be unaware of their own subordination. However, the researcher's task is to pay due attention to people's accounts, to impute meanings to them based on her own values and to discuss the relationships between accounts and values.[9]

The uses of research

Finally, the discussions in the following chapters suggest that the uses of research vary according to circumstance, as well as to topic. In the field of health promotion initiatives, properly conducted evaluations are rare and, as Greet Peersman shows, examination of studies of these initiatives indicates the urgent need for re-theorizing the concepts on which health promotion is based. The currently popular notion of 'empowerment' is a facile way of avoiding the socioeconomic determinants of health. But some research has more direct policy implications. For instance, Sandy Oliver's work on lay participation in service design and delivery, suggests that immediate modifications to planning procedures are necessary. Yet another facet to research policy relationships is highlighted by Susan Williams, who points out how our understandings about the social order, past and present, are structured through historians' emphases, their ignoring of some (minority) evidence, their silences and the silences of some people in the past, notably women.

The chapters

Each chapter focuses on a particular minority group or topic and the editors asked authors to observe a common ordering of their material. This request was at a broad level, since we did not wish to distort the material; rather to enable readers to see their way through each chapter and the book. Thus the authors explain firstly how and why their chosen group or topic is understood or defined as problematic, as deviating from 'the norm' or as a minority. Secondly, they provide a critique of the main disciplines used to study this group or topic. Thirdly, they consider the goals of research and their implications, if any, for method. Fourthly, they describe and discuss important features of the research process. Each chapter ends with a discussion or set of conclusions.

In Chapter 1, Berry Mayall proposes that children be regarded as a minority group *vis-à-vis* adults, who order and control their lives. She discusses the dominant theoretical paradigm for the study of children – developmental psychology – and argues for the complementary merits of sociological approaches with their distinctive methodologies. She describes recent explorations into methods of collecting data with and for children and considers the researcher's power to interpret children's knowledge and experiences compared to children's relative powerlessness.

The prestige of psychological theories developed in Anglo-American contexts as *the* knowledge about children is taken up in Chapter 2 by Helen Penn, who discusses the globalizing ambitions of some Western, or Minority World, agencies. Through discussion of her work on early childhood services in many countries, she shows how competing ideas about children and childhood are culturally distinctive, and she analyses the sometimes difficult position of the Minority World researcher employed to advise Majority World policy makers on the development of these services.

After listening to children with learning disabilities and their families, Christopher Goodey shows in Chapter 3 how people's genuine understanding of their own needs can be distorted and even overridden by the power of the medical profession and the law. Professionally diagnosed 'needs' are matched by professionally appointed services, which are not offered as a right in response to requests for help, but are imposed on individuals and families even in the face of their opposition. In such circumstances, research invokes both passion and politics and the researcher as advocate can be dismissed as partisan. Christopher asks how this affects the goal of emancipatory research to influence policy.

Priscilla Alderson argues in Chapter 4 that psychological and medical paradigms and associated methods have led to isolation and special treatment for some groups of 'emotionally disturbed' young people. This treatment can be damaging and ineffective. It happens when people are treated as collections of symptoms, which can be modified through disciplinary regimes. Using ethnographic methods, she suggests the inadequacies of treating people primarily as disturbed, and the importance of recognizing that each person has a range of abilities and characteristics, and contributes as well as receives.

The unrecognized contributions by people in the past is Susan Williams's topic in Chapter 5. The dead cannot influence the ways in which the living portray them, and the least powerful leave behind little evidence about their lives. Susan discusses the challenges faced by the historian who tries to uncover the lives and contributions of women. She shows how women are largely absent from male historical accounts, and how standard sources of evidence represent the history of public life, from which women are also absent. To understand more about women we must study the informal or 'private' domain – the family – as well as workplaces and popular culture. But it is also necessary to develop models of social interaction that include both men and women, and that analyse interactions between the 'public' and 'private' domains.

Individuals' behaviour in relation to health-related risks has become an important research issue in the wake of governmental emphasis on personal responsibility for health status. But although people's knowledge and understanding may seem to be key topics, much health research is clinical, and epidemiological. In Chapter 6 Penelope Scott reports on her attempts to raise money for qualitative, exploratory research in a social and political context where such medical research paradigms are dominant. She discusses issues of access to a hidden and marginalized group, and of relationships with the people accessed in the context of ethnic and social class similarities and differences.

Access to the understandings of elderly people is the theme of Valerie Hey's chapter (7). She was employed by a charitable trust to enquire how 'frail elderly' people understood and valued 'community care'. Her conversations with these people revealed how different were their knowledge, experiences and concerns from those of service providers and policy makers. Valerie discusses the social position of the researcher during the interview process, including complications such as the emotionally loaded nature of the exchanges in the context of power inequities. She thus addresses questions about the place of researcher's and interviewees' subjectivity in interview contexts; this clearly has implications for other interviewers, such as service providers engaged in 'needs assessment' procedures.

Understanding why people behave as they do is arguably essential to effective policy initiatives. In Chapter 8 Chris Bonell considers the case of gay men, sexual activity and risk-taking to highlight the importance for policy initiatives of tapping into and understanding the knowledge and experiences of the men themselves. Quantitative social research methods have often been identified as oppressive to gay men. But Chris argues that the value of a method depends on careful preparatory work to establish and harness the conceptual frameworks of the researched.

Assessing needs and enabling people to take control of their lives are currently emphasized in the area of health promotion, as means of developing appropriate services. But in Chapter 9 Greet Peersman points out that: discourse about empowerment in health promotion is mostly rhetoric and ignores inequalities in power; most health promotion does not start from the agendas of ordinary people; most is not about empowerment at all; and most is poorly evaluated. Rather, health promotion professionals set the agendas for needs assessment and service development and they are the gatekeepers to evaluative research. In turn, service providers work with political constraints. Greet favours developing and evaluating a range of approaches to health promotion while guarding against some individualistic approaches that persist merely because addressing social contexts is more challenging and more costly.

Disparities between the agendas of service users and those of health professionals is the starting point for Sandy Oliver in Chapter 10. She explores how health services research could be reshaped if it were to draw on the insights of service users, and could thereby better respond to their circumstances and priorities. She presents examples of research funded and conducted by 'lay' people, and highlights its emphasis on social and emotional well-being. She argues that involving service users as equals to plan and conduct research is revolutionary, but will only reach its potential when lay people take leading roles in such partnerships and in the evaluation of those partnerships.

In Chapter 11, Ann Oakley examines issues of power embedded in research methodologies themselves. She argues that current choices between 'qualitative' and 'quantitative' methods reflect a gendered history in which different ways of knowing have been aligned with minority and majority groups. Research methods, like everything else, are socially constructed. An awareness of this process is essential for social science researchers, particularly if they wish to avoid falling into the trap of condemning 'quantitative' methods on ideological grounds. Cutting across all research methods is the fundamental issue of tailoring the method to the research question, and of creating knowledge in a reliable and trustworthy way.

Notes

1 See B.G. Glaser and A.L. Strauss (1967) *The Discovery of Grounded Theory: Strategies for Qualitative Research*. London: Weidenfeld and Nicolson; see also C. Wright Mills (1959) *The Sociological Imagination*. London: Oxford University Press (1967). Wright Mills provides not only a critique of 'grand theory', but a proposal for linking the macro to the micro, by simultaneously building up from the micro and deducing down from conceptual elaboration (see especially Chapter 6).

2 H.S. Becker (1963) *Outsiders: Studies in the Sociology of Deviance*. New York: Free Press. A general discussion of deviance and labelling is in Chapter 1.

3 Among the many discussions of political minorities, a good early example of theoretical and empirical work is J. Rex and R. Moore (1967) *Race, Community and Conflict: A Study of Sparkbrook*. Oxford: Oxford University Press.

4 Each chapter refers to relevant literature.

5 See also for discussion D. Silverman (1997) The logics of qualitative research, in G. Miller and R. Dingwall (eds) *Context and Method in Qualitative Research*. London: Sage.

6 J. Qvortrup (1993) Children at risk or childhood at risk – a plea for a politics of childhood, in P.-L. Heiliö, E. Lauronen and M. Bardy (eds) *Politics of Childhood and Children at Risk: Provision, Protection, Participation*. Eurosocial Report 45/ 1993. Vienna: European Centre; G.B. Sgritta (1997) Inconsistencies: childhood on the economic and political agenda, *Childhood*, 4 (4): 375–404.

7 D.E. Smith (1988) *The Everyday World as Problematic: A Feminist Sociology*. Milton Keynes: Open University Press.

8 S. Lukes (1974) *Power: A Radical View*. London: Macmillan.

9 J. Holland, C. Razamanoglu, S. Sharpe and R. Thomson (1998) *The Male in the Head: Young People, Heterosexuality and Power*. London: the Tufnell Press; S. Harding (1993) Rethinking standpoint epistemology: what is 'strong objectivity'? in L. Alcoff and E. Potter (eds) *Feminist Epistemologies*. New York: Routledge; A. Gitlin (ed.) (1994) *Power and Method: Political Activism and Educational Research*. London: Routledge.

▶ 1

▷ Children and childhood

▷ **Berry Mayall**

Defining the focus of the research: children as a minority group

Among the many disadvantaged groups in the UK population, children occupy a specific social position. Adult policy and practice on, for and with children is based on the proposition that they lack essential abilities and characteristics of adulthood, but that adult work may successfully steer them through dangerous waters towards adulthood. Through their designation as inferior they are denied the ability to transform themselves but through submission to socialization they may reach acceptable standards of adulthood. For 'child' is a relational category and children are those whom adults designate as rightly subordinate to adults. Children are indeed best regarded as a minority group in their social positioning within local and national power structures. Within families, schools and localities, children have little power to participate in decision making. They have no say in the political processes that affect their lives. Adults control children's lives – how their time is spent, and where it is spent – through the established customs and social policies that structure their access to social and physical worlds.

Research traditions: disciplines, goals and methods

Research on any social group has to be considered in the light of its purposes. In the case of research relating to children, specific issues arise from the dominance in the Anglo–American (Minority) world, over at least the past hundred years, of certain psychological theories about children and childhood. Child development theory is so dominant that, as

Helen Penn describes (Chapter 2), some Majority World policy makers also think that they should modify their established policies and practices in line with it. Understandings of what children are and of what knowledge about them is needed are assumed and promoted by powerful social groups, and these understandings have been allied to certain methods to produce a strong research tradition. Psychological paradigms have focused attention on the character of children's otherness, and their progress towards sameness, that is towards adulthood. Children have belonged to psychology, which, a century ago, developed out of biological enquiry. It established itself as an experimental, testing, fact-finding discipline, focusing on the mental life of people, and especially on the mental development of children. The mental and the social were split apart, with the mental, now recast as the cognitive, and deemed the central focus of study, and the social relegated to the status of descriptive backcloth.[1]

The development of this discipline coincided with the emergence of children on to public agendas in health, education and welfare. And an important reason for the continuing dominance of psychology has been its ready acceptance in those fields as the essential, factual body of knowledge about children. Theory and practice have been mutually reinforcing; academic psychology has provided the knowledge to help practitioners and their reliance on it has helped to promote its high status.

Over the years, with the goal of healing the split between the cognitive and the social, psychologists have tried alliances with both sociologists and anthropologists, but collaboration has commonly foundered on incompatibilities of approach.[2] However, since the 1970s, psychologists' explorations of children's lives in a range of countries have led them to reconsider universalist paradigms of child development. In the past 20 years, Anglo–American work has built on the work of Russian psychologists, notably Vygotsky, who argued for intersections between children's learning and social contexts. Rogoff defines the social activity of learning as apprenticeship.[3] Research in the cultural psychology tradition has sought to consider interactions between children and environment as the basis for understanding how and what children learn.

So Anglo–American psychological approaches to children are moving closer to those of sociologists and anthropologists. However, they remain distinctive. They are also dominant, since they are promoted through high status professionals, and inscribed in social policies. The questions psychology asks centre on individuals and on future time: how do individual children develop towards adequate adult status, what factors ensure good development, what are children's needs from the social environment? These central questions inform the parameters of understanding, both about what is interesting about children, and about what issues need attention. Thus, interest in children's cognitive development throws emphasis on normality as a key issue and individual children's deviation from norms raises questions about what treatment or control is appropriate. Adult roles in meeting children's 'needs' emerge as important.[4] In complement to this individualizing focus, the social tends to be seen as a set of contributory factors; and power issues are defined as second order issues. Another key theme is the process of socialization. Since children are, by definition, inferior to adults, the socialization process is defined essentially as adult intervention with children; the status of children as social actors is dubious. It has been said that children as a phenomenon disappear in this formulation.[5]

In recent years a number of initiatives have compounded to provide alternative sets of understandings of children and childhood. The Childhood as a Social Phenomenon project – a 16-nation macro-level study in industrialized countries – has been concerned with the status of children: their legal and socioeconomic position, the distribution of resources between the generations, and the activities of children.[6] Reconsideration of children as citizens and as actors has been promoted across the world through the United Nations Convention on the Rights of the Child. Work on local implementation of its articles has led to investigation into methods of tapping into children's knowledge and views. The 'new childhood studies' start from broadly social constructionist premises: that the child is not a natural category and that what a child is and how childhood is lived is structured by adult norms, aims and cultures.[7]

Recent sociological and anthropological approaches to children and childhood have certain distinctive features. Firstly, childhood is regarded as a constituent part of the social order, and not as a preparatory stage. Secondly, children are understood as constituting a social group, with their own specific relationships with other social groups, notably with adults and, more generally, power structures; and, complementary to those relationships, their own specific experiences and understandings of childhood. Thirdly, within interactive paradigms, children's learning and experience are understood as the site of complex political tensions between children, parents and the state.[8] Intersections and interactions between agency and structure are invoked to consider children's social positioning and activities. Fourthly, children are regarded as social actors, who have purpose, and who influence as well as being influenced; as people who construct relationships and childhoods, and who can report on and discuss their experience.

On the basis of these understandings, current research questions within the new childhood studies are: what are the features of children's participation in the process of becoming social; what are the characteristics of child–adult interactions and relationships; what is the character of childhood as lived experience; what are the interpretive competencies of children in making sense of their social worlds and in reconstructing childhoods; and how are we to tap into children's understandings of these issues?

Goals of research

I have suggested that psychological theoretical traditions, sustained and promoted by powerful social groups, have constituted accepted knowledge about child-related research issues, both in the Minority and Majority Worlds. With its roots in positivist sciences, psychology has sought to prove its points. Measurement, observation and testing have been dominant methods; large-scale studies have been commonplace, in order to establish relationships between phenomena. Such goals and methods have been complementary to the concerns of funders in the UK. Much research about children is funded through the agencies responsible for children's welfare and education, whose staff appear to regard children as constituting a social problem, rather than, as in many countries, as the nation's best resource. As a result, funded researchers are asked to investigate and, preferably, solve the problems caused by and to children. The Department of Health wants to know how effective its preventive and protective policies are in helping individuals and groups identified as deviant from norms. The Department for Education and Employment is concerned above all with the child as product – children's future, not their present. The Health Education Authority asks whether its programmes lead, as intended, to behaviour modification in children. Children are understood by these agencies as objects of adults' activity; the goal is to turn out adults who fit certain norms. Children's own experiences, understandings and goals are immaterial, except in so far as they affect outcomes.

My own position is that research about children should increase knowledge about children's experiences, knowledge and views; these data can then contribute to policy-oriented work towards improving the social condition of childhood. Therefore, as I see it, the critical research issue in the study of children and childhood is how to link theoretical study with exploration of children's experiences. It is necessary to work up the everyday experiences of the minority into sociological theory. By exploring experience, you uncover the political processes that shape it. In Dorothy Smith's words,[9] you identify how the 'relations of ruling' operate. Then you deconstruct dominant theory, by imposing on it experience. The standpoint of the minority not only provides a critique of theory, but serves as the principal basis for reconstructing theory. Thus the research process engages with societal processes through insiders' understandings of their own lives. If we follow the feminist track, then we should go through the following steps:

- mount a critique of children's social position;
- devise concepts that help understanding – a key concept here is that of generation;
- deconstruct knowledge by studying the concepts and categories in conventional views, showing how ideas implicit in 'generation' structure ideas about children and childhood;

- develop a child standpoint, and use it as the basis for restructuring social theory.

In carrying out these research processes, we need to devise ways of putting together child standpoint and adult understanding of children's social position.[10] This means aiming for more than children's descriptions of what they see and experience; it means also eliciting their interpretation and knowledge of what it is to be a child in the society they live in. Then, in turn, adult interpretation of the conditions of childhood, the rights and wrongs of childhood, has to remain sensitive to the accounts given by children. An important means towards linking child and adult stories is to think of research for children as being research with children; an interactive, participatory, reflexive activity.[11]

However, just as women found that women's experiences were diverse, especially in association with class and ethnic factors in a range of societies, so we have to face the diversity of childhoods. How important then is cultural relativity? Are we happy with the idea that childhood is culturally constructed, that there are many childhoods, no universal constituents of being a child and no core components of childhood? These issues surface most dramatically for people faced with implementing the UN Convention on the Rights of the Child, which sets out basic, universal rights. International work on implementing it also provides pointers to what may be an acceptable compromise. The general principles seem to have a general application (although some articles are extremely problematic), but the local interpretation, understanding and implementation can be worked out in the light of local social and cultural conditions, through local consultation exercises, including the participation of children.[12]

The research process

Although established bodies of knowledge tell us that children are not competent witnesses to their own experiences, researchers are learning otherwise, by respecting children's views and using a wide range of methods. These include questionnaires, discussions, interviews, structured activities, participant observation and written accounts. Researchers can and do use with children most of the methods used with any social group. Research with children is teaching adults some key lessons for any research about people's knowledge. Researchers cannot assume they share the world experience of the researched, so they must try to address people's own concerns and to devise means of getting at people's understandings of their own designated social position; what it means to be, and to act as, that designated person; and what it means to be an individual within and in tension with that social position. I outline here various ways of tapping into knowledge in these matters, depending on the precise question.

Study of the general picture

Recent large-scale statistical data on the distribution of resources among social groups has been used to investigate children's social position. Across the world, in all but the Nordic countries, the share of national resources allocated to children has decreased in the past ten years.[13] Such information provides a context for study of children's understandings of their social position. Recent examples are structured questionnaires and interview schedules providing quantifiable data about children's rights, views on consent to surgery and out-of-school activities. Such data may be contextualized in and interrelated to smaller scale, qualitative data. For instance, a recent study collected data on the status of children's health in primary school through a 1-in-20 survey of schools in England and Wales; and through case studies in six schools. Individual comments and descriptions both endorsed and explained findings from the large-scale data.[14]

Study of process

Where sensitive topics are addressed, researchers are developing supportive research environments where research is organized as a participatory process, which gives children space and time to reflect on and discuss issues, with each other and with adults. For instance, one study aimed 'to understand how children aged between 5 and 12 describe their emotional experiences and to ascertain their perceptions of how people both do and should respond to their emotional experiences and needs'.[15] The research team used interactive group discussions. These allowed children to express feelings and have them recognized by and shared with other children. Groups of six children engaged with a researcher in a discussion, designed in such a way that the children contributed to decisions about the agenda, at different stages throughout the discussion. For example, the session included brainstorming to list important emotions. The children then voted on which were the most important and should form the basis for the next stage of the discussion. At a later stage children took part in short role-plays to illustrate what they saw as typical interventions by adults when a child was, for instance, unhappy or frightened. This allowed for follow-on discussion about child–adult relationships.

From the researcher's perspective, study of processes, including bodily and verbal interactions, is a key way of getting at how children construct their social identities. Participant observation gives children 'a space for vocalization', and helps the researcher understand how children construct their childhoods through action. In James's study of how children become friends, participant observation allowed her to reflect on field notes, and on the process of 'noting' the field. 'As I watched and listened to the children interacting with one another and with me, they literally enacted for me (and for each other) the structuring processes through which their friendships are given form and meaning.'[16]

Observation of children in action gives the adult the chance to witness children learning what it is to be a child, in the social and political contexts they operate in. When children interact in a playground one can see them learning both how to be children, and how to be particular children in particular settings. For instance, Prendergast and Forrest describe the activities of boys in the playground, how the larger ones enact violence towards each other in the centre, while the smaller ones practise violence round the edge.[17] Their observation taught them about boys' learning processes. The advantage of participatory observation – minimum intervention by the adult – has to be weighed against the point that the children may have little part in directly addressing the research agenda; the researcher structures the research activity and decides what issues are important. However, the researcher may use ongoing consultation with the children on interim findings as a basis for later stages in the research process.

Watching children in action can include study of children talking with each other and with adults.[18] One way in which children learn to make sense of their social worlds and of their own individual positions in those worlds, and of the appropriate ways of being a child and doing childhood, is through talking with each other; working through the points and arguing. I have found it productive to encourage children to talk in twos and threes. This somewhat reduces the salience of the researcher, and gives children an opportunity to take up each other's points, argue them further and present other points of view. In some cases, using this method, one is looking at the process whereby people are constructing and reconstructing their ideas.

Bob: In the infants it was more fun. Because you weren't sat down all the time, you were doing things, like painting.

Jack: Now[adays] you don't do painting. In the infants we built the Great Wall of China. We made it go right round the room. With the big bricks.

BM: You liked doing that?

Jack: We did then! We're not allowed to do it now. We did this big thing – we made a big catapult, across both classrooms and . . .

Bob: . . . we made it, it (joint laughter), it didn't work in the end.

BM: Whereas now?

Jack: We're doing more of: sit down, write down, write up!

Bob: The teacher reckons we're too big to do running around, because we hardly ever do. We hardly ever go out. We usually work.

In this snatch of conversation the boys are exploring their ideas about how time is and should be spent at school; about what constitutes work; and about congruence then and now between children's and teacher's wishes.[19]

Study of intergenerational issues

I have suggested that the critical concept in helping us understand children's lives and how childhood is constructed and lived is that of generation. The social worlds of children are determined by adults, both locally – in homes, schools and neighbourhoods – and through the impact of social policies and political understandings of children and childhood. If we use this idea as a basis for research, then it follows that we need to explore childhood from a generational standpoint, including children's own understandings of the generational order.

It has been relatively easy for researchers to study children's own social worlds (although of course they are not their own, but structured by adult goals and practices). And there is also research in the socialization tradition on what parents and teachers do to and with children. These strands need to be supplemented with work starting from children's own standpoints on generational relationships. But it is difficult to study generational issues through ethnographic methods; hanging around in homes and schools tends to lead to adult enquiry about one's purposes and methods. Goodnow and Burns organized a large number of informal small group discussions with children in Australia, across a range of schools and ages, in order to encourage children to discuss the relative merits of home and school.[20] So their data are both qualitative and capable of being analysed quantitatively. Their data include children's understandings of what makes a good mother and a good teacher and of rules and responsibilities in each setting. An example of children's discussion on such issues comes from my own small-scale study of children's understandings of life at home and at school.[21]

BM: What do you like best about being at home?
Sandra: Um, nothing much.
BM: Nothing much? Do you prefer being at school?
Sandra: Yeah, I prefer being at school. Do you, Rita?
Rita: Well, not really.
Sandra: I do, because it's fun. It's not all fun, because sometimes we do boring work.
Rita: Sometimes we have to do really boring things and . . .
Sandra: [Shouting] . . . and sometimes we have to do really hard things that we can't even do!
Rita: And sometimes when we don't want to do something, the teachers won't let us not do it.
BM: So you have to do things at school?
Rita: Yeah. Sometimes we don't have to.
BM: Do you have to do things at home?
Sandra: No, not really.
Rita: Well, my Mum tells me to put my stuff away. I don't really.
Sandra: I don't really either.

These girls explored with each other how group characteristics (as well as individual characteristics) of parents differ from those of teachers, and how these characteristics constitute the structures in tension with which children act.

Similarly, in a recent study on children's use of television the researchers aimed to show how discourse is an arena within which children construct their ideas, in this case about childhood, and about child–parent relations. Study of the transcripts indicates that talk about television:

> provides an arena in which relationships between adults and children are established and defined. In talking about their tastes and preferences, and in asserting their right to have access to them, children are actively negotiating with, and often resisting, the constructions of childhood that are made available to them.[22]

Generational issues arise in the triangle of researcher, children and carer–gatekeepers. Adult gatekeeping may take effect at any stage in research (compare Alderson, Chapter 4). At the outset, adults may wish to give consent. During the course of data collection, parents, teachers or nurses may regard their presence as appropriate. Because these adults shape children's daily lives, children themselves are not entirely free to choose to participate or to refuse. Adults may wish to vet dissemination. Researchers generally have to accept the status quo, that adults control children's lives, and so they collude with adult permission-giving. Moore gives an interesting example of adult worry; he had adult permission to talk with children at school about their favourite playspaces, but when he went a step further and asked children to take him to these, an angry mother confronted him.[23]

Our study, 'Children, Parents and Risk',[24] exposed generational issues in the interviewer's positioning in people's homes. First, although we regarded children as our principal informants, we spoke first (on the phone or at the door) to a parent, usually the mother, and so could gain access to children only through parents. As we progressed, we found ourselves exploring the implications of holding joint discussions with children and their parents. We had not aimed to do joint discussions, but had asked each prospective interviewee to choose whether parents and/or other children should also be present at interviews. Study of the transcripts of these joint discussions showed us several phenomena.

One was that during the interview, the researcher often sided with the adult view, or tried to drag the interview back to research topics. It was hard to listen carefully to children and encourage the development of their train of thought. This was perhaps partly because the interviewer had her or his own agenda, and also because it was hard to turn from parents to the child and privilege the child's comments over those of the parents. The interviewer often felt bound to pay tribute to the parents' contribution, in recognition of generational power issues: that is, the interviewer regarded herself or himself as a guest in the parents' home, not the child's, and parental views ought to have high status, even if parents and interviewer also gave space to the child. Here Frederick, aged 3, struggles to make his voice heard against three adults. He continues with the topic he was asked about (his favourite thing – the zoo) even though they try to move the discussion on to nursery, friends and his character.

I: And what do you like to do, Frederick? What's your favourite things to do?

Frederick: To go swimming.

I: And what else?

Frederick: To go to the zoo.

I: And what do you like about that?

Frederick: Cause there's monkeys.

I: Do you like nursery?

Frederick: I like Beeches

Mother: Beeches Nursery

I: And what do you like doing there?

Frederick: Playing.

I: And your Mum says you've got lots of friends there.

Mother: Who are some of your friends?

Frederick: John.

Mother: Who else?

Frederick: Jack, Sam.

Mother: So many you can't remember them all.

Frederick: I know somebody I'm going to his house.

Mother: Who?

Frederick: Peter who's my friend.

I: And what sort of things does Frederick not like doing?

Frederick: I don't like sharks.

Mother: You're not likely to meet many of them. I don't think there's anything that he doesn't like.

Father: He's a very amiable child. The thing that he doesn't like is that he can't get what he wants. That's the only thing he doesn't like. [Laughs.] Most of the time he's very amiable.

Mother: Yes, he's very easy, he gets very excited about things

Frederick: [Louder] I know what I don't like to do, I don't like sharks or crocodiles.

Here the parents' inclination to work with the interviewer, by trying to be co-operative and by presenting the child in favourable light, restricts Frederick's contributions. The interview process also showed the dynamics of intergenerational processes in action, with the interviewer as catalyst. Strikingly, too, the transcripts showed us that data collection through joint interviews commonly resulted in child and parent(s) presenting a family front. Faced with an outsider (and perhaps because face-to-face with each other), they joined forces to downplay difficult intergenerational issues they had encountered in family life.[25]

I: What sort of things have you had to decide then, Harry?

Harry: Just recently my Mum and Dad said that I could have an allowance for my thirteenth birthday, so I have to buy all my clothes, not my school uniform, so I had to make that decision.

I: So what did you decide, what things you'd use it for?

Harry: Yes.

I: And are there any rules about what things you use it for?

Father: Well, yes, basically – I don't want to speak for you – but, it's his money, his clothes, but there are still parental control over what he buys, and we will have to give advice as to value – if you know what I mean. Also particular designs which we will discuss and talk about. I tend to have some fairly strong views on those sort of things, but at the end of the day a discussion takes place and a compromise is reached.

Mother: But also decisions like if he is allowed to go to London on his own, if he's allowed into town, where – how he's allowed to go.

Harry: It's pretty much very easy. They let me go into town because there's always two or three of us. And we have to go with people who know London.

The topic of the allowance caused embarrassment to the parents, judging by their expressions and their comments. The interviewer's introduction of decision making leads to an intervention by Harry's father, whose usage of the impersonal mode ('a discussion takes place') and the passive voice ('a compromise is reached') seems aimed at smoothing over a history of conflict. Then his mother shifts the ground from clothes to travel. By intervening, the parents deter the interviewer from focusing further on the topic that has caused family conflict. Harry is able to reassert family solidarity, also using the impersonal mode: 'It's pretty much very easy'.

Analysis and presentation of data

These are the areas where the people researched have least power. This is true for adult minorities as well as for children. However, adult minorities have formal rights that make it somewhat easier for them to strike back – through commenting publicly and conducting their own research. It is because of the specific character of their political minority status that children cannot access public debate except through adults. As children, they are not regarded as having a legitimate independent voice.

In our Risk study,[26] we tried to give weight to children's accounts by comparing them with those of their parents, in order to identify children's specific 'take' on their social positioning at home. This meant opening up difference; emphasizing the changing and negotiated character of the contract between children and their parents. Other methods include reflexivity – checking back the researcher's understanding with the children – but this requires lengthy access, which is not always possible.

As regards enabling children to comment on findings and engage in further discussion of them, various schemes have been tried out. Researchers are devising ways of carrying out reflexive research: reporting back to their child informants to check the accuracy of findings and of interpretations; reporting back, more widely, to groups of children not involved in the research to discuss with them implications of findings. A recent action study has used discussion data with children and school staff as the basis of a book on how they reformed the social ethos of their school.[27] Such books can be used by children as a jumping-off point for advancing their interests. There are also initiatives to enable children to set their own agendas, both for public action and for research.[28] For instance, a school newspaper – edited by an adult – employs children to write articles.[29] Children's conferences are held, to discuss and report on social issues identified by children.

In conclusion

Two broad methodological approaches to research about children relate to their distinctive essential purposes: to understand children's trajectories towards adulthood, or to understand the social condition of childhood. I have explored some aspects of the more recent paradigm, the new childhood studies, which, within sociological and anthropological frameworks, aims to relate the empirical to the theoretical. In order to understand the condition of childhood, it is necessary to explore children's own knowledge: their understandings of what it is to be a child and to do childhood. These data can help in the construction of a child standpoint. Complementary theoretical work is required on children's political and socioeconomic positioning and on the structures that condition or intersect with children's agency. Slotting together the empirical and the theoretical may help us understand the condition of childhood in a given society.

Our understandings of children and of child–adult relationships certainly could do with reconsideration. Psychological theory has positioned Minority World children as vulnerable, dependent and incompetent; children have become women's work; children are economic and social burdens to parents and the state, compared to contributing adults. This vision has always looked inaccurate, and is doubly so once one starts to consider children as social actors; as contributors to the social order. A wider vision encompasses Majority World children as economic contributors to households and to communities more generally. Rethinking children's contributions to human activity requires us to reformulate our ideas about what is work, and indeed to reconsider what word to use to describe socially useful human activity. Feminists insist that women's unpaid work is work. Nine-year-olds in my current study describe their daily lives at school and home as work, and hard work at that.[30] From a theoretical point of view, therefore, we need to reconsider child–adult relationships and the character and value of diverse human contributions to social welfare.

In the UK, such rethinking is urgent. Children can be said to suffer oppressions; whether or not these are intentional, they are certainly damaging. Children suffer from 'structural inconsiderateness'[31] – a blindness at the centre of government towards the implications of policies for the quality of their lives: traffic policy is a clear example. Education policy is either blind to its impacts on the quality of children's daily lives, or regards quality as of lesser weight than children's future usefulness as a workforce. So research with the minority group children is ultimately a political activity. Although research cannot and should not engage directly with policy making, it can provide knowledge that may help to shift paradigms of thinking about children and about how childhood might be lived.

Notes

1 S. J. Williams and G. Bendelow (1998) Introduction, in G. Bendelow and S. J. Williams (eds) *Emotions in Social Life: Critical Themes and Contemporary Issues*. London: Routledge.

2 M. Cole (1996) *Cultural Psychology*. Cambridge, MA: Harvard University Press.

3 B. Rogoff (1990) *Apprenticeship in Thinking: Cognitive Development in Social Context*. Oxford: Oxford University Press.

4 M. Woodhead (1997) Psychology and the cultural construction of children's needs, in A. James and A. Prout (eds) *Constructing and Reconstructing Childhood: Contemporary Issues in the Sociological Study of Childhood*. 2nd edn. London: Falmer Press.

5 R.W. Mackay (1991) Conceptions of children and models of socialisation, in F. C. Waksler (ed.) *Studying the Social Worlds of Children: Sociological Readings*. London: Falmer Press.

6 J. Qvortrup (1994) Childhood matters – an introduction, in J. Qvortrup, M. Bardy, G. Sgritta and H. Wintersberger (eds) *Childhood Matters: Social Theory, Practice and Politics*. Aldershot: Avebury Press.

7 C. Jenks (1996) *Childhood*. London: Routledge.

8 D. Ingleby (1986) Development in social context, in M. Richards and P. Light (eds) *Children of Social Worlds*. Cambridge: Polity Press.

9 D. Smith (1988) *The Everyday World as Problematic: A Feminist Sociology*. Boston, MA: Northeastern University Press.

10 L. Alanen (1998) Children and the family order: constraints and competences, in I. Hutchby and J. Moran-Ellis (eds) *Children and Social Competence: Arenas of Action*. London: Falmer Press.

11 G. Lansdown (1995) *Taking Part: Children's Participation in Decision-making*. London: Institute for Public Policy Research; V. Johnson, J. Hill and E. Ivan-Smith (1995) *Listening to Smaller Voices: Children in an Environment of Change*. London: ActionAid.

12 Childwatch International (1996) *Research Project: Indicators for Children's Rights*. Cambridge: Centre for Family Research and Childwatch International.

13 G.B. Sgritta (1997) Inconsistencies: childhood on the economic and political agenda, *Childhood*, 4 (4): 375–404.

14 B. Mayall, G. Bendelow, S. Barker *et al.* (1996) *Children's Health in Primary Schools*. London: Falmer Press. The study was funded (1993–5) by the Economic and Social Research Council (ref. no.: R000234476).

15 M. Hill, A. Laybourn and M. Borland (1996) Engaging with primary-aged children about their emotions and well-being: methodological considerations, *Children and Society* 10 (2): 129–44.

16 A. James (1996) Learning to be friends, *Childhood* 3 (3): 314.

17 S. Prendergast and S. Forrest (1998) Shorties, low-lifers, hardnuts and kings: boys, emotions and embodiment in school, in G. Bendelow and S.J. Williams (eds) *Emotions in Social Life: Critical Themes and Contemporary Issues*. London: Routledge.

18 I. Hutchby and J. Moran-Ellis (1998) Situating children's social competence, in Hutchby and Moran-Ellis (eds), op. cit.

19 B. Mayall (1994) *Negotiating Health: Children at Home and Primary School*. London: Cassell. This study of children's daily lives at home and in one London primary school was funded by the Institute of Education, London University and the Nuffield Foundation.

20 J. Goodnow and A. Burns (1985) *Home and School: A Child's Eye View*. London: Allen and Unwin.

21 Mayall op. cit.

22 D. Buckingham (1994) Television and the definition of childhood, in B. Mayall (ed.) *Children's Childhoods: Observed and Experienced*. London: Falmer Press, p. 94.

23 R.C. Moore (1986) *Childhood's Domain: Play and Place in Child Development*. London: Croom Helm.

24 S. Hood, P. Kelley and B. Mayall (1996) Children as research subjects: A risky enterprise, *Children and Society*, 10 (2): 117–28. The study 'Children, Parents and Risk' was funded by the Economic and Social Research Council (ref. no. L211 252022) from 1995–6, as part of the Risk and Human Behaviour Programme. The researchers on the study were S. Hood, P. Kelley, B. Mayall and A. Oakley.

25 Ibid.

26 Ibid.

27 Highfields Junior School (1997) *Changing our School: Promoting Positive Behaviour*. P. Alderson (ed.). London: Social Science Research Unit.

28 C. Nevison (1997) *'A Matter of Opinion': Research with Children and Young People's Participation Rights in the North-East*. Youth Issues North: Save the Children.

29 Kids can hack it. *The Guardian*, 5 November 1997.
30 This study, *Negotiating Childhoods*, is funded (1997–9) by the Economic and Social Research Council (ref. no. L129 252032), as part of the Children 5–16 Programme.
31 F.-X. Kaufmann, quoted in J. Qvortrup (1993) Children at risk or childhood at risk – a plea for a politics of childhood, in P. L. Heilio, E. Lauronen and M. Bardy (eds) *Politics of Childhood and Children at Risk: Provision, Protection, Participation*. Vienna: European Centre.

▶ **2**

▷ # Children in the Majority World: is Outer Mongolia really so far away?

▷ ## Helen Penn

Defining the focus of the research: constructions of Minority–Majority Worlds

America constitutes about 5 per cent of the world's population, Europe about 12 per cent. For this reason I will use more recent terminology to refer to what is sometimes called the 'developing' or 'third' world and call it more appropriately the 'Majority World'. By the same token I will call America and Europe the 'Minority World'. This point is important because Anglo–American norms of childhood – and for that matter womanhood and manhood – are assumed to be normal, natural and universal, just as capitalism and industrialism are assumed to be a normal and natural progression towards a better universally desired future, and a nation state that has not achieved a certain level of capital accumulation and industrial development is regarded as half-formed and in need of intervention. There is now a substantial literature on what may be called 'post-development', which explores the paradoxes of relationships between the Majority and Minority worlds, in terms of unequal distribution and consumption of environmental and other resources, and the one-way cultural flow of ideas from the Minority World to the Majority World.[1]

As Burman has pointed out, images of children from Majority World countries constantly portray them as helpless and suffering.[2] In my doctor's surgery there is a big – no doubt well-meaning – notice, which says, 'Please let us have your old medicines to send to third world deprived countries'. This notice illustrates neatly the prejudices and stereotypes that characterize our attitudes to the 'third world' – that these are poor, helpless, even feckless countries, which cannot provide for their own populations, and will be grateful for our out-of-date cast-offs, and whose children are innocent victims of mismanaged societies.

Another example of a distorted vision of childhood is offered by the World Bank (commonly regarded as the most pervasive instrument of market ideologies), which has been persuaded that it is a good investment, which will produce a profitable rate of return, to invest in early childhood and to loan money to countries that have some kind of early childhood scheme. This is their rationale for doing so:

> A quarter of a century of US pre-school research has identified several features that successful, centre-based pre-school programmes share . . . both research and experience have taught us that many principles of early education are universal . . . thus the Western studies detailed here are presented not so much as models to be imitated but as examples of 'best practice' with much to offer anyone interested in helping young children learn.[3]

The gist of the position expressed by the World Bank is that 'quality' early childhood education inoculates against poverty, delinquency, early pregnancy and a host of other ailments that we normally think of as having a societal causation. The World Bank report on early childhood draws heavily on US longitudinal research comparing groups of children who had experienced some kind of cognitively based early childhood programme with a group who had not. Weikart claims that differences between the two groups persisted into adulthood, adults who had received preschooling being less prone to criminalization, and more likely to be in employment.[4] However, the World Bank (as do many other organizations and researchers) overlooks the culturally specific circumstances pertaining in the USA: a nation with a very high per capita income, yet with a great income inequality, which is justified by a rhetoric of individual striving, success and self-esteem; and with a particular racial history, which includes a very high rate of incarceration of black youths. Using the evidence about cognitive gains is analogous to using the evidence about high yield grain crops in the USA and assuming the findings can be transferred without taking any notice of land tenure, soil types, climate, irrigation, crop variet-ies, pest resistance or traditional farming methods; in other words without allowing for local complexity and diversity. Or to put it another way, equity and inequity, social justice and solidarity, are not part of the balance sheet that the World Bank and market philosophies have generally taken into account, although they may well be important goals for other commun-ities and countries.

In the Majority World, just as there are many cultural constructions of communities, and the place of individual lives within them, there are also many different and complex understandings about children and childhood. But the hegemony of Anglo–American research, particularly an interventionist model of medical and educational research into childhood, is so consumingly powerful that alternative voices are rarely heard. A few studies attempt to point out the nature of this globalization of childhood and show how even something frequently taken for granted like the rights of the child (although rarely implemented!) can have a very different and not always helpful meaning in Majority World contexts.[5]

Research traditions in the Majority World

Unease with universalist and conventional models of development, whether in economic or ecological terms, is already expressed in social science disciplines. Clifford Geertz, for example, one of the most famous of contemporary anthropologists, argues that we have a great deal of hard work ahead of us in order to do documentary justice to the diversity of man- or womankind.[6] As he points out:

> The Western conception of the person as a bounded, unique, more or less integrated motivational and cognitive universe, a dynamic centre of awareness, emotion, judgement, and action organized into a distinctive whole and set contrastively against other such wholes, and against its social and natural background, is, however incorrigible it may seem to us, a rather peculiar idea within the context of the world's cultures. Rather than attempting to place the experience of others within the framework of such a conception . . . understanding them demands setting that conception aside and seeing their experiences within the framework of their own idea of what selfhood is.[7]

Geertz does this in looking at male society in three very different places, Java, Bali and Morocco, and shows very succinctly how selfhood differs enormously, from what he calls 'a bifurcate conception of the self, half ungestured feeling, and half unfelt gesture, an inner world of stilled emotion and an outer world of shaped behaviour' which characterizes Javanese selfhood, to '*nisba*', the Moroccan system of a kind of nested hyperindividualism. In other words there are many and profoundly different ways of being in the world, and in the Minority World we are shockingly ignorant of most of them.

Another recent theoretical framework is called 'cultural psychology'.[8] Very briefly, this abandons the universalist conceptions of process and learning set out by Piaget and others, which permeate child development theory. Cultural psychology instead posits a view in which learning is seen as an increasing familiarity with a very particular community of practice. Shweder maintains that in cultural psychology:

> Thinking through others in the first sense is to recognize the other as a specialist or expert on some aspect of human experience, whose

reflective consciousness and system of representations and discourse can be used to reveal hidden dimensions of ourself. Some cultures of the world are virtuosos of grief and mourning, others of gender identity, and still others of intimacy, eroticism and ego striving . . . selections from the arc of human possibility.[9]

Recognition and acceptance of 'the other' is a major philosophical and epistemological issue. The political philosopher Benhabib cogently argues for 'a discursive, communicative concept of rationality', or what she calls 'a discourse ethic', which seeks understanding amongst humans while considering the consensus of all to be a counterfactual illusion.[10] She posits a universal search for values and experiences but one that 'reforms universality in terms of the model of reversibility of perspectives and the cultivation of "enlarged thinking"'.[11]

The theoretical inroads of anthropology, cultural psychology and ethics, so briefly described here, have as their goal to arrive at universal understandings through paying close attention to and engaging with local particularities. But recognition of and engagement with other ways of viewing the world is not sufficient. The challenge, as Benhabib claims, is to 'perspectivize'; to see oneself and one's prescriptions for action from the standpoint of the other, and to enter into mutually respectful dialogue about it. Although donor agencies and those from the Minority World working in the Majority World are increasingly trying to find methodologies in which local views can be identified, the notion of equal dialogue is far less frequently raised.

Goals of research

The disparities and power imbalances of the Majority and Minority worlds dramatically raise the question of *research, for what and for whom*? As Susan George pointed out some time ago:

> Meanwhile not nearly enough work is being done on those who hold power and pull the strings . . . let the poor study themselves. They already know what is wrong with their lives, and if you truly want to help them, the best you can do is give them a clearer idea of how their oppressors are working and can be expected to work in the future.[12]

How can the *act* of research by Minority World researchers on Majority World peoples be justified? What methods are most appropriate? The theoretical paradigms of the Minority World are routinely applied (or imposed) in Majority World countries. This problem is slowly beginning to be addressed, at least in the fields of agriculture and health, where there is a new emphasis both from within Majority World countries, and by a very few external agents and donors from the Minority World, on the importance of understanding and recording indigenous knowledge systems.[13]

There is now a trend towards 'participatory research', in which local people are asked to express their views and opinions on the issues under investigation. For example, the World Bank commissioned a study in Swaziland of poverty assessment by the poor, in which rural villagers were enabled to define need and poverty, through a ranking system, as a basis for a poverty alleviation programme. These methodologies are mainly used for assessing the likely impact of aid packages. This is not so much on ethical or moral grounds but because the consequences of getting aid wrong are so dire, with misused and wasted resources, degradation of the environment, and increased inequalities, power struggles, fraud and bitterness in the communities where the aid is (mis)directed. An estimated two thirds of all aid packages are failures.[14] There is a burgeoning literature on these participatory approaches.[15]

Even with participatory research there are many problems – apart of course from the (frequently economic) theoretical paradigm in which the research is located. Such research is more appropriate than so-called 'objective' methods, where Minority World researchers appear with their own agenda for research, and their own predetermined interventionist methodologies, and proceed to apply these in the name of scientific enquiry, with little if any reference to local conditions or understandings.[16] But even participatory research is expensive because Minority World aid workers usually have to set it up, even when they rely on local support. There are always competing claims for money, because the target populations are so poor that what seems to us from the Majority World like a rational exercise in determining efficacy may be seen as an impossible luxury to some of those on whom the research is being imposed. Moreover, Minority World investigators are rarely fluent in the local languages of the Majority World, although they may well expect the reverse; that is for local people to converse in a European language – English, French, Spanish, Portuguese. There is invariably a problem of translation and of finding ways to compensate for the absence of a shared language. Methodologies that rely on written material may founder because of illiteracy. (It is of course possible for people in a local community to be illiterate *and* subtle and ironic.)

The preferred methods in such circumstances rely on visual techniques such as mapping, ranking and sorting with very basic visual aids such as sticks and stones on a mud surface. Sometimes it is possible to extend such visual aids by using drawings, diagrams or matrices, to encompass mutual reflections on the meaning of events to the appraisers and the appraised. Because of the problems of money and language these research methods are usually short and quick – in the jargon, 'rapid participatory appraisal'.

Finally of course, participatory appraisal is not a cast-iron guarantee against the foolishness of donors. The most bizarre programmes have been justified on the basis of participatory appraisal. For instance a UNICEF programme in Namibia, led by Americans, aimed to teach 'Better Parenting' to bushmen (or, rather, to bushwomen).

Dissemination – that is having a local audience to whom one can explain and justify one's findings – is usually part of the project of research in Majority World countries. However, 'local' may mean the people who have been directly participating in the research and whose conditions of life and daily practices are being investigated, or, at another level, government officials from the country in question, who may be far removed from and have relatively little sympathy with those conditions and practices. (In fact the question of exactly *who* benefits from aid packages is another painful debate in the aid community).

As a researcher, one is expected to make decisions and give advice that is often eagerly and humbly awaited. The gulf between researcher and researched is far greater than in a typical Minority World study; but the goodwill and respect from those being researched to the foreign researcher is sometimes unearned. The research is often classified (by the donor as well as the recipient) as 'technological assistance' (a typical classification of the World Bank for example). On this technological model, derived from engineering, the researcher is supposed to have diagnosed the problem, and to proffer solutions for sorting it out. The problem for the researcher is in *not* being seen as a guru, in being modest, in presenting oneself as someone with an open-ended set of ideas for feedback and discussion; in Benhabib's words, 'to promote a discourse ethic'. As Hancock's book *Lords of Poverty* shows all too clearly, Minority World consultants and researchers in Majority World countries frequently exhibit arrogance, and import solutions from the Minority World, imposing them on an audience over disposed to accept them and in any case required to pay for them.[17] As de Waal commented, we would do well to remember that alongside the concept of 'donor fatigue' there is a parallel concept of 'recipient fatigue';[18] of officials so conditioned to outside intervention by donor agencies that their tactic has been passive compliance – face-to-face agreement but with a minimum of action – since the next set of consultants or aid packages will not be long in arriving.

The research process

These are the discussions and debates in which I try to locate myself when I work in countries of the Majority World. Starting off as a policy maker, and ending up as a researcher, I have had a substantial track record in the UK and Europe looking at models of provision of services for young children – what Minority World countries think should be provided for young children and why. I have been concerned with policy and practice as well as with theory.

Over the past two years I have begun to work increasingly in the Majority World. Most of this work has been for Save the Children UK (SCF). It is a remarkable charity, partly because of their focus on and advocacy for children, and their sustained criticism of market philosophies, but also because they respect research and theory, and frequently commission work from the academic community to try to site their practice against a theoretical focus. Their education adviser has attempted to adumbrate some principles about practical work in Majority World countries with regard to early childhood.[19]

I am interested in working in the Majority World for a number of reasons. Firstly, I believe there is an issue of profound injustice concerning the distribution and consumption of resources between Majority and Minority Worlds that we have a moral obligation to address, in whatever way possible. Secondly, in the particular field in which I work, I am concerned that Minority World views of childhood and young children are limited and limiting, and I – and others – have much to gain from learning about other, very different, ways of bringing up young children and providing for them. Thirdly, although I have many reservations about the aid trade, it exists, and it may be possible to use the knowledge and skills, the cultural capital, that I possess as a privileged Minority World researcher, for the benefit of those I visit.

I have been doing research/consultancy work for SCF, spending a relatively short amount of time in a country – one or two months – and in that time working intensively, collecting as much information as I can from a variety of sources, written, oral and based on observation. I try always to be open to any possibilities; to any small trails that might lead me to unforeseen conclusions. I also try to read whatever I can before I go, and again ground my findings and opinions when I get back by further reading. Increasingly I have found that I have to understand development economics – to begin to understand the financial circumstances of the countries I visit and to read financial statistics – since the reasons for the provision or non-provision of services for young children are not merely ideological, and there may be very real and harsh economic constraints on what can be collectively provided. In short, as a Minority World researcher, one needs to be intensely reflective and reflexive, but also as well informed as possible about the Majority World countries one visits.

A number of donor agencies, mainly based in the USA, sponsor programmes in early childhood in Majority World countries. These include UNICEF, World Bank, the Soros Foundation, the Aga Khan Foundation and the Bernard van Leer Foundation, as well as the various Save the Children Alliance members. These early child development programmes are usually based on a Minority World prescription of intervention, in particular on various 'parenting' and 'child-centred' approaches. This proselytizing approach is not compatible with seeing childhood as a complex phenomenon. Moreover, since the intellectual traffic is perceived to be one way: those in the Minority World teaching those in the Majority World, reciprocity is rare. There are held to be no implications for Anglo–American childrearing.

Researching in Mongolia

I will use the example of Mongolia as an illustration of the points made so far. Outer Mongolia, to distinguish it from inner Mongolia which is part of China, is a highly unusual country. It is about three times the size of France, with a population of 2.5 million, very thinly dispersed over the terrain. Most of the country is high steppe, and temperatures in winter are commonly −40°C or below. More than 50 per cent of the population are pastoral and/or part nomadic, and live in transportable felt tents called *gers*. They herd cattle and sheep and, in the desert areas, camels. The capital city, Ulaan Baator, has a seasonally fluctuating population of approximately 500,000.

With a Gross National Product per capita of $390,[20] Mongolia is one of the poorest countries in the world (compare this, for example, with the UK figure of $18,060) but on conventional figures for education, mortality of the under-fives and other poverty indicators, it used to rate surprisingly well. For 70 years, although nominally independent, the country was part of the Soviet block, and its subsidy from the USSR amounted to about 35 per cent of gross national product. Since the fall of communism, the Soviet income has been withdrawn. Donor agencies have stepped in to fill the gap, but typically the donor intervention is fragmented and often ineffective, and all the poverty indicators now show an increase in severity. The infrastructure of the country – schools, energy, water supply and sewage – is degenerating. On the other hand, after years of suppression, the National government in power has been able to stress its nomadic cultural history and heritage.

Low population density, the extreme remoteness of some of the settlements, the nomadism, and the hostile winter climate, present unusual problems for the education system. Partly for these reasons, children do not start school until the year in which they are eight. Instead there has been an extensive preschool system, operating at village or *sum* level and on an outreach basis, as well as in towns and cities. The education and preschool system was heavily influenced by Soviet ideas, and was geared to providing a service for working parents as well as an educational service. Despite considerable financial difficulties and international pressures since transition, the preschool system has endured and even, in a few places, expanded. I was asked by SCF to undertake a review of early childhood services in Mongolia for the Ministry of Education, Science and Culture (MOSE). In the period of structural adjustment following transition from a communist to a non-communist government many aspects of government were opened to scrutiny by Westerners for the first time. I went in November 1996 and returned again briefly in 1997.

The report I wrote was based primarily on observations and discussions during a series of visits, both formal and announced and informal and unannounced, to kindergartens within Ulaan Baator, and in Zavkhan and Tov *aimags*.[21] I was able to visit a small number of *ger* homes, and talk (with the help of an interpreter) to nomadic families as well as to more articulate middle class parents. I had meetings with various officials, politicians and non-governmental organizations (NGOs) at national and provincial level, and consulted a wide range of documents, situation analyses provided by a variety of agencies, conference reports, curriculum requirements and legal documents. I made use of statistical evidence – which in Mongolia is relatively sound – drawing on demographic and household surveys, as well as on education statistics. I also tried to read Mongolia's equivalent of the *Bhagavad Gita*, called *The Secret History of the Mongols*, which is a semi-mystical account of the life of Chenngis Khan. The full list of sources is given in the references.[22]

I was invited to Mongolia for two reasons. Firstly, SCF wanted to increase access to the preschool system for very low income families. They considered that the system could mitigate some of the worst excesses of structural adjustment policies,[23] although any increase in access had to be secured at little or no extra cost. Secondly, the Mongolians were concerned about the quality of the system in transition. There was real ambiguity about this. Teachers and administrators perceived the system to be very good and well developed, and there were sustained protests at any proposals to reduce levels of provision. But there were considerable uncertainties about the curriculum, and in particular whether or not a more child-centred, Westernized curricular model should be adopted. This dilemma is common to many countries in transition and reflects the overwhelming hegemony of Anglo–American (rather than Euro–American) traditions. Experiments were underway in two kindergartens to introduce these child-centred methods. I was asked to examine the system and to comment on both access for poor parents and curriculum and pedagogy.

The Mongolian system of kindergartens is closely based on the Soviet system, and indeed most of the senior staff were trained in Russia or in East Germany. But now the Soviet system is being modified, and the East German system has been more or less abandoned in favour of the much freer methods practised in West Germany,[24] and Singapore has paradoxically become a new base for overseas training. In a recent article, *Chinese Daycare in Cultural Change*, Limin Gu explored the changes in the preschool education system in China, which was also closely based on the Russian system, and has provided a useful analysis of the Soviet educational model.[25]

Table 2.1   *Differences between Anglo–American and Soviet models of kindergarten care*

Soviet	Anglo–American
Historicity – a society in transition. Kindergartens have a key role in the transition period from one mode of production to another.	Ahistorical – kindergartens a peripheral service with no particular role to play.
Dual care and education – starting point care for working mothers with education.	Education and care as separate systems – cognitive development as a separate and distinct issue, unrelated to daycare.
Knowledge consciously defined and prescribed by education system.	Emphasizing the individual construction of knowledge; constructed by the individual child in her own particular way.
Importance of educators in delivering knowledge; educators highly trained using carefully described methods.	Education of young children a marginal occupation; children create their own knowledge.
Importance of educational institutions over family.	Emphasizing the importance of family upbringing. The child is seen firstly as the product of her family, and more particularly of her mother.
Collective character of education; the group is more important than the individuals within it.	Education is only the education of individuals and not a welding of the group. Young children are seen as individuals for whom group life is an imposition.

Following on from her paper, I tried to clarify and contrast for MOSE the differences between Soviet and Anglo–American assumptions in the provision of kindergarten systems.

Using this analysis as a basis for discussion, I tried to clarify what aspects of the Soviet inspired system my Mongolian colleagues wished to see changed. Basically the discussions centred on the intensely collective and didactic approach to learning within the kindergartens, and the exclusivity of the system towards the poorest parents and towards children with disabilities.

The curriculum of the kindergartens was systematized to the extent that it runs to 106 pages, in which the detailed content of each lesson is carefully spelt out. Rote learning and copying were used as the core method for instructing children. Children, even very young children, were required to memorize and recite poems and songs, and give performances of what they had learnt. The curriculum also included regular sessions of vigorous callisthenics. The children were very fit and moved gracefully (but in any case it is commonplace for very young children to be roped to horses or to ride bareback, and there is an annual nomads' festival of horseriding and wrestling, which is a focus of civic life).

The curriculum is the repository of acceptable and allowable practice, and teachers are judged by their ability to impart knowledge to a group of children in a previously prescribed way. The teachers I saw were conscious of themselves and the effect they had on children, and the best performed very well: they were able to stimulate and hold the attention of their children; they were kindly towards them; and they did not often, if at all, appear to be irritated or angry. When I asked teachers if there was anything they would like to see changed, although they made minor suggestions, no one was prepared to question the dominance and prescriptive nature of the curriculum. When I probed further, I was often told that it was designed by experts who had drawn upon the best scientific knowledge to formulate it, and therefore, by implication, it was not within their remit to question it.

The curriculum was highly prescribed, and was not open to modification by teachers or children. Yet it had its good points. The regularity of the routines, an approach that combines meeting physical needs – for exercise, diet and rest – with cognitive needs, is an all-round approach that is frequently lacking in the USA and UK, where despite a much higher standard of living, children are often under-exercised and ill-fed.

Children who attended kindergarten were primarily children of working parents who could afford the food costs. Children of non-working parents and disabled children were excluded. In Mongolia, disabled children are frequently regarded as diseased or defective, and therefore as incapable of joining in with other children and liable to harm them. The service currently available for disabled children is essentially a separate and medically oriented service, and because it is also city based, very few children can get there.

Although poor and vulnerable children are not seen as being as damaged or inferior as disabled children, if they come at all they are frequently treated differently from other children in the kindergartens. All children are excluded from ordinary kindergartens if they are not in perfect health, since even where there are doctors in the kindergarten, it is not considered appropriate to treat minor ailments or skin infections. Poor children are most vulnerable to infections, and their parents least able to deal with them, for even the provision of hot water and soap at home, let alone medicine, can be problematic in the poorest households. Part of my report explored and rejected the arguments for exclusivity, and linked such arguments to the wider work being undertaken by SCF for poor and vulnerable families.

The kindergarten system in operation in Mongolia has very different priorities and rests on very different assumptions from those we are used to in Minority World countries. Within that cultural and institutional framework what change is possible or desirable? Like most transitional countries there is an assumption that change is necessary, if nothing else in order to attain a higher standard of living with more consumer choice.[26] However, the traditions I have described were clearly enduring, and could not be modified easily. Nor was I able to do more than very lightly outline current practice, and reflect back to MOSE what had most struck me, as an outsider to Mongolia.

Any sustainable change would have to be based on dialogue. To support and extend such dialogue, more local research into understandings about children would be helpful – for example the treatment of poor children and children with disabilities. Systematic comparison with over-admired and somewhat mystically interpreted Minority World models of child development would also be useful. Working with First Nation peoples in Canada, Pence and McCallum have given one model of how this might be done, by rigorously exploring and contrasting value systems and requiring students in childcare and early years education to understand the nature of the divergences.[27]

Conclusion

Whether or not the research/consultancy was of use to the Mongolians in trying to illustrate how they stood in relation to Anglo–American systems of childcare, and in making suggestions for the development of the system, the findings were relevant to my ongoing work in trying to explore the parameters of childhood and the services that are provided for young children.

In Mongolia, for example, expectations of children differ profoundly from ours. Nomadism is an utterly remote way of life to us. The constant movements, the symbiosis with an often hostile terrain, the reliance on animals for survival and the closeness of family units, produce what Cable called 'the harsh social discipline of the nomad'.[28] It produces a very different kind of childhood. As an outsider it appeared to me that young children, whether in kindergarten or outside of it, had a constructive understanding of being in a communal setting, where maintaining the harmony of the group meant that it was antisocial and offensive to cry, whine, demand or disobey. This was achieved without any obvious chiding or hectoring by adults – a radically different approach from that of a liberal, Minority World parent, who would regard crying, whining, demanding and disobeying as normal behaviour in a young child. Very young children were also seen as being much more physically capable and morally responsible than we in the Minority World conventionally assume to be possible, for instance in relation to the care and management of domestic animals – camels, goats, horses, dogs – or in the concern and commitment expressed to siblings.[29]

Moreover, Mongolia's health and welfare systems, once so precariously pieced together, are falling apart because of a new economic philosophy, which preaches survival in a world marketplace in which Mongolia must negotiate entry on whatever terms are dictated by international financial institutions. Can lessons be learnt from these abrupt and dramatic changes in social policy? And what may we infer when a country as poor as Mongolia, and undergoing such radical transition, still attempts to maintain a publicly funded kindergarten system, which combines care and education in the remotest of places, and even seeks to expand it? Can we draw out any connections between countries like Mongolia and the systems we uphold, explicitly or implicitly, willingly or unwillingly, in our own countries?

How can an account be told in such a way as to lead to genuine discussion, rather than being seen as a traveller's tale from an exotic land? As Burman has shown, most Western attention is paid to children in Majority World countries at times of acute crisis.[30] In the interests of fund raising, children are invariably portrayed as victims in need of rescue, a kind of Dickensian sentimentality that serves to confirm the prejudices of the audience about the Majority World as a nasty, deprived, squalid sort of place from which orphan children need to be saved; rather than recognizing that the lived childhoods of children in countries such as Angola and Mozambique, with their legacy of war as a consequence of apartheid and the arms trade, are as irredeemably complex as in the Minority World, or even more so.

I try to raise such issues both within the donor community and more widely, and have been talking and writing about them in academic, professional and even political forums. But interesting and challenging as these issues are, it is hard to pierce the parochiality of the Minority World. In terms of straightforward public or even scholarly recognition of the diversity of children in the world, and the circumstances in which they grow up, there are, cliché as it is, no easy answers. As a Minority World researcher working in the Majority World, there is merely a long scholarly haul of documentation, a building of networks and a 'discourse ethic': and, one should add, a more vivid appreciation of ourselves as part of a minority, but intensely privileged, world.

In the end one is faced with the fact that representing the voices, whether of children or adults, from the Majority World and in some way relaying them to the Minority World is intensely political, since it requires us all to accept that our assumptions of universality are in fact reflections of deep privilege and, frequently, shocking exploitation.

Notes

1 S. George (1994) *Ill Fares the Land*. London: Penguin; G. Monbiot (1994) *No Man's Land*. London: Macmillan; M. Warren, L. Slikkerveer and D. Brokensha (1995) *The Cultural Dimension of Development*. London: Intermediate Technology Publications; R. Chambers (1997) *Whose Reality Counts? Putting the First Last*. London: Intermediate Technology Publications; M. Rahnema and V. Bawtree (1997) *The Post Development Reader*. London: Zed Books.

2 E. Burman (1996) Local, global, or globalized? Child development and international childrights legislation, *Childhood*, 3 (1): 45–66.

3 M. Young (1996) *Early Child Development: Investing in the Future*. Washington: World Bank.

4 D. Weikart (1996) High quality preschool programmes found to improve adult status, *Childhood*, 3 (1): 117–20.

5 A. Armstrong (ed.) (1995) *Towards a Cultural Understanding of the Interplay Between Children's and Women's Rights: An Eastern and Southern Africa Perspective*, working paper no. 11. Harare: Women and Law in Southern Africa; J. Boyden (1990) The globalization of childhood, in A. James and A. Prout (eds) *Constructing and Reconstructing Childhood*. Sussex: Falmer Press; E. Burman (1994) Innocents abroad: western fantasies of childhood and the iconography of emergencies, *Journal of Disaster Studies and Management*, 18 (3): 238–53; M. Woodhead (1997) *In Search of the Rainbow*. The Hague: Bernard van Leer Publications; S. De Vylder (1996) *Development Strategies, Macro-economic Policies and the Rights of the Child*. Stockholm: Discussion paper for Rädda Barnen.

6 C. Geertz (1996) From the native's point of view: on the nature of anthropological understanding, in N.R. Goldberger and J.B. Veroff (eds) *Culture and Psychology*. New York: Columbia University Press.

7 Ibid., p. 27.

8 R.A. Shweder (1990) Cultural psychology, what is it? in J.W. Sigler, R.A. Shweder and G. Herdt (eds) *Cultural Psychology: Essays on Comparative Human Development*. Chicago: Chicago University Press; M. Cole (1996) *Cultural Psychology*. Cambridge, MA: Bellnap Press/Harvard Press; J. Lave and E. Wenger (1992) *Situated Learning: Legitimate Peripheral Participation*. Cambridge: Cambridge University Press.

9 Shweder op. cit., p. 33.

10 S. Benhabib (1992) *Situating the Self*. Cambridge: Polity Press.

11 Ibid., p. 12.

12 George op. cit., p. 289.

13 Warren *et al.* op. cit.; H. Penn (1997a) Inclusivity and diversity in early childhood services in South Africa, *International Journal of Inclusive Education*, 1 (1): 101–14.

14 A. de Waal (1997) Is aid redundant? Paper given at London School of Economics Debate on Aid Policies.

15 B. Pratt and P. Loizos (1992) *Choosing Research Methods: Data Collection for Development Workers*, Oxfam development guidelines no. 7. Oxford: Oxfam; N. Nelson and S. Wright (1995) *Power and Participatory Development*. London: Intermediate Technology Publications; Chambers op. cit.

16 Chambers op. cit.

17 G. Hancock (1989) *Lords of Poverty*. London: Mandarin.

18 de Waal op. cit.

19 M. Molteno (1996) *Starting Young*. London: Save the Children UK.

20 UNICEF (1996) *State of the World's Children* (based on 1993 figures). Oxford: Oxford University Press.

21 The *aimag* is equivalent to a province or region. Zhavkan aimag is in the north west of Mongolia and is poor and mountainous. Tov Aimag borders Ulaan Baator.

22 *Curriculum Workbooks* (1995) Mongolia: Save the Children Fund (UK); *Herdsmen's Pre-School Curriculum Book* (1995) Mongolia: National Educational Institute; *Mongolia Demographic Survey* (1994) Main Report, Mongolia: Population and Teaching Centre, Mongolian National University; *Mongolia: Poverty in a Transition Economy* (1996) Draft Report, Bangkok: The World Bank Rural and Social Development Operations Division, Chines and Mongolia Department, East Asia and Pacific Regional Office; *Mongolia Household Income and Expenditure Statistics* (1995–6) (sample data only), Mongolia: National Statistical Board; *Mongolia Education Statistics* (1995–6) Mongolia: Ministry of Enlightenment.

23 In all cases in developing and transitional countries structural adjustment policies appear to have resulted in widening income inequalities.

24 P. Calder (1996) After the wall: the experiences of childcare in East Germany, *International Journal of Early Years Education*, 4 (3).

25 L. Gu (1996) *Chinese Daycare in Cultural Change*. Paper given at the European Educational Research Association Conference, Seville, Spain.

26 There is very little consumer choice in Mongolia – it is very difficult even to identify a shop exterior, since most shops look like any other apartment.

27 A. Pence and M. McCallum (1994) Building a generative curriculum, in P. Moss and A. Pence (eds) *Valuing Quality*. London/NY: Paul Chapman/Teachers College Press.

28 M. Cable (1942) *The Gobi Desert*. London: Hodder and Stoughton.

29 J. Holst, C. Kruchov, U.A. Madsen *et al.* (1995) *School Development in Mongolia 1992–4*. Copenhagen: Royal Danish School of Educational Studies.

30 E. Burman (1994) op. cit.

▶ 3

▷ Learning disabilities: the researcher's voyage to planet Earth

▷ Christopher Goodey

Defining the focus: interview and identity

What is the relationship between research and power? Of course the researcher has to be some kind of politician to nurture referees, attract fund holders and publicize results. But the research process is political in the deeper sense that it *starts from* a realm of shared ethics and human community, and not from the external script against which we dispassionately tick off normal vs. pathological, lay vs. professional and methodology vs. response. Like it or not, research is participation in social change and in mutual, reflexive exploration. This is apparent in the kind of qualitative research that involves talking with people, but paradoxically is best illustrated by talking with people with whom it is difficult to talk: those with severe learning disabilities or elderly dementia. Funders and professional audiences already circumspect about the value of small-scale qualitative work may want to know how interviews or any kind of interaction with supposedly non-rational respondents can be taken seriously. An in-depth interview already has more obvious connections with the researcher's subjectivity than, say, a multiple-choice questionnaire. But what if the outcome is not something to be interpreted this way or that but, by the specific criterion of rational communication, virtually nothing at all: does the outcome then lie wholly in the sphere of the researcher's subjectivity? The question implies an inverse proportionality, between quantifiable amounts of the respondent's rationality and quantifiable amounts of interpretation: the less our respondent says the more we say, or the less rational our respondent the more rational we are. Just as quantitative work may be said always to have a qualitative component, the analysis of in-depth interviews may rest on an unwittingly quantitative assumption that they are tidy individual units that yield amounts of something; it is an abstraction that suits the funding mechanisms. Transgression of the boundary between individual and context is implicit in all qualitative research, but especially so in the case of learning disabilities.

The definitional problem extends from the interview to the group identity, 'people with learning disabilities'. Although the phrase is used for the purposes of this chapter, we need to challenge its meaningfulness. Learning disabilities exist, of course, but they are specific to individuals more than to medical or psychological conditions, and they shade into the general population. Baljinder speaks no more than two words at a time, but they are deployed to the point.[1] He answers questions willingly and initiates social interaction and warmth by getting out of his chair and coming to sit next to me on the settee; a subversion of the physical arrangement of the interview. Stephen is 14 and has little verbal communication; the behavioural checklist would reveal minimal social skills. He relies on others to interpret what he is feeling. He spits at me a couple of times; he can however do Level 2 maths and has an understanding of French using flashcards. Alison is 15 and cannot do single-digit arithmetic, and her television viewing consists entirely of videos for very young children; however, she has fully social speech with an above average vocabulary dramatically deployed during our interview. No definition encompasses them all, as many clinicians would acknowledge. Similarly, there is no clear connection between types of impaired communication among the elderly, for example between Alzheimer's and Parkinson's diseases.

The boundary problem is not just conceptual, it is subverted from within. Maria is an autistic 11-year-old with no speech. She can communicate a little using flashcards; I can ask her what her favourite lesson is at school. But this is clearly limited, and in any case there are other children with her condition but without this skill, whom I could not interview in this way. On my first visit I arrived at her mainstream school playground at breaktime, at a loss because I didn't know anybody. She was the first person to spot a new face through the crowd, ran over and pumped my hands up and down. In the resource room where Maria was withdrawn for some of the day with children like herself, she picked up the card saying 'Class 6L' (her mainstream class) and walked around waving it impatiently. Yet people with autism are routinely defined by experts as belonging in their own world, separate from that of others. In my research relationship with Maria quantifiable amounts of response were substituted not by amounts of interpretation but by her power of strategic intervention. She was establishing for me and her schoolmates a social terrain that we could all manage, the realm that I want to suggest is the starting point of the research process, and she was challenging the clinical diagnosis of isolation and uncommunicativeness applied to her condition.

A sceptical response is therefore possible both to the ontological question (what is really there?) and to the sociological question (how does what is really there come to be classified and institutionalized?), and therefore to positive theories about learning disability. At the same time disadvantaged groups arouse empathies in us; we feel driven to do something 'positive' (in the everyday sense) ourselves, to become their advocates or to persuade others to listen to them. Research is politics in this sense too. Whether or not we are organic members of the population we research with, the feelings induced by research activity in our fields are those characteristic of political activity, of what Weber called its 'passion' and 'violence'.[2] Extreme scepticism induces quietism, but our research arouses a desire for action, a desire to develop theories and perspectives of our own that are not at odds with the feelings but which nevertheless have some prospect of being effect- ive in the real world of policy making. The oscillation between scepticism and hope is a source of anxiety in all stages of the research process; to use the vocabulary of political thought, it manifests itself as a search for *trust*, for firm ground.

Research traditions: between theory and value

Although qualitative research with learning disabled people may be seen as problematical, specific psychiatric theories are certainly applied to parents and families. Unlike their children, or perhaps any children, parents have the appearance of rational beings; but in medical discourse to classify a category of people with learning disabilities is automatically to pathologize, and this sometimes casts pollution over families too. Sandra is talking to the paediatrician about her infant son Richard as if he is a normal member of the family and will go to his local school. The paediatrician interrupts, 'You do realize that Richard is not like other children, don't you?' Rich- ard's grandmother turns to Sandra after the consultation and asks, about the paediatrician, 'Who does he think is mentally handicapped, Richard or you?' Child and family are somehow united as recipients of labelling and abstract classification. Secondary differentiations exist within this: a behaviour management programme for the co-operative family but drugs for the child of a 'feckless' one, for example, and sometimes nothing at all for the Asian child and family because they have 'different values'. To be a rational being does not necessarily mean to be accepted into a community of trust, already qualified as it is by social class, gender and ethnicity.

Medical theories have found it difficult even to see those parents who may present themselves or their children as non-pathological. Any view that manages to include them at all may then seem impressive and even radical. One such approach has been phenomenological; that is, it has stressed the families' need to make a coherent interpretive account that will adjust events to what they already know about the way the normal world works. These families are said to 'present' normality, the premiss being that they present the child's *pathology* as normal; a presentation that is itself implicitly a pathological act. This approach clearly rests on a medical–statistical model of normality, by which the subject is in denial: she says no but really she means yes.

Another stock item of the psychiatric literature, almost ubiquitous among practitioners, is acceptance theory, derived historically from Charcot's theory of female hysteria. All parents given a diagnosis of disability in their child are said to undergo a natural and necessary process of distress, measured by an index divisible into specific numbered stages (denial, guilt, anger towards professionals, and so on) until the final stage, acceptance, is reached.[3] This discourse was legitimized by the 1997 High Court judgment *Spendiff* v. *North Tyneside Council*, which determined that a local education authority has the power to prevent a disabled child from attending an ordinary school in spite of the child's or parents' wishes. The judgment told the Spendiffs to accept their child's disability, since their appeal for an ordinary school was proof that they had not; they had to 'swallow the bitter pill'. In some variants of this theory acceptance has a subcomponent called mission orientation. If organic researchers are perceived as mission-oriented, their results can thus be pre-emptively discussed like those of the 'hysterical woman' in feminist research.

Parents relating their experience of receiving the diagnosis frequently use the word 'acceptance'. Only concentrated listening tells us that it is being used in diametrically opposite ways by professionals and parents. In the psychiatric view, a parent starts out denying the reality of the child's pathological nature, its clinical 'monstrosity', which the parent eventually comes to accept. In the parental view, however, acceptance seems to involve realizing that the child is not the monster that had been described to them, and that its 'difference' simply expands the variety of the normal environment. The received discourse of acceptance is the only one parents know, but (*pace* Foucault) they may convey through it an underlying social reality that is not dictated by that discourse, and access to which is available only to them. The researcher can learn from it, but learning is difficult unless we trust our respondents to be telling truths about social reality rather than denying it, just as they trust us with their thoughts and trust our reassurances about confidentiality. Trust in our research subjects comes first. Without it we will not go looking for those truths and no critique of existing theories or elaboration of new ones will be possible. The phenomenological and acceptance theories clearly do not take this step, and in this sense could be said to suppress truths that are, as we shall see, of broader social significance than our own particular topic.

While it is often admitted that a single generic boundary cannot be drawn for learning disability, a covert unifying theory actually exists: that of incurability, and of the 'mind' and 'mental development'. These apparently transhistorical medical–scientific concepts in fact constitute a theoretical framework that is also a set of values. They have a past, a genesis. 'Learning disability' is unthinkable without a specifically *modern* concept of psychology, mind and intelligence and a correspondingly modern sociopolitical context. The Greeks had words for woman, lay, disturbed, ethnic and gay, but not for anything like our 'learning disability'. Whether the mind itself is something that is really there in the sense that the body is or whether it is (in Wittgenstein's phrase) an occult medium, is a question the sociological researcher cannot just leave psychology to assume. Research activity starts out already embroiled in the messy relationships of real people in the real world. To stay upright requires a conceptual footing firmer than that provided by a discipline born a mere 300 years ago to support a new ruling political theory; that of individual consent. Constructions of race, sexuality and gender at least assume a common humanity: constructions of incurable learning disability, in the terms of that political theory, challenge the very definition of the person as human and the validity of the research interview as an inter-human activity. Historically, doubt about the humanity of our interviewees has undergone a seamless process in which modern scientific psychology has not dispensed with but merely subsumed theology. In seventeenth-century belief, cures for the mind were providential; they came directly from God. If God is benign, incurability (especially when associated with congenital conditions) can only be demonic in origin, and this questions the humanity of incurables. One of religion's tasks is to make things vanish and reappear and to make the ordinary extraordinary in this way. Psychology plays these same tricks with the concept of 'the mind' and its 'development'.[4]

Sociology and history contextualize these value-laden theories about learning disability and mental development, showing that construction of an outer boundary for what it is to be human impinges on internal constructions of childhood, race, gender and sexuality. Severe learning disabilities may thus be paradigmatic, providing a critical focus on the goals of social policy and healthcare as they relate to all disadvantaged groups. These goals are inseparable from the research techniques and methodologies employed in each of them, central to which is the concept of 'need' and needs assessment and its accompanying ethics of benevolence and utilitarianism.

The goals of research: needs assessment and difficulties

The classic position on benevolence was given by Hume. Its utilitarianism consisted in the belief that 'moral obligation holds proportion with usefulness', although he was franker than his modern descendants about utility being a function of existing class and power relations:

Were there a species of creatures intermingled with men, which, though rational, were possessed of such inferior strength [of] mind, that they were incapable of all resistance, and could never, upon the highest provocation, make us feel the effects of their resentment, the necessary consequence . . . is that we should be bound by the laws of humanity to give gentle usage to these creatures, but should not, properly speaking, lie under any restraint of justice with regard to them, or of right or property exclusive of such arbitrary lords.[5]

He continues by asking whether the hypothesis applies to colonized people or women. He is unsure about the answer, but this is precisely because his feeble-minded human was a baseline abstraction. To us, feeble-mindedness (what we call learning disability) seems to be a watertight category against which the inferiority of women or colonized peoples is measured; emancipation movements have in this sense emancipated their members from their pollutant association with a category that they themselves still regard as positive and transhistorical. Yet the passage quoted shows that this category is merely an abstraction. General feeble-mindedness could not have been hypothesized without pre-existing concrete relations of subordination which are class-oriented, gendered, racialized, age-grouped, and so on.

Hume says we should treat this category with benevolence. But we have added to his hypothesis a correspondingly abstract concept of need. The power relationship is such that we, not they, know what they need. According to Hume, feeble-mindedness encompasses all those who are incapable of forcing us to give them what they ask (and to whom we give something else instead). Researchers and professionals who listen to learning disabled adults will know how insistently they express two particular dissatisfactions: one is with the enforced tutelage ('gentle usage') of having their needs prescribed for them, the other is with labelling. Their social situation enables them, however they express it, to perceive and challenge this close relationship between disadvantage and abstract classification.[6]

Some social policy theorists have criticized the concept of need, but their only strategy has been to redefine it. As our paradigmatic group shows, more radical action is required. The legal category of special educational need is an example. At its core is a subspecies that we define broadly by mental characteristics: the 'special needs child', who carries a resource-allocation tag and, usually, a segregated placement and who comes to be defined by those characteristics. Here, need just means lack. In the case of learning disabilities this is a lack both of the necessary additional resources and of the defining characteristics (mind, rationality) that entitle one to have normal needs. Thus there arises a circular 'theology of lack':[7] first we take something away; then we complain it isn't there; then we invent a theory of (special) need grounded in – and compensating for – its very absence.

On the one hand this rabbit-and-hat procedure is characteristic of the fiscal power play of the last quarter century: the verb to need conjugates *we* need *x*, *you* need *x*, *they* lack resources. On the other hand quantifiable algebraic needs are generalizable and, as such, fundable in concrete instances – but also controllable, with funds channelled to powerful specialisms and institutions. Research not oriented towards needs fulfilment may not be seen as generalizable, and threatens to escape control. History illustrates the values implicated in government-funded research goals and methodologies: 'need' is another specifically modern concept the Greeks didn't have a word for. Nor did Beveridge, as late as 1942. The word, which has become a locust in health, social services and education, migrated only recently from economics. The value term that we do find in Beveridge, in the context where professionals today use need, is 'great evils'.[8] There is a utilitarian link between the two terms: that is, what constitutes an evil or a need for the individual is determined by an ideological account of social dysfunction. This is unproblematical if, as is frequently the case with poverty or physical health, policy makers' assumptions about need match those of the individual recipient. But if they assume, on behalf of the whole society, that certain people are suffering when those individuals say they are not, then to prescribe their needs is to assert power over them: when they say no they mean yes. Merely to have a learning disability, it seems, constitutes suffering and thus a need, although people with learning disabilities may maintain (or behave as if) it is not their lack of understanding that causes them suffering but other people's belief that this is the case. This point is also expressed sometimes by parents: 'the only problem I had was people thinking I had problems'. Thus research with disadvantaged and socially excluded groups has to engage with the possibility that the very concept of need may positively generate exclusion.

The process from evils to needs, from value to method, is self-reproducing. A case study will illustrate. Chloe was not observed to have any problems until she was 3 years old, when it began to be noticed that she did not interact with other children. A year later she was diagnosed as autistic. Her parents were offered a consultation at a national centre specializing in the condition. They discussed the offer of a place for Chloe by a local mainstream school. The psychiatrist's report, attached as medical advice to the local education authority's statement of special educational need for Chloe, said:

> We would not recommend that [Chloe] attends a mainstream school . . .
> We would recommend that she should go to a school for autistic children
> where the focus could be on her problems with social interaction . . . She
> has good fine motor co-ordination. This means that Chloe does not
> have any learning disabilities. We would recommend that her parents
> attend a TEACCH course.

The first part emphasizes segregation, on the assumption that a child with a severe communication disorder will learn social interaction from the exclusive company of other children with a severe communication disorder. The second part offers a casuistry (that this is not a learning disability) and a falsehood (that it has a cure, which an expert programme will supply). The intention may be benevolent, to soothe an anxious parent, but Chloe's mother, asked previously to describe her daughter, had begun with the words, 'She's lovely' and clearly did not need soothing. The proffered possibility of cure may actually generate anxiety, since no programme will make Chloe 'normal' in the restricted individualist sense the psychiatrist is using, and the parents advised to conduct it may blame themselves for its failure. Chloe's father asked the psychiatrist about the significance of the birth complications, but she replied that, 'these were likely to be due to the autism rather than to have caused the autism'. This remark may be connected with the fact that genetic researchers at the same institution are currently looking for a causal link between genetic causes of autism and difficult labours. Seventeenth-century doctors cited the Old Testament to explain how foetuses that kicked heavily in the womb were malevolent, and predicted mental disorder in the child.

Figure 3.1 illustrates the process. The dominant premiss about learning disability is the connection between needs and evils, between a method of resource allocation and the historical values from which it emerges. In the (vertical) political and ethical dimension my work as researcher is represented here as exposing and undermining this premiss. I am constrained by an opposite force, also operating as 'ethics', in the name of protocol and confidentiality. That the psychiatrist's head of unit sits on several research grant committees in the social sciences is a further constraint. The policy apparatus imposes the premiss from above but is itself subject to an opposing force in the form of public discussion and potential links with other emancipatory movements. In the horizontal dimension, the historical origins of the values appear on the left. They are transformed into the social policy abstraction of 'needs', mediating the concrete interests and power of a separate autistic specialism. That is why the criteria for segregation are fiscal rather than purely financial, the question being not 'Do we have the resources?' but rather 'In whose fiefdom do the resources exist?' Chloe's segregation from normal school life, tortuously perceived as facilitating her individual normality, ensures that the historical values will be reproduced, since there will be no accommodation of difference, no expanded concept of normality and no next generation of schoolchildren growing up in an inclusive environment, and therefore no fresh values. Thus while in its short-term political dimension the diagram shuttles from top to bottom and back in a kind of stasis, the longer-term historical dimension from left to right closes a professional and institutional circle.

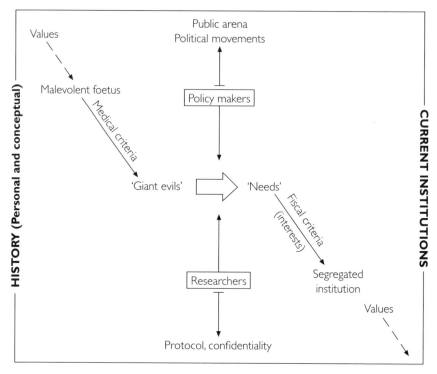

Figure 3.1   *The process from evils to needs*

Is it possible to reorient research goals when a situation is seemingly closed? The notion of difficulty, fortuitously provided by the label 'learning difficulties' in education law, provides some leverage. While the concept of need is algebraic, difficulties are concrete. In qualitative work difficulties must be critically probed rather than just ticked off, whereas research methods based on a concept of need tend to forestall reflexivity or mutual understanding. The notion of difficulty thus has a clearly interactive character. It enables us to see something 'not purely as a consequence of specific characteristics of the child, but of the encounter between child and [context]',[9] and thus to question the supposed division between 'special' (pathological) and normal needs.

We can also use the notion of difficulty to 'study up' the professions and the funding bodies. What constitutes a difficulty for them is partly a private vision, distorting public realities. In the sociology of knowledge, Utopian thought is identified as false consciousness stemming from a particular niche in class society and producing a restricted, ideological account of social reality; we might say the same about dystopian thought, an expression of anxiety just as Utopia is an expression of hope. Dystopian visions of disability are trademarks of clinical and educational assessment. While not every professional may be possessed by such visions, parents often identify them with the professional class as such. They may see professionals as 'not living in the real world' and their own understanding as approximating more to the reality in front of both sets of people, and implicitly as ethical on just those grounds:

> I wouldn't plan a life out for my child . . . My priorities in my mind's eye is better. Their priorities to me is out the window, if you understand my meaning. My priorities in life is smaller, more compact, but their priorities is for about ten, fifteen years from now. God forbid anything should happen to their children, never mind their house, or their car.[10]

Prenatal testing for learning disabilities was justified ethically by the high costs of care for the person who would have been born; this was seen as a hindrance to social progress, expressed in terms of cost effectiveness.[11] This narrowly financial utilitarianism is nourished by a dystopian vision of individual psychology as producing social malaise. It is a descendant of religious utilitarianism, by which the aetiology of the 'idiot' or 'changeling' (the offspring of a sexual liaison with the devil) was a demonic intervention aimed at subverting efficient rule by the godly. Much research funding on learning and other disabilities, not only in health but in social welfare and education, is still informed by such visions, which have passed into modern thought as the pathology corresponding to political norms of autonomy and rational choice.

Certainly we have needs; the abstract concept of need, however, may be a policy device for failing to meet them. This seems particularly true of 'special' needs as a health or social services resource heading. When Jake was born with Down's syndrome and additional physical problems, his parents were told that he would not survive beyond six months. The doctors, while making it clear that this would be for the best, also supplied as much expensive advanced technology as they could towards his survival. At six years old, with a gastrostomy and progressive breathing problems, Jake finally seemed to have only a few weeks to live. The allocated social worker discussed respite care with the parents, who politely expressed reservations, but he arranged it anyway. When they refused to take it, he stopped visiting and later justified this action on the grounds of their refusal. Jake had an ordinary cold, and the doctors' behaviour indicated that they did not want to treat him; his parents insisted, and the doctors' response to this insistence indicates that they perceived it as the parents' failure to accept his impending death. The willingness and ability of both services to prescribe for special needs seems to correlate with a refusal or inability to help with normal needs. The qualitative notion of difficulty, with its concrete focus, challenges the distinction between special and ordinary, between a dystopian and a real world.

Passion and the research process

The prevailing discourse about learning disability combines conservative and liberal traditions of political thought: on the one hand it fulfils needs benevolently, albeit abstractly and at a distance, and on the other it sees people with learning disabilities as a hindrance to progress and works for their elimination. Hence everyday discourse too is contradictory, presenting them as icons of charity in which is hidden a narrative about their incomplete humanity: 'People call us loveable and cuddly. This makes us feel like babies or toys and not adult human beings'.[12] One alternative view is offered by Maria and Baljinder: to be human does not presuppose 'rationality'. Rather, their initiations of social interaction within the research process rest on the supposition that to be human consists in being in the world with other humans. In this respect they demonstrate both understanding and a capability for being agents of change.

A view of community membership as entailing this shared ethics, rather than as being read off from psychological assessment, can inform and unify projects with other disadvantaged groups. (Conversely, research projects with learning disabled people that imitate the model of autonomy and rational consent, can only be limited; grants from the Rowntree Trust currently require that learning disabled people collaborate on research design and aims, but this stipulation is not generalizable because it applies only to people with skills that others within the putative group might lack.) The theoretical framework of development, mind and mental age forces us to think of learning disabilities as a 'developmental plateau'. Current theories speak about 'infantile autism' as the normal condition of all newly born humans; a few do not escape from it, and thus the adult with learning disabilities is said to have the mind of a child. A critique of this theory might also be a critique of received notions of childhood in general and of its disadvantaged status.

Incurable learning disability can also help with anti-relativist arguments, which seem aimed against the distinct cultures of disadvantaged groups. Defining our species by mental ability suits ideas of absolute truth (and absolute power): if the species is defined by rationality and intelligence, these cannot be relative or changeable for different members of the same species. However, the very existence of learning disabilities in someone could be seen as the defining criterion of their species membership; precisely because they are disabilities in those respects which define us as human, they show that such people have a human 'form of life' and not that of some other species.[13] This allows us the insight that beyond the idea of a unified rationality and intelligence and also beyond the postmodernist perception of these as dependent anthropologically upon 'cultures', there can be a unifying, absolute characteristic to the species that is still nevertheless cultural.

We might call this 'deep culture'.[14] With national and local authority resourcing, the relativistic cultures of disadvantaged groups may turn into competition between them. The abstract concept of need has instilled a belief that additional resources for the disabled or elderly must be withdrawn from, say, sickle-cell or HIV–AIDS funding, or vice versa. There seems to be a set of corresponding localist ideologies: black activists who are homophobic; misogynistic gay men; feminists defending abortion rights with demonic perceptions of disability; physically disabled campaigners dissociating themselves from the learning disabled; and any number of groups denying the radical qualifications that social class imposes upon their own make-up. Some of these images are themselves stereotypes, but if academics working with or from within a particular group assert the identity and difficulties of their own group by trivializing those of others, they risk reinforcing those stereotypes. The path from postmodernism to the market is hardly difficult. Researchers operating with a notion of 'deep culture' can avoid the competitive politics that needs assessment sometimes imposes. To assert that this notion is supplied by people with incurable learning disabilities and their defining humanity is not to claim pre-eminence for a particular group yet again. The paradigm is simply illustrative, with practical indications for other groups. Positivist notions of learning disability are a fundamental problem for women and black people, for example. Some psychologists continue to say that black people have lower IQs than white; as the claim is buried, so it rises again. The sterilization of young women with learning disabilities is a well known issue;[15] single motherhood has its accompanying psychological stereotypes. It would clearly be more helpful for all socially excluded groups to have a critical view of what constitutes a learning disability than just to deny that one's own group deserves to be tarred with it. A positive category of learning disability is one that can be drawn on in future to render any other group, in Orlando Patterson's phrase, 'physically alive but socially dead'.[16]

The political character of the research process extends inwards, to the 'passion' and 'violence' which, Weber claimed (*The Profession of Politics*), result from the lack of ultimately determining rules or sanctions in politics. Members of disadvantaged groups need passion and a kind of violence to be included in mainstream life and social institutions. Researchers too, constantly jostled off balance by the external compulsions described above, may be driven by empathy and anger. Even where researchers are not organic members of the group they research with, the term 'disadvantage' inevitably evokes justice, which is an emotional prompt to become (if we were not before) facilitators and advocates. However, our motives are also perceived in this way by policy makers, and our partisanship may cause us not to be taken seriously. Citing researchers' passion in order to deny their credibility may go beyond appropriate caveats about objectivity; it can suggest that questions of justice are irrelevant to social policy, or deny that social science is also interactive and ethical. By contrast, for the research and advocacy roles to unify could mean that our work would be not just emancipatory of particular groups, but effective and influential on a broader policy scale.

Conclusion

How can we ensure that policy makers take us seriously while we still take seriously the group we research with and their lives? How do we persuade them that this group may have theoretical understandings and perceptions of social reality that could cure policy makers' special anxieties about the very dysfunction that they think the group embodies? How do we do this without neglecting any 'needs' the group may actually have? In Tarkovsky's film, *Solaris*, humans land on a distant planet expecting to find aliens, but simply find themselves entangled in the moral consequences of the Earthly lives from which they have run away. Policy makers and professionals sometimes have a dys/Utopian vision of themselves as approaching a planet inhabited by strange, inferior and untrustworthy beings, when in fact they need to learn that this planet just consists of themselves and their society as they really are. The job of the researcher landing with them is to help them trust and learn from the inhabitants. Or perhaps this is a Utopian view of research.

Notes

1 Examples drawn from P. Alderson and C. Goodey (1996) Research with Disabled Children, *Children & Society* 10 (2): 106–17.
2 M. Weber (1920) *The Profession of Politics*.
3 For an example see J. Bicknell (1988) The psychopathology of handicap, in G. Horobin and D. May (eds) *Living with Mental Handicap*. London: Jessica Kingsley.
4 See C. Goodey (1996) The psychopolitics of learning and disability, in A. Digby and D. Wright (eds) *From Idiocy to Mental Deficiency*. London: Routledge.
5 D. Hume (1777) *An Enquiry Concerning the Principles of Morals*. London: Macmillan, 1948, p. 190.
6 People First (1995) *Oi, It's My Assessment*. London: People First.
7 D. Shapiro (1996) 'If Only I Had a Brain'. Internet: University of Washington.
8 J. Bradshaw (1995) The conceptualization and measurement of need, in J. Popay and G. Williams (eds), *Researching the People's Health*. London: Routledge.
9 S. Hart (1996) *Beyond Special Needs*. London: Paul Chapman. I am also indebted to Tony Booth for discussions on this subject.
10 C. Goodey (1991) *Living in the Real World: Families Speak about Down's Syndrome*. London: Twenty-One Press.

11 N. Wald (1988) Maternal serum screening for Down's Syndrome in early pregnancy, *British Medical Journal*, 297: 883–7.

12 People First (1996) *Not Just Painted On: A Report on the First Ever Conference Run by and for People with Down's Syndrome*. London: People First.

13 L. Wittgenstein (1980) *Remarks on the Philosophy of Psychology*. Oxford: Blackwell.

14 C. Goodey (1997) Learning difficulties and the guardians of the gene, in A. Clarke and E. Parsons (eds) *Culture, Kinship and Genes*. London: Macmillan.

15 People First (1996) *Women First*. London: People First.

16 O. Patterson (1994) *Slavery and Social Death: A Comparative Study*. Cambridge, MA: Harvard University Press.

4

▷ Disturbed young people:
research for what,
research for whom?

▷ **Priscilla Alderson**

Introduction

Each year, thousands of young people are permanently excluded from
school for being disruptive. Official figures rose from about 3,000 in 1989–
90 to over 13,500 in 1995–6.[1] While disabled pupils are moving from special
schools into mainstream ones, special schools are filling up with pupils
assessed as having emotional and behavioural disturbance, difficulty or
disorder (EBD).[2] The questionable term 'EBD' is used generally, and also for
brevity in this paper, to refer to individuals, special schools and their staff,
and general EBD services and policies. Many EBD students have a statement of special educational need (SEN) written by teachers, psychologists
and doctors. The involvement of doctors shows how EBD is perceived as a
partly medical condition. Public concern about quasi-medical conditions like
attention deficit hyperactivity disorder, and its treatment with drugs like
Ritalin, has recently increased. In some American states, 3–5 per cent, and
in the UK maybe 1 per cent, of all primary school children are estimated to
be taking prescribed stimulants.[3]

The apparent increase in behaviour problems raises these questions.
Have many more young people become badly behaved and disturbed? If
so, why? If not, why have measures of disturbance, such as school exclusions, risen so much, and what part has research played in these increases?
What does EBD actually mean, and how can it best be defined, assessed
and treated? Research about EBD mainly measures incidence through psychological tests and teachers' and parents' estimations,[4] which, as discussed
later, raise and construct problems. Why has there been so little of the
alternative 'micro-level' research about young people's own perspectives,

linked to 'macro-level' research about the social and political context of rising rates of EBD? These questions are discussed in relation to two main traditions in research: positivism linked with functionalism; and social construction linked with critical theory. The latter pair is illustrated by a few examples from our recent research about students' and adults' views and experiences of special and ordinary schools.[5] The contrasting research processes and conclusions about EBD are considered.

Traditions in research methods and theories about EBD

'Theories' here include explicit research questions and also implicit assumptions about the nature and purpose of behaviour and disturbance in people and schools. Choice of theories and methods is crucial and shapes all later stages including research findings, although the choice is often assumed and its effects unacknowledged. This section contrasts two broad research traditions and defines them through comparing them. It begins with a note on the achievements of positivism in medical research. With tuberculosis, for example, positivist research has:

1 identified the bacillus;
2 developed methods of diagnosis;
3 shown predictive factors that cause or increase incidence of the disease in order to aid prevention;
4 developed effective drugs;
5 tested them in trials.

Yet complications arise when positivist methods are used in research where:

1 the 'disease', like EBD, is not visible or even clearly definable;[6]
2 diagnoses vary widely and are contested;
3 'predictions' that stigmatize and work as negative self-fulfilling prophesies risk increasing the incidences;[7]
4 there is no agreed treatment;[8]
5 and it is impossible to test such ill defined, complex and elusive phenomena through rigorous trials.

The following summaries briefly define the two broad research approaches by comparing them.

Positivist functionalist research

Positivist functionalist research tends to assume the following. Disturbed behaviours are quantifiable facts to be recorded in surveys and some behaviours are grouped into diagnoses.[9] Experts decide which diagnosis fits each person and the person can be fitted (reduced) to a genetic or behavioural type.[10] The disturbed person is the problem, and the function-alist intention of diagnosis is benign: to contain, care and perhaps cure and restore normality. The overriding concern is to ensure the efficient func-tioning of society, for instance by removing a small disruptive minority from mainstream schools. A biological model of cause and predictable effect is favoured, preferably according to general laws such as physiolo-gical or familial patterns, to explain EBD. Complicated, varied 'macro' details of the social and political contexts and 'micro' details of individual responses and motives tend to be ignored. Standardized, impersonal approaches are also recommended in 'objective' methods of enquiry in ques-tionnaires and interviews. Parents' and teachers' estimations are recorded and measured. Disturbed young people's views are seen as irrational and their protests are simply evidence of disturbance. After assessment, in accordance with the medical model, treatment is provided in centres of expertise. The whole EBD system of special and excluding schools is based on these solid assumptions.

Social construction and critical theory research

In contrast, social construction and critical theory research tends to assume the following. Many phenomena are fluid social constructions rather than firm facts, and all the above positivist assumptions are questionable the-ories, which researchers have to examine critically. Critical theory questions functionalist assumptions about power: that professionals are inevitably benign experts and that disturbed people are a deviant minority who must be excluded or restored to 'normality'. EBD is a social construction in the way it is identified, perceived and evoked by relationships and situations.[11] A single act, such as striking another person, can be seen as reasonable self-defence or dangerous provocation, prudent or crazy, trivial or serious, due punishment, play, sport, aggression or unacceptable violence. If beha-viours are recorded without reference to context, purpose or motive, as in many positivist accounts, they easily look bizarre. An example is a psychi-atric report of a girl throwing a chair at her stepfather, with no mention of what he did before the action.[12] She might have been acting in self-defence. Teachers' reactions vary, as their pupils reported, according to pressures on them, personality, their moods and favouritism. Classes in EBD schools behave well with one teacher and disrupt another's lessons. Many 'dis-turbed' young people see themselves, and are seen by others, as 'normal', and some stoically endure severe difficulties not of their own making.

It then follows that the way behaviours are defined and assessed can be contentious, and more so when they are grouped into vague, broad diagnoses. A behavioural diagnosis can be influenced more by the assessor's beliefs than the actual behaviours or how intense or frequent disturbed episodes are, so that claims to expertise in EBD rest on questionable knowledge and not on solid research or textual or empirical knowledge. People are far more complex than any category they are assigned to, and their many capacities and interests may be forgotten if there is undue attention to a few of their ascribed negative qualities. Problems arise through interactions between people, so that one individual alone is not the whole problem and remedies depend on also addressing the context. Interventions to diagnose (and blame) and to treat (often by control and punishment) can harm the person; they can increase and even create disturbed behaviours.

To remove a few disturbed students allows mainstream schools and society to ignore the need to improve excluding schools in order to prevent and reduce problems that affect many other students adversely. Before they can do this, professionals have to move from impersonal cause–effect predictions towards examining individuals' motives and reactions, including their own, as well as possible broader influences such as the great increase in poverty among children and teenagers, the demands of the new education 'market', and pressures to meet government targets.[13] This involves willingness to learn from disturbed young people and respect their views. Impersonal mass questioning methods can alienate them and evoke disturbed responses. Some degree of mutual respect and trust is essential for any honest communication, so that relations within interviews are part of the research methods and data.

Parents', teachers' and psychologists' estimations, the bases of positivist surveys, are known to differ; they are not neutral and may exaggerate reports of disturbance to gain more resources. Therefore effects on research of adults' own motives and vested interests should be acknowledged. Special EBD schools, as 'centres of expertise', are limited by being unable to address the problems that initiated the disturbance, and the staff rarely have greater insight, skill or techniques than skilled mainstream teachers. Also, to return to the first point, knowledge about EBD mainly consists of opinions not facts.

The goals of research: for what, for whom?

The contrasting approaches have complex and broadly different goals, which are here roughly summarized. Positivism and functionalism dominate research, the funding bodies and journals. These traditions observe justice by affirming the authority of benevolent expertise to diagnose, survey and treat pathology, and ensure compliance.[14] The goal is to increase professional expertise in order to maintain the normal functioning of a well-regulated society. Punishment may be advised to deter and reform the deviant few, but research is assumed to be in everyone's interests, or at least the interests of the great majority.

Social constructionists' main goal is to develop knowledge, partly by deconstructing positivist assumptions. They tend to avoid making explicit judgements or policy recommendations, by eschewing the question 're-search for whom?', although they initiate important debates.

Critical theory observes justice by advocating a more equal redistribution of power and resources towards disadvantaged groups. It does so by interpreting social construction theories within a view of a divided society where professional expertise is used to further powerful interests. The question 'research for whom?' only really arises if the interests are seen to conflict, for example, between professionals and their clients, students or patients.[15] The question then raises disturbing dilemmas: whether and how to report and analyse conflict; how to demonstrate that the evidence supports critical and unpopular findings; and how to reconcile the important values of impartial research on the one hand, with honest accounts of injustice informed by explicit value judgements on the other. One dilemma is how strongly to word critical research reports so that they identify problems without simply provoking angry dismissal. Positivists tend to avoid these dilemmas by denying that their research is value-laden, or by assuming that their values are an uncontroversial consensus. This makes it harder for critical theorists to report their research when it runs counter to the complacent 'evidence' of most research, and also when it appears to betray traditions of mutual support between researchers and practitioners.

I started research about special schools expecting most to cater for physical, sensory and learning disabilities, but found that they mainly relate to EBD. All my previous research had been in health areas and not in education. The visits were so disturbing that critical theory appeared to be the only relevant research approach. The research goals became to explain the great discrepancies between the rhetoric and the reality in EBD schools, and to compare our observations of segregating systems with more efficient integrating ones.

The research process

The stages of our research about EBD are reviewed here to illustrate critical theory research.

Research design and setting

We began at the 'micro-level', talking with students aged 8 to 15 and their parents in their homes about their experiences and views. We met young people with physical or sensory disabilities and learning or emotional difficulties, and observed them in their special and mainstream schools, and interviewed school and LEA staff. On a 'macro-level', our research compares policy and practice in two very different local education authorities (LEAs). The semi-rural West County is an affluent and almost entirely white area with many schools that select for ability, sex and religion, including special, grammar, grant maintained and private schools. In the other LEA, East City, average family incomes are far lower and many people belong to ethnic minority groups. This LEA has closed all but one special school and redirected funds into all-ability-range schools that are very well resourced, with much staff support and training for inclusive and differential teaching methods, aimed at making lessons relevant and challenging to all-ability-range classes. Despite closing all the EBD schools and including EBD students in mainstream classes (with extra staff support for the most disturbed ones), this LEA has reduced exclusion rates, and has risen to the top of the government's school improvement table.

The term 'EBD' was rarely used by families in East City. Philip and Sean, now doing well in mainstream secondary schools, and their parents gave typical accounts of initial problems in infant school. These were resolved by support from special assistants in mainstream classes, where class teachers encouraged and negotiated with them, instead of 'winding them up'. Although they still quickly become stressed and angry, Philip and Sean have learnt to manage their feelings and to enjoy an ordinary school and social life. In West County, hundreds of pupils attend EBD schools and hardly any return to mainstream school.

Funding

The research was funded by the Gatsby Trust, who considered our 50-page final report on the inadequacies of special schools, and the benefits of integrated education in the schools observed, to be controversial. They decided that evidence and analysis to support the critical conclusions should be presented in greater detail, to allow readers to draw their own conclusions, so they provided us with funds to write a book and related papers.

Access

We aimed to approach 45 families through informal networks, because we wanted to hear their independent views, and did not want to be identified with the education services or seen as authority figures. A few families were found quickly and interviewed and they referred us to others, but eventually we had to approach some through the schools. Families responded warmly through East City comprehensive schools and through informal contacts in both LEAs. For example, Lucy's father responded to a telephone call, 'Yes, come round now,' and the family talked for over three hours. However, no parent contacted through special EBD, autism and learning difficulty schools, including Lucy's school, replied. This may relate to their feelings about being associated with the school. One argument advanced for referral to special schools is that staff and parents can work more closely together. All the parents interviewed about EBD schools spoke of the great gulf between them and the staff, as if having a child classified as EBD made parents feel, and become, distanced and excluded; one effect was to silence and exclude them from research when formal opt-in methods through schools were used.

Access to schools varied, and in some cases took months. Given the many demands and stresses on teachers I was grateful for their permission and help. However, schools are the main access route for researchers to young people, and teachers can present formidable barriers to such research. Some teachers were very friendly and helpful, but in the EBD schools they tended to be somewhat hostile and defensive. It is as if they see themselves as guardians of morality, with such disturbed students that the value of the teachers' work is self-evident, and any questioning of it must be discouraged.

Consent and ethics

Formal ethics requirements intended to protect vulnerable people can also exclude them. With the pupils' and parents' consent, we taped interviews and made home visits. Without parents' consent we only observed and talked informally with pupils at school. Ethics guidelines advise obtaining the parents' consent in research with minors under 18, as well as the minors' consent.[16] Opt-in methods are preferred by ethics committees, who assume that these enable people to decide much more freely whether to take part in research, but these can silence many minors, as well as groups who prefer informal personal spoken contact, who seldom read or reply to formal notes or book future appointments.

Informal contacts can set people at their ease and avoid the embarrassed or disturbed responses that formal approaches, including those required by ethics committees, risk provoking. In East City, the researcher called on families and they spontaneously gave a detailed interview; at one home other callers casually dropped in, including one who was selling dresses. The interview (we believe) occurred on terms the family was used to. The conversation was as between neighbours, with jokes about the dresses, in which Stacey, who has learning difficulties and also appears to be obviously different at school, joined on an equal level with everyone else at home.

One example of how conventional ethics standards can silence seldom heard groups was given by Elizabeth. At her EBD school at lunch time, she offered to show me how to buy a lunch ticket and took me to sit next to her. She showed me round the school, the grounds and the boarding areas, and agreed to tape two interviews. She lives with her father in the holidays but is worried that 'he'll chuck me out anytime'. From interviews and observations (which there is not space here to relate), she seemed, like other students, to be at the school because of her disturbed family rather than because she was disturbed. Initially the head teacher, care staff and her father agreed to the interviews but later, although Elizabeth, by now 16, was keen to continue, they withdrew permission, without regard for her wishes, right to freedom of expression or right to share in making decisions that affect her.[17] There is an impasse, in that barriers imposed by adults will remain until researchers, among others, enable young people's views to be more widely heard and policies to change, and these barriers partly prevent the research and changes that could shift them.

One solution to rules of consent is that, as long as the research has been approved by an ethics committee as respectful of teenagers and not against their interests, parents' consent need not be sought. Ethics committees could raise standards of research with young people by involving them in reviewing protocols and by asking, 'Who is this research for? How might it help young people? Whose interests will be served?'[18]

Data collection

I gave short leaflets to all potential interviewees and staff and explained the research to classes and staff. In the leaflet, *What school is best for me?*, we said we were looking at young people's views about their special or ordinary school in two different LEAs. I sat with the pupils during lessons as unobtrusively as possible, while gaining vivid examples of the experiences and relationships in each school. Despite my explanations, the staff did not seem to realize that all they said or did could be relevant. Paradoxically, the more the EBD staff exerted their own power, such as by shouting reprimands and insults, the more they exposed themselves. And the more powerless they perceived me to be and tried to make me feel, the more they revealed themselves. They were far less guarded than they would be with, say, an Office for Standards in Education (Ofsted) inspector. Consciously or not, they tried to control me and sometimes put me in the position of the EBD students. The most disturbing were examples of what I thought of as the 'lynch mob syndrome'. All observers were drawn by an angry teacher to share in condemning a culprit for an offence, sometimes after an unjust accusation: 'What are you? You are a very, very naughty girl. The whole class [looking round the room] thinks that you are very, very naughty.' I felt angry to be used in this way, anger the sullen students appeared to share, and I felt trapped into being used as a jury through powerfully revealing psychodynamics that are the essence of the construction of EBD.

Another challenge was to maintain the permission and reasonable co-operation of EBD staff, but also the goodwill and trust of the students, and it was hard to satisfy both sides. Paradoxically, the most feared teachers seemed to have less confidence about their power, as if they constantly had to reassert it through rows. Some appeared to resent my presence but perhaps felt that if they sent me away they would lose face. If I sensed such reluctance among pupils I would move away from them, but I left people in authority to tell me their preferences.

In a system of compulsory education, all schools share in some forms of enforcement, but special schools are the only ones to which LEAs can legally force parents to send their children.[19] They illustrate Luke's first and least type of power: enforcement against obvious resistance.[20] The second type is mis-framing choices, and the third most powerful type is concealing knowledge so that people comply because they are unaware of choices they would otherwise make. The two latter types occur when professionals who write SEN statements tell parents they 'have no alternative . . . this is the only school that will take your child'. The least powerful people are the students when EBD is assumed to be their fault and adults do not inform or consult with them about options. Our evidence shows that students at EBD schools can be informed and reasonable.

The harder EBD school staff punish resistant students, the more obdurate some of them become. Examining this partly invisible power play became the key to understanding how innovative, inclusive schools succeed in resolving behaviour problems where EBD schools, which emphasize students' failings, inevitably fail. Inclusive schools exploit positive aspects of power such as the creative energy of staff and students, by treating everyone in the school as potentially a responsible agent and involving everyone in setting and helping to maintain high standards in the school, instead of pitting staff against students.[21]

Examples from interviews and observations

The following examples from an EBD boarding school illustrate conflicts between staff and students. A head teacher explains the discipline system, then some girls describe the system, followed by a research note.

HT: We try to create as stress free an environment as possible. We appreciate that many of the girls have a background of conflict and abuse, they really struggle with rejection by their families . . . It is a boarding education coping with all the factors which prevent learning behaviour . . . A child may refuse to learn and we try to get to personal development through that. We quite often find that we can make a break-through in the classroom; you've seen yourself that there is a continuity through the day, that they get used to being the butt of jokes, bullying. That affects their confidence. When they first come they are badly affected and then they blossom, those that have reached that plateau. We are mindful of their needs. We're kind to them, we look after them, we like them, and in a way this cushions their behaviour. We're trying to fill in all the gaps, repair all the damage . . .

PA: How do you reduce stress?

HT: Confidence is one thing. We've got girls who for years overreacted to people teasing them. And now because they've developed, and become more confident, more mature, what people say to them doesn't matter now. They've moved beyond that . . . Just over a year ago we decided to work on personal behaviour more . . . We were trained in behaviour management.

PA: You were trained?

HT: Yes, by X, a local educational psychologist . . . and he advised a behaviour modification system (BMS), to give added structure and security for the girls. So right at the beginning we thought we'd involve the girls, and we asked them, 'In what way do you want us to reward you and in what ways do you want us to sanction you? Do you want to be treated separately according to your behaviour?' Yes. There was a massive reaction. Some of the suggestions were quite outrageous, some of them were very sound, and we'd take some of the girls' suggestions and we put together a continually emerging package.

Girls commented on the BMS.

Someone tells a teacher you've done something and you get a cross, and when you try to say you didn't do it you get another cross, so it's not worth trying.

I'm often on one star, I get up a bit and then go down again. I'd rather be on three star, then you can go out of the school with your friend.

I've been trying all week to get enough ticks to move up a star, but they count them all up today and I won't get enough.

They have BMS on the floors [boarding areas] so you never get away from it.

If we get one single cross we stay on base for an extra week unless we get 11 ticks. On five star you only have to get one cross to go down, on four you only have to get two crosses, and on three star you have to get ten or more crosses, I think.

Crosses cancel out ticks but ticks don't cancel out crosses, you can't do it that way . . . There's a new rule, if you go down you don't go back to the level you came from, you have to work your way back up . . . It is easier to go down because if you're on five stars and you get one cross you go down to four; if you're on four stars and you get two crosses you go down to three. If you get 10 crosses you're base, or two; I can't remember, and to go up you can only go to two anyway. And it is hard.

When the teachers shout at you, the girls get so angry they shout back and the teachers don't like it. And if you say something and the teacher shouts and you say, 'Don't shout,' she takes it the wrong way and says, 'Right, you get a cross!' And one teacher said, 'You get a cross,' and the girl turned round and said, 'I haven't done nothing.' The teacher said, 'You're still getting a cross.' It's like, a person wants to go to the toilet. She asks the teacher can she go? The teacher doesn't answer, so they walk off and go to the toilet. And when you get back and the teacher says, 'Right, you get a cross.' And everyone thinks it's so stupid, 'cause every time you do something you get a cross for it. We don't like it. We think it's stupid. For the little ones, yes, but the grown ups, no, 'cause I think we should behave ourselves. We should learn without needing this.

My research fieldnote commented on the BMS system.

The complications in BMS could increase its power (Foucault on appropriating rules of power,[22] Seligman on learned helplessness) so that the more confused and therefore helpless the girls feel, the more control the staff have.[23] The girls' uncertainties and constant sense of being watched appeared to make them feel cautious, anxious, intro-spective and self-doubting, rather than secure as the head teacher believed. When asked about permitted activities, the typical reply was, 'I don't know, you have to ask.' The staff seemed to be much less self-conscious than their pupils, who repeated, 'I must keep my anger.' Teachers shouted furious reprimands, as when one reproved a girl for spreading false accusations about someone. 'Don't you dare tell any-one else! That is one cross, and another for everyone you have told!' The reprimands continued during break time in front of the whole school for several minutes, ensuring that everyone would know about the accusation. The girl looked down. 'Look at me!' shouted the teacher, glaring at her. The pupils tried to look impassive, but they were in a double bind; if they cried they looked guilty, if they did not they seemed hardened impenitents.

Contradictions are raised by differing definitions and assessments of EBD, and by the head teacher's account of BMS as a 'secure' system but also a 'continually emerging one'. His reference to girls learning to tolerate bullying could be his justification of taunts by staff, which another teacher described as 'being friendly'. The teacher who advert-ises a secret while punishing a girl for spreading it contradicts herself.

Even when staff try to measure a girl's behaviour by counting ticks and crosses they are actually measuring staff reactions.

Data analysis and writing up

Researchers have the power to misrepresent and abuse subjects when they interpret, selectively report and publicize the data, and when the media, for example, broadcast derogatory research findings that further stigmatize vulnerable groups. Almost everyone in EBD schools is drawn into stressful, self-exposing animosities, which the head teachers, at least, gave us permission to observe. We have obligations to conceal the individuals' and schools' identity, and to report them as fairly as possible, which we do mainly in their own words, in our longer research reports.

Yet we also have obligations to show adverse aspects of EBD schools, injustice and inefficiencies, and to question the language of 'special' schools: special resources, special staff training and expertise, special liaison with families, a special haven from ordinary school stresses and special whole school policies. 'Special' implies something extra and better than ordinary, and yet the EBD schools we observed were less and worse. The central problem is not individual teachers' attitudes, but inevitable structures in special and excluding schools and most LEAs that label and herd away together groups of pupils with difficulties, and provide meagre resources and mediocre staff so that students then lose the chance to be ordinary people.

Conclusion: whose interests are served?

Despite lip service to inclusion, the language of exclusion, misleadingly dressed up as 'special' and 'parental choice', now dominates policy. The current education literature under-reports the parlous state of EBD schools, and the very high cost of EBD schools places, and glosses over special education experts' vested interests. Positivist approaches dominate research programmes, funding and academic journals, public policy, the mass media and public opinion. Politicians prefer to present uncomfortable political value choices as an expert technical decision: 'Of course, we are for social inclusion and experts assure us that the best way to achieve this is to have special EBD schools.'

Some reports cited in this chapter examine the problems we report yet in the current concern with efficiency and effectiveness, adult leadership and fast practical solutions to EBD, policy makers and professionals appear to have little time for analysis of the assumptions on which policy is based.

These mistaken assumptions include the following: that EBD is a psychological fact and not a social construction; that EBD is a helpful diagnosis and not a political device for managing non-conforming students; that rates of EBD are rising, although they have been fairly constant for the past century;[24] that school records accurately record the incidence of EBD, although they contribute to the apparent increase through new pressures to record truancy and examination failure among students who were formerly hardly visible.

EBD schools are very disturbing to witness, analyse and report. It is disturbing to grasp and convey these complex problems, and the urgent need for new solutions. Critical research helps educators to move beyond misleading assumptions, to examine the views and experiences of the teenagers most directly involved and to consider how to work with them in more positive ways.

Acknowledgements

I am grateful to the Gatsby Charitable Foundation for funding the research; which I conducted with Chris Goodey, and to the hundreds of people who helped with the project.

Notes

1 Clear official records are not kept. Schools Minister's report to National Children's Bureau Conference. *Guardian*, 10 July 1996, p. 10.

2 B. Norwich (1994) *Segregation and Inclusion: English LEA Statistics*. Bristol: Centre for Studies in Inclusive Education.

3 F. Levy (1997) Attention deficit hyperactivity disorder. *British Medical Journal*, 315: 894–5.

4 M. Rutter, J. Tizard and K. Whitmore (1970) *Education, Health and Behaviour*. London: Longman.

5 P. Alderson and C. Goodey (1998) *Enabling Education: Experiences in Special and Ordinary Schools*. London: the Tufnell Press.

6 House of Commons (1997) *Child and Adolescent Mental Health Services*. London: HMSO.

7 F. Musgrove (1984) *Youth and Social Order*. London: Routledge; R.P. Dobash and R.E. Dobash (1986) *The Imprisonment of Women*. Oxford: Blackwell; P. Alderson (1996) Sociological aspects of adolescent health and illness, in A. MacFarlane (ed.) *Adolescent Medicine*. London: Royal College of Physicians.

8 NHS Health Advisory Service on Services for Disturbed Adolescents (1986) *Bridges Over Troubled Waters*. London: HMSO.

9 Classifications include the ICD-10 (World Health Organisation 1992) one or the DSM-IV (American Psychiatric Association 1994) one.

10 S. Rose (1995) The rise of neurogenetic determinism. *Nature* 373: 380–82.

11 D. Galloway, D. Armstrong and S. Tomlinson (1994) *Assessing Special Educational Needs: Whose Problem?* London: Longman.

12 In re R (a minor) [1991] 3 WLR full legal report of the case.
13 T. Jeffs (1996) Children's education rights in a new era?, in B. Franklin (ed.) *The Handbook of Children's Rights*. London: Routledge.
14 S. Tomlinson (1982) *A Sociology of Special Education*. London: Routledge.
15 A. Gouldner (1977) *The Coming Crisis of Western Sociology*. London: Heinemann.
16 Royal College of Physicians (1990) *Research Involving Patients*. London: Royal College of Physicians.
17 Children Act, 1989. London: HMSO; United Nations Convention on the Rights of the Child (1989) Articles 12 and 13.
18 P. Alderson (1995) *Listening to Children: Ethics and Social Research*. Barkingside: Barnardo's.
19 Education Acts 1974, 1981, 1988. Department of Education, London: HMSO.
20 S. Lukes (1974) *Power: A Radical View*. Basingstoke: Macmillan, Chap. 1.
21 Highfield School (1997) P. Alderson (ed.) (1997) *Changing Our School: Promoting Positive Behaviour*. London: Institute of Education/Plymouth; Highfield School; S. McNamara and G. Morton (1995) *Changing Behaviour: Teaching Children With EBD in Primary and Secondary Classrooms*. London: David Fulton.
22 M. Foucault (1979) *Discipline and Punish*. Harmondsworth: Peregrine.
23 M. Seligman (1975) *Helplessness*. San Francisco: Freeman.
24 T. Williams (1985) *Troubled Behaviour*. Milton Keynes: Open University Press.

5

'Unhistoric acts': women's private past

A. Susan Williams

The 'growing good of the world is partly dependent on unhistoric acts', observes George Eliot in the final sentence of *Middlemarch* (1871–2), her novel of provincial life in mid-nineteenth-century Britain. These 'unhistoric acts' are the stuff of her narrative, which celebrates the unsung contributions of ordinary people in their daily life: 'that things are not so ill with you and me as they might have been', she writes, 'is half owing to the number who lived faithfully a hidden life, and rest in unvisited tombs'. The heroine of the novel, Dorothea, exemplifies this faithful and hidden life; she is extraordinary in terms of her gifts and humanity, but is destined to live an ordinary life because of the limited opportunities available to her as a woman. When her husband Will becomes 'an ardent public man', Eliot comments wryly: 'Many who knew her, thought it a pity that so substantive and rare a creature should have been absorbed into the life of another, and be only known in a certain circle as a wife and mother. But no one stated exactly what else that was in her power she ought rather to have done'.[1]

This raises an important question about the meaning of 'historic' and 'unhistoric': what criteria should be met by the acts of the past in order to qualify for entry into the pages of history? This chapter will attempt to examine this question, exploring the role of the historian in relation to 'the number who lived faithfully a hidden life, and rest in unvisited tombs'. It will equate this 'hidden life' with the private and domestic sphere, to which Dorothea was confined, away from public space. The full-time inhabitants of the private sphere are nearly always the least powerful members of society – women, children, the poor and unemployed – whose world lies outside official institutions and operates in domains like the family, workplace, street and popular culture. Women in Britain have been made the specific focus of this chapter, as a way of probing a large and problematic area within a limited word count.

Defining the focus of research

The history of women can be seen in many ways as the history of an invisible sphere running parallel to that of men. Fifth-century Athens offers an instructive illustration of this: although praised as the cradle of *demo*cracy (ruled by the people), it was actually an *andro*cracy (ruled by men, at least those occupying the more powerful strata of society). Most of the population – women and slaves – were excluded from civic life. They produced virtually none of the ancient Greek literature that informs Western culture,[2] and it is impossible to know much about their lives except through the eyes of men; and even this source of information is limited, since men mostly chose to write about themselves. When women *were* their subject, they were also their object: as mothers, wives, lovers, daughters and sisters.

'Public' opinion has prioritized the public world over domestic space. 'Personal relationships', comments Ann Oakley, a feminist sociologist and novelist, 'have no political significance only to those who deny the importance of private lives in shaping identity and moral values. The home doesn't matter much, except as a retreat from the public world, only to those who aren't responsible for it'.[3] This observation is made in *Man & Wife*, an account of the relationship before and during the Second World War between her parents, Kay Titmuss and Richard Titmuss, the social policy analyst who helped to found Britain's welfare state. The book is effectively a case study of the private and public spheres and examines the relationship and conflict between the world of the home and the world outside.

Despite a widespread ambivalence towards domestic life that often verges on contempt, the private sphere of society has been increasingly scrutinized over the twentieth century, especially by sociologists. Interest in social scientific research between the wars led to the founding of Mass Observation in 1937, which observed and reported on contemporary social phenomena. After the war, feminist researchers gave a new recognition to the private world of women, through a respectful scrutiny of the daily routine of ordinary women's lives. Typical of this approach is Ann Oakley's *Housewife*, published in the mid-1970s, which examines the housewife role and the ways in which housewives are seen by society and how they see themselves.

Historiography too has embraced the idea of making visible a strand of life that was previously hidden from view. Socialist historians and those working in the area of women's black history have established social history as an authoritative field of inquiry that seeks to give an account of ordinary people's lives.[4] Previously, their cultural reality had not been documented by the writing elites, the powerful or the state, whose history had been overwhelmingly and falsely represented as the history of the whole community.[5] Now, at the end of the twentieth century, any scholar wishing to qualify as a feminist historian will treat with respect the history of the private and 'ordinary' past. Sheila Rowbotham, whose research and analysis has pushed forward feminist historiography since the publication in 1973 of *Hidden From History*, published *A Century of Women* in 1997, which contains a detailed section on 'daily life' for each period of the twentieth century. Rowbotham observes that, 'The growth of women's history in the last twenty-five years has fused personal memories and oral testimony, shifting the focus of interest and highlighting women's experience. This has been part of an ongoing recasting of historical "knowledge"'.[6] This recasting has in most cases been deliberate: the feminist historian Carol Dyhouse writes that one of her major purposes in writing *Girls Growing Up in Late Victorian and Edwardian England* was 'to show that the majority of girls living in the period 1860–1920 received at least a crucial part – if not the major part – of their education in the family, and not through schooling of any kind'.[7] Her work is self-consciously different from most histories of women's education, because it looks closely at girls' experiences in the non-public sector and attempts to place these in a broader social context.

This work has been exciting and ground breaking – but it also tends towards the simply anthropological. The time has now come for historians to look afresh at the operation of the private sphere and to extend and deepen their analysis. What has been its role in the functioning of society? Has it contributed overall to the 'growing good of the world', to use Eliot's words, or held it back? The interwar novelist and feminist Virginia Woolf argued in her essay *Three Guineas* that the 'private figure' is as important as the 'public world'.[8] Eleanor Rathbone, a contemporary of Woolf and a feminist social reformer who was an Independent member of parliament, underlined the dynamic nature of this private sphere when she described the spread of information about birth control as the passing of 'the torch from hand to hand',[9] at a time when the state sector and 'public' opinion were opposed to contraception. Mary Chamberlain has written about this type of popular knowledge in *Old Wives' Tales*. She argues that although it has been increasingly superseded over the century by the formal institutions of modern medicine, which are mostly dominated by men, it was of enormous value to earlier communities.[10]

It is reasonable to argue, indeed, that throughout history, the value of the private sphere has been *greater* than that of the public sector. Female civilization, for example, which has been handed down between grandmothers, mothers and daughters over generations, and between female members of a community, has been absolutely fundamental to the processes of human and social survival. Through the transmission of knowledge and culture and the production of domestic work like nurture, feeding and cleaning, it has inhabited a more central space in society and been more indispensable than the public sector in maintaining the population of the country.

The private sphere has a further impact on the functioning of society through various forms of direct intersection with the public sector: 'the public and the private worlds are inseparably connected', wrote Virginia Woolf.[11] Even before the extension of suffrage at the beginning of this century, some upper-class women had already enjoyed a long history of influence on public life, even if they wielded this influence through indirect channels. Edith, Marchioness of Londonderry, the notorious Fifth Columnist and intimate of Hitler, who according to her biographer was 'the foremost social and political hostess of her day – a dazzling symbol of wealth, power, glamour and influence',[12] acknowledged the extent of her own power in a letter to *The Times* in 1913. Although she actively supported demands for the female vote, she took the view that women like *herself* did not really need it: 'It is not "for the noblest women in England" as such', she said, 'that the vote is really desired, *except for the recognition of the principle*'.[13] Lady Londonderry enlarged her political influence through her close relationship with Ramsay MacDonald, Prime Minister of the National government and leader of the Labour party, which was characterized by affection on her side and besotted love on his. 'With MacDonald under her spell', observes her biographer, 'she could be more effective than ever.' Her husband Charles was dependent on her social cachet and political cunning for his success in public life: so effective were his wife's skills as a hostess, that Lord Birkenhead accused him of 'catering his way into the cabinet'.[14]

Research traditions

Traditional historiography (nearly always written by men) has located public life (nearly always managed by men) at the centre of perceived meaningful activity. This tradition is still vigorous at the end of the twentieth century: for example, *A Monarch Transformed*, Mark Kishlansky's recently published history of Britain between 1603 and 1714, is almost entirely a history of men.[15] Women and their habitual territory of domestic life have rarely been documented by the writing elites. When their existence *has* been acknowledged, it has been in the margins – or the footnotes – of the history books. In the case of *A Monarch Transformed*, this acknowledgement takes up only seven lines of a lengthy and comprehensive index. Women are barely mentioned by Francis Fukuyama in *The End of History and the Last Man*, which argues that the twin triumphs of capitalism and democracy have brought an end to history.[16] Remarkably, his chapter title 'Men without chests' is presented without any apparent sense of irony.

David Cannadine's *Aspects of Aristocracy*, a substantial and impressive historical study of 'Grandeur and Decline in Modern Britain', is informed by the same male-centredness. Calling for a study of British aristocrats that goes 'beyond the country house', Cannadine advocates an examination of 'the things that have always preoccupied aristocrats throughout history: getting and spending money, accumulating and wielding power, and revelling in prestige and authority'.[17] But his own examination is a partial one: he scrutinizes a set of individual aristocrats in modern Britain who are all men, with the single exception of Vita Sackville-West, who qualifies for inclusion as one half of a marriage. Cannadine is presumably not aware of this partiality (since he does not acknowledge or explain it), which is a pity: the absence of women is inappropriate to the subject and limits the possibilities of analysis. For instance, the statement that 'Londonderry owed his job to [Ramsay] Macdonald's [sic] favouritism', ignores the central role of his wife in generating this favouritism.[18]

But 'male-dominated history' is not the only culprit. Feminism, too, with its overwhelming concern to celebrate women's achievements and to mourn female suffering, has tended to prioritize some areas of female existence and communities over others. Feminist historians in the UK have tended to neglect the influence of aristocratic women, especially those who identified their own interests with those of the Conservative party. In *Forever England*, Alison Light has observed that, on the whole, feminists 'have preferred to believe that feminism and conservatism are mutually exclusive'. She explains, 'Right-wing women were felt to be another breed, a subject too distasteful or remote to take up time in a movement whose driving energies have been largely spent recovering and reclaiming collective achievements and progressive struggles'.[19] But as Sheila Rowbotham points out, belonging to a 'subordinated sex is not an automatic ticket to ride with the angels'.[20] Nor does it qualify one as a victim: numbers of rich and privileged women have been oppressed less than many men, and have had enormous investments in the status quo. To be *less* powerful than some others does not mean you are the *least* powerful members of society overall.

In fact, a number of women closely associated with the Conservative party in Britain were active feminists. Prominent among these was Mrs Baldwin, wife of the Conservative leader Stanley Baldwin, who was Prime Minister of Britain for a long period between the wars. She contributed substantially to the cause of the Conservative party and to the interests of her class. During the General Strike of 1926, which 'displayed all the overtones', claims one of Baldwin's biographers, 'of a class war as between "We" and "They"', Mrs Baldwin harnessed support from ordinary citizens to help the state maintain essential services, by organizing a special convoy of motor cars to assist business women and girls living in the suburbs of London to reach their places of work. Car owners were asked to communicate immediately with Mrs Baldwin in writing or by telephone to 10 Downing Street. The response 'was considerable, owner-drivers willingly putting their vehicles at Mrs Baldwin's disposal as a patriotic duty'.[21]

Working-class women, on the other hand, mostly backed the General Strike; like Mrs Baldwin, they did so through the channels of their own, domestic world. They ran soup kitchens, raised £300,000 for boots and clothing for miners' families, adopted miners' children during the period of absolute deprivation and organized meetings of up to 10,000 miners' wives.[22]

Goals of research

The goal of the historian is to uncover and to interpret the past with integrity, as fully and as accurately as possible. This is an especially formidable challenge for historians investigating the private past, for not only do they have to unearth a strand of the past that is obscured from view, but they also need to be aware of and to shed a political ideology that tends to privilege the public sector over private and domestic life. Many feminists since the 1970s – writing books with titles like *Man's World, Woman's Place*[23] and *Woman's Consciousness, Man's World*[24] – have colluded with this tendency by placing men and public life at the centre of events and uncritically locating women and private life on the margins. This is an understandable perspective, given the long history of the subordination of women by men, who kept women firmly in the home and refused their attempts to enter public life or even, until relatively recently, to have an equal vote. But now that women are achieving some success in the public arena, the time has come to reassess the value and contribution of the domestic sphere to the social order.

The production of history and culture is intricately bound up with the empowerment of dominant groups and their wish to advance their own self-interest: an elite can establish its power only if it exerts a cultural domination over other social classes, as Antonio Gramsci argued in his discussion of the concept of 'hegemony' in his prison notebooks of the 1920s and 1930s.[25] In the case of political propaganda, this is usually a conscious wish involving a deliberate strategy; but this wish is not always conscious and its manifestation in cultural forms may simply reflect unquestioned convictions, which serve as blindfolds. One illustration of this is the neglect by mainstream medical historians of informal providers of healthcare working outside the public realm, notably in the area of maternity. These workers, such as handywomen, monthly nurses and unqualified abortionists, who were trained within an informal apprenticeship system and were key members of female communities, have now disappeared from British society. They have also disappeared from consciousness, because the history of maternity service provision has been largely retrospective, using as its yardstick the development of consultant care (by obstetricians who are mostly male) within the state health service.

In fact, there was resistance to this development by women campaigning for better maternity care. When the administration of the Midwives Act

1936 (which was responsible for abolishing the role of the handywoman) was being negotiated, many women said they were unhappy about the proposed control of midwifery care by the state. Eleanor Rathbone wanted to see the role of the voluntary organizations maintained because they were 'naturally very largely women', compared with the local authorities. During debate on the Midwives Bill in the House of Commons, she said that:

> an honourable Member who objected to this work being left to volunt-ary organisations told me a few minutes ago that his particular local authority has only one woman on it among 50 men, and he claimed that she was an expert on this subject. *There you have the case of a local authority with one woman among 50 men dealing with a prob-lem which the most ardent anti-feminist must admit to be a woman's problem*, and it is suggested that all the expert work of the voluntary organisations should be swept away because of a stupid, old-fashioned, musty prejudice against voluntary organisations [emphasis added].

Miss Rathbone accused the Labour Opposition ('with which I very often find myself in agreement') of doctrinaire prejudice that neglected the needs of women. 'Even Mr and Mrs Sidney Webb, and if ever there were people who believed in the bureaucrat, they do', she said, were not taking the Opposition's line regarding voluntary organizations.[26]

Mrs Baldwin, a prominent figure in maternity campaigns, used the same sort of argument as Miss Rathbone to oppose state-run maternity care: that because the public sector was dominated by men, it was not an appropriate domain for the care of women in pregnancy and labour. 'Now, we women are temperamental', she told her audience at a fund raising event in the mid-1930s, 'as I think a good many men friends here would agree – (laughter) – some of us more so, some less, but never more so than when a baby is on its way. You are up against that mystic psychology of motherhood. And therefore I venture to think that you cannot run the maternity services the same way as you can the health services'.[27] Mrs Baldwin and Miss Rathbone were making a valid point, since women were by no means proportionally represented in either local government or parliamentary politics: it was as recently as 1919 that Viscountess Astor had become the first woman MP to take a seat in parliament, following which the percentage of women MPs had been as low as 2.3 per cent in 1929 and 1.5 per cent in 1935.[28] But it is significant that they were less concerned with increasing the numbers of women in politics or state-run healthcare provision, than with keeping the care of pregnant women within a private and womanly sphere that was independent of the public sector.

Current mythology about so-called 'back street' abortions suggests that all abortionists before the Abortion Act 1967 – who inevitably worked within a private sector that was kept separate and secret from the state – were wicked quack doctors and mostly male. But in fact, most abortionists were women,[29] many of whom were motivated by a sense of vocation and did not charge a fee. Evidently there were some abortionists who did prey on vulnerable women, but many local abortionists were valued members of a close network of women: 'one elderly woman . . . confessed that until she heard of the birth control clinic she used to keep a jar of slippery elm and pennyroyal in the oven for the neighbours . . . She did not make any charge – did it from kindness of heart'.[30] Their confidentiality was usually protected by the female subculture: 'there is a death and everyone knows who has done the abortion, but no one will tell'.[31]

The dispensing of nutrition advice in 1930s Britain offers another example of confused historiography that privileges the public over the private sphere; in this area, 'public' is associated with science and scientific knowledge, while 'private' is associated with folk and popular knowledge. Historians have accepted without question the value of advice handed out by government funded 'experts' to women of the working classes whose families were suffering from malnutrition in the years of the Depression. One example of this dispensation of advice was the free weekly classes given by the Durham Federation of Women's Institutes, which were funded by the so-called Commission for the Special Areas, where almost the whole population was unemployed and dependent on insurance benefit and help from the Unemployment Assistance Board. The notice advertising these demonstration classes gave clear instructions to mothers:

Buy without waste,
Cook with great care,
Serve with good taste,
Enjoy your fare.

The so-called 'experts' on nutrition and family welfare assumed that the targets of these classes welcomed this 'scientific' instruction and benefited from it. But a study of letters to the editor in local newspapers reveals a different story: that most women believed they already knew how to cook for their families. As far as they were concerned, they needed money, food and fuel, and they resented this undervaluing of their skills by representatives of the 'outside' world. 'We can cook so long as there is something to cook', wrote one mother in 1936, 'and even when there is not so much to stir on we still manage to keep our men in health and strength, hoping against hope for work some day. Let [the Commissioner for the Special Areas] give our men work. He can save the talk.' Another letter exclaimed in anger, 'My husband has been out of a job three years. Little money has come into the house . . . Then [the Commissioner] says we don't know how to cook! How do we manage? *The evidence is there all the time, else we would all be dead*' [emphasis added].[32]

The research process

Given the complex difficulties in producing a full and accurate historical account of any moment in the past, there are good reasons for historians to take on board the scepticism of the postmodern era – to scrutinize and to question the old certainties of faith and ideology. According to post-modernist thought, which questions the possibility of human access to any certain knowledge of what happened in the past, one such construct is as valid as another, whether it can be backed by logical evidence or not. But as Richard J. Evans has pointed out in his end-of-century study, *In Defence of History*,[33] this postmodernist view of history can lead to dangerous doctrine, for if all historical arguments are equally valid, then a fascist or racist or Stalinist view of the past is as valid as any other. If history is invented, then the histories of Auschwitz are invented, too. The feminist historian Linda Gordon has recently observed that 'It is wrong to conclude, as some have, that because there may be no objective truth possible, there are not objective lies. There may be no objective canons of historiography, but there are degrees of accuracy; there are better and worse pieces of history'.[34]

But how does one manage to produce better pieces of history? The answer to this question involves the unearthing and the evaluation of the evidence upon which an interpretation of the past can be based. This presents a particular challenge for the researcher who aims to unearth the history of the private realm: the history of those who have left behind little evidence of their lives and work. This difficulty is aggravated by the fact that the terrain of historiography is largely inhabited by dead people, which means that the subjects of the research are unable to impact upon the research or to negotiate with the researcher and their agenda. They cannot say, for example, 'No, that's not true', or 'What about us?'

Standard sources of evidence for historians are archives, government documents and artefacts. But because these sources represent the history of public life, they contain little evidence about domestic and private life. The boxes of government files in Britain's Public Record Office contain letters and memoranda that document the evolution of an increasingly public society; if there were a *Private* Record Office, presumably it would be full of data about women's endless labour over centuries to deliver babies, to feed and clothe families and generally to keep the nation going.

It has been necessary, therefore, to develop new methods of unearthing the history of women's private domain and a revaluation of what counts as evidence, which has been recently broadened to include songs, recipes, cartoons, games, costumes, pictures, photographs, rituals and children's books. Pioneering feminist historians, such as Deirdre Beddoe in her book *Discovering Women's History*, have investigated alternative sources of evidence like the syllabuses of courses for girls on cookery, housewifery and laundry work in the nineteenth century.[35] In *The Unexpected Revolution*, a study of the history of the education of women and girls in the nineteenth century, Margaret Bryant turns to fiction, autobiography, couplets, paintings, photographs and magazines.[36] Oral testimony is also invaluable as a method of unearthing information about past attitudes and events.

But it is important to guard against a romanticization of private and domestic life. Historians need to accept and deal with conflicts between what they *expect* to find, and what they actually *do* find. Linda Gordon writes that as an historian who has been active in the women's movement, 'It frequently happened to me that the women's movement offered questions and topics, but my answers did not confirm all the slogans I had helped write'.[37] Without this kind of awareness, there is always the risk of a grossly inaccurate interpretation of the past.

Conclusion

This chapter has focused on the challenge of producing historiography relating to the role of women in the private and domestic sphere. Investigating this sphere will not only lead to a fuller history of women and their place in society, but will also generate a better understanding of men and of society as a whole. For even though men as a sex tend to identify themselves and to be identified by others with the concerns of the public arena, there are numbers of men – notably the unemployed and the sick – who are relegated to the margins of this territory or are excluded from it altogether. Furthermore, the roots of masculinity are largely produced within the private space that is generally managed and maintained by women. Most fundamentally, writes John Tosh, 'masculinity is formed within the family, in intimate relations of desire and dependence. How those relations are structured affects both the gender conditioning of boys and their subsequent attitude to family life as adults'.[38]

In any case, the private sphere in twentieth-century Western society does not and cannot function in and by itself, but is wholly dependent for its survival on the material resources produced in the public arena and made available for the needs of domestic life. While women continue to take responsibility for children and families, they are dependent on the work of the state and of industry and business, which are predominantly male arenas of activity. As yet, the female separatist Utopia of Charlotte Perkins Gilman's novel *Herland* (1915) remains just that – a Utopian fantasy. A comprehensive picture of society, therefore, is bound to incorporate men and masculinities and the relations between these and women's lives. The 'unhistoric acts' that are the stuff of George Eliot's *Middlemarch* – and the stuff of history itself – are far more complex and interesting than one might guess from a historical account that simply removes women or men from the story of the past or prioritizes the activities of one sex over the other.

Acknowledgements

The author is grateful to Gervase Hood, Berry Mayall, Sandy Oliver and Helen Penn for their valuable comments on earlier drafts of this chapter.

Notes

1 G. Eliot (1871) *Middlemarch*. Harmondsworth: Penguin (1994), p. 896.
2 An exception was the lyric poet Sappho; however, she lived in the late seventh century BC and on the island of Lesbos, not in Athens.
3 A. Oakley (1996) *Man & Wife. Richard and Kay Titmuss: My Parents' Early Years*. London: HarperCollins, p. 4.
4 For a discussion of the influence of Karl Marx on historians, see Eric Hobsbawm (1969) *On History*. London: Weidenfeld & Nicolson (1997), pp. 141–56.
5 W. Frikjof (1996) 'Education's memory', in *Education and Cultural Transmission: Historical Studies of Continuity and Change in Families, Schooling and Youth Cultures*, Gent, CSHP. Paedagogica Historica, International Journal of the History of Education, p. 343. Supplementary series volume II.
6 S. Rowbotham (1997) *A Century of Women*. Harmondsworth: Viking, p. 6; S. Rowbotham (1973) *Hidden from History*. Harmondsworth: Penguin.
7 C. Dyhouse (1981) *Girls Growing Up in Late Victorian and Edwardian England*. London: Routledge and Kegan Paul, p. 1.
8 V. Woolf (1938) *Three Guineas*. London: The Hogarth Press (1986), p. 162.
9 E. Rathbone (1927) *The Ethics and Economics of Family Endowment*. London: The Epworth Press, p. 114.
10 M. Chamberlain (1981) *Old Wives' Tales: Their History, Remedies and Spells*. London: Virago.
11 Woolf op. cit., p. 162.
12 A. de Courcy (1992) *Circe. The Life of Edith, Marchioness of Londonderry*. London: Sinclair Stevenson, p. 141.
13 *The Times*; Letter to the editor by Edith, Marchioness of Londonderry (1 April 1993).
14 de Courcy op. cit., p. 226.
15 M. Kishlansky (1996) *A Monarch Transformed: Britain 1603–1714*. Harmondsworth: Penguin.
16 F. Fukuyama (1992) *The End of History and the Last Man*. London: Hamish Hamilton.
17 D. Cannadine (1994) *Aspects of Aristocracy*. Newhaven: Yale University Press, p. 244.
18 Ibid., p. 70.
19 A. Light (1991) *Forever England: Femininity, Literature and Conservatism Between the Wars*. London: Routledge, pp. 13–14.

20 Rowbotham op. cit., p. 578.
21 H. Montgomery Hyde (1973) *Baldwin: The Unexpected Prime Minister*. London: Hart Davis, pp. 270–1.
22 P. M. Graves (1994) *Labour Women*. Cambridge: Cambridge University Press, pp. 163–4.
23 E. Janeway (1971) *Man's World, Woman's Place*. London: Michael Joseph.
24 S. Rowbotham (1973) *Woman's Consciousness, Man's World*. Harmondsworth: Penguin.
25 As explored in J. Appleby, Lynn Hunt and Margaret Jacob (1994) *Telling the Truth about History*. New York: W.W. Norton, pp. 220–1.
26 *Parliamentary Debates* (Hansard), 7 July 1936, 1109; emphasis added.
27 Report of Speeches at fund-raising dinner at Guildhall (8 May 1934), National Birthday Trust Fund archives held by the Contemporary Medical Archives Centre at the Wellcome Institute for the History of Medicine in London (hereafter CMAC), G7/4(1), p. 22.
28 M. Pugh (1992) *Women and the Women's Movement in Britain 1914–1959*. London: Macmillan.
29 M. Woodside (1966) 'The woman abortionist' in the Family Planning Association, *Abortion in Britain*. London: Pitman Medical Publishing Co., p. 36.
30 Cunnington to Pyke (8 March 1937), Abortion Law Reform Association archives held by CMAC, B3.
31 Statement by Mrs M. Williams of Leeds, quoted in 'The Report of the Conference of the Abortion Law Reform Association' (1936), Eugenics Society archives held by CMAC, D1.
32 Notices advertising cookery demonstrations and cuttings from newspapers (1936), Public Record Office, LAB 23/8; emphasis added.
33 R.J. Evans (1997) *In Defence of History*. London: Granta.
34 L. Gordon (1991) 'What's new in women's history', in S. Gunew (ed.) *A Reader in Feminist Knowledge*. London: Routledge, p. 75.
35 D. Beddoe (1983) *Discovering Women's History*. London: Pandora Press (1987). See especially Chapter 3 on 'The education of girls', p. 48–107.
36 M. Bryant (1979) *The Unexpected Revolution*. London: Institute of Education, University of London.
37 Gordon op. cit., p. 74.
38 J. Tosh, 'The making of masculinities. The middle class in late nineteenth-century Britain', in A.V. John and C. Eustance (eds) *The Men's Share? Masculinities, Male Support and Women's Suffrage in Britain 1890–1920*. London: Routledge, p. 40.

▶ 6

▷ Black people's health: ethnic status and research issues

▷ Penelope Scott

Defining the focus of the research

The Health of the Nation (HON) brought into public and policy focus the specific health issues of minority ethnic groups.[1] The HON policy stressed that 'research is essential to any strategy to improve health'.[2] This has given health policy research a new lease on life although not a 'carte blanche' as the policy clearly defines the research agenda. Much of the research informing the HON and stemming out of it has been clinical and epidemiological in nature. This type of research, however, does not always engage with the issues of power and socioeconomic circumstance that are integral in structuring the health experience of minority groups, including minority ethnic groups.

Giddens defines power as 'the ability of individuals or groups to make their own concerns or interests count, even where others resist'.[3] He further elaborates by noting that power and inequality are closely associated. Certainly by this definition minority ethnic groups in the UK can generally be considered both powerless and disadvantaged. Studies of the socioeconomic experience of minority ethnic groups[4] have shown that members of these groups experience high unemployment rates, have low paid occupations and poor working conditions and suffer poverty and poorer housing tenure. Their under-representation in the political process not only reflects their lack of political power but also serves to reinforce it.

These characteristics of minority ethnic groups in general are the basis for prevailing social definitions and perceptions of Caribbean people as a minority group in the UK. However, this construction is further defined by views of them as 'deviant' with reference to their over-representation in school exclusion rates,[5] the incidence of mental illnesses and involvement in crime.[6] Doctors and health professionals also collude in the labelling of Caribbeans as deviant by pronouncing them as 'non-compliant'.[7] These perceptions coalesce into an establishment view of Caribbean people as a dysfunctional social group failing to fit the norms and expectations of mainstream society.

In this chapter I shall be raising some issues inherent in researching minority ethnic health status by discussing current research, including my own on diabetes in the Caribbean community. This disease has a high prevalence rate among Caribbean people,[8] and is associated with poorer health outcomes and higher mortality for members of this group compared to their white counterparts.[9] Through examples taken from research I will firstly make the more general points that the 'power' of the researcher is constantly challenged and that the research process itself is not a fixed, controlled activity governed solely by the 'how to' rules of standard methodological texts. Secondly, I will demonstrate that data collected are products not only of the methods used but also of the various contexts and actors that together constitute the process. In considering these two points I will argue that research is both 'experiential' and 'reflective' practice: in the 'research economy' all processes, activities and experiences need to be considered for their potential value in the analysis and interpretation of data.

Research traditions

Epidemiological and clinical studies with their largely positivist/empiricist methods constitute the majority of research done on Caribbeans with diabetes.[10] The strength of such studies is that they provide useful information for health planners and health professionals treating the clinical aspects of the disease. On a more general level also, the quantitative research methods used by such studies have proved invaluable in revealing the extent and systematic patterning of social inequalities in health and illness. However, the major weakness of these studies is that the information they offer is rigidly biased towards the physiological. The biological determinism of the medical sciences fails to acknowledge the complexity of the challenges faced by the person with diabetes, who, as a social and cultural being, must undergo radical dietary and lifestyle changes. Consequently, the data yielded by these disciplines present only a partial picture of the disease's impact on the individual and cannot offer a complementary in-depth understanding of the social and cultural factors affecting diabetes management.

By contrast qualitative research, which is often grounded in a more critical epistemology, brings into sharp focus the real life issues and contexts structuring the experience of individuals with the disease. However, very little research attention has been directed towards an examination of the health experience and beliefs articulated by minority ethnic groups themselves and to date no sociological studies have looked in depth at the experience of Caribbeans with diabetes. Among the limited number of studies that have examined general health beliefs and knowledge, most have been conducted among Asian populations,[11] while a few others have presented findings on beliefs among West Indians.[12]

Goals of research

The study of diabetes among Caribbean people lies at the intersection of interests between the medical/scientific community, social research, health planners and Caribbean people themselves. However, as most of the research conducted to date has been epidemiological, it serves primarily the needs of health managers planning the provision of services and other scientific researchers who are interested in the distribution of the disease and in generating hypotheses about its possible causes. This is not to deny that all this has relevance to Caribbean people with diabetes. However, it does little to effect real change in the health status of this ethnic group. It is also likely that from their perspective this type of knowledge would be considered remote and as not engaging in issues that are relevant to them and that have an impact on their ability to manage the disease. Only qualitative research methods can more faithfully articulate these concerns and bring into public policy focus the issues which Caribbeans view as important.

The examples and discussions presented in this section are the product of two research projects on diabetes that I have undertaken here at the Social Science Research Unit. The first of these was an exploratory qualitative study (1994–5) funded by the Economic and Social Research Council (ESRC) which examined the lay health beliefs and service use experience of both White Britons and Caribbeans with diabetes. The second project (1996–7) was funded by a medical charity, the British Diabetic Association (BDA), and followed up on the findings of the exploratory study. The second project used both quantitative and qualitative research methods to study the issues being addressed. The decision to use a quantitative method was in part influenced by a recognition of the need to use a research method which proved familiar and acceptable to the clinical gatekeepers at the BDA.

The first and most obvious way in which the powers of the social researcher's concepts and methods are challenged is on that tortured journey to secure research funds. I initially tried to find funding for the first diabetes project from the BDA. This project, costing £21,691, aimed to conduct in-depth interviews with a sample of 24 Caribbean and White British patients with diabetes and key informant interviews with a range of health professionals selected from GP and outpatients clinics in Cambridge and London. This application to the BDA's Research Grants committee was unsuccessful; the unattributed comments by the sole referee quoted below are a salutary reminder of the chasm that exists between the goals and methodological outlooks of medical and social scientists:

> It is hard to see that the present protocol demands 10 months support: I would anticipate that a maximum of half this period of time would be required both to perform the necessary interviews and provide the appropriate documentation . . . The plan of investigation proposed will not yield any decisive results, nor is it apparently intended to . . . I would like to see a more probing and definitive study planned: although more expensive, it would have the potential of providing a definitive answer and in the long run would be more cost-effective.

The definition of research here, that it provides 'definitive' answers, is grounded in a positivist understanding that the reality being investigated and the data so produced are observable facts that can be explained in terms of general laws governing their relationship to each other. Research, as the term is used in this extract, is therefore conceived of as the very linear activity of providing solutions to problems, a definition which has its epistemological roots in positivism/empiricism. The expressed concern about the cost-effectiveness of the study is an instructive reminder of the economic imperative, which features significantly in decisions regarding research funding. In a sense this 'commodifies' research; defines it as a product but unlike the general marketplace of goods and services, which is subject to fairly established and predictable laws, what counts as 'cost-effective' by funders is often subjective and not transparent.

The referee's comments that the time allocated to do the research is excessive is also significant as it betrays a more general ignorance about qualitative research endemic in the medical scientist/scientific community. A recent article in the *British Medical Journal* on qualitative research methods is an encouraging breakthrough in trying to advance the merits of these methods in health research.[13] However, there is still a tremendous amount to be done to educate the medical scientific community on the contribution these methods can make.

The poor understanding among medics about what qualitative researchers do is manifest in several ways. At a most basic and crude level this lack of understanding is rooted in the different starting points of enquiry between the medical scientist and the social researcher. Although both are concerned with how to improve health, the former sees the individual's illness or disease as the main focus of concern whereas the latter sees the individual within the context of his/her cultural and socioeconomic environment as the necessary beginning of any serious investigation leading to improved health status. Added to this are the different epistemology and methods of enquiry, which further separate the worlds of the medical and social scientist. These differences inevitably raise the question: how does the qualitative researcher 'situate' her/himself and respond to the dominant methodological paradigm in health research?

My own experiences of interacting with health professionals, particularly doctors, and attempting to explain what I am researching and how, has been instructive in revealing the pervasiveness of the scientific worldview and the ways in which it is self-perpetuating. Explanations of the research, in my best lay 'sociologese', usually elicited professionals' response that I was looking at 'how people's culture affected the management of their disease'. What is striking about their interpretation is the way in which they uncritically constructed culture as a variable. To do so logically fits the positivist framework of biomedical sciences. This is potentially dangerous however, as the inherent reductionism of positivism, reflected in such an interpretation, reinvents culture as a static, homogenous factor that can somehow be influenced or changed wherever it is perceived as dysfunctional in diabetes management. What was also apparent from health professionals' discourse on their Caribbean patients was that they used culture as a term denoting 'otherness': it was a term that was applicable to other people. Subsumed under the 'culture' terminology was a hodge-podge of different food habits and lifestyle behaviours; in effect anything that in their perception was different or unfamiliar. The inherent ethnocentrism of this use of culture is also, as Smaje argues, one face of racism in the health service.[14] It has the potential to create stereotypical and victim blaming views of the role of culture in chronic disease management. On a more general level, the emphasis on culture deflects attention away from the more fundamental issues of inequality in access to material and other societal resources, as well as from socioeconomic and gender differences in health experience.

The existing gulf between the medical and social scientist and the slippage in communication that inevitably arises is quite amusingly exemplified in the following telephone conversation I had with a general practice doctor in Cambridge. I had written to him asking whether I could recruit a subsample of diabetic patients from his clinic. As time passed and I did not receive a reply to my letter I rang him. The following is a paraphrase of the conversation.

PS: I'm ringing up in connection with a letter I wrote to you about a research project I'm doing entitled 'Ethnicity, lay beliefs and the management of disease among diabetics'.

Dr: Could you repeat the title again for me please.

PS: 'Ethnicity, lay beliefs and the management of disease among diabetics'.

Dr: Oh, yes . . . hmm . . . ethnicity . . . what's that?

PS: Well, ethnicity . . . it's from the word ethnic . . . it refers to the shared background, traditions and culture which identify one group of people as distinct from another.

Dr: So is ethnicity a word then . . . is it in the OED [Oxford English Dictionary]?

PS: Well, yes, when I last checked it was.

Dr: Okay, and lay beliefs, that means patient expectations, doesn't it. Right, I'm with you now.

This extract also introduces a question which is perhaps at the heart of any discussion of minority ethnic health. What exactly is meant by 'ethnicity' and how reliable is it as a category or variable in research? Ethnicity is now to a large extent used instead of race to study and understand human differences. Race has been discredited as an acceptable and meaningful category in health research for a number of reasons, including the argument that no race possesses a discrete package of genetic characteristics; genetic diseases are not restricted to certain racial groups although risk varies by origin; there is more intra- than interracial genetic variation; and the genes responsible for features such as skin colour are few and atypical and not responsible for disease.[15]

As a concept, ethnicity is not easily defined. Generally social scientists use ethnicity to embrace all the ways in which people seek to differentiate themselves from others. These markers include language, religion and historical or territorial identity,[16] as well as what Wallman terms 'symbolic identification',[17] which includes dress, diet and kinship systems. In many instances also, another important marker of ethnicity is physical appearance; in particular skin colour. As a result, defining ethnicity is closely associated with the ideological construction of race.

An increasing number of researchers have drawn attention to the problematic way in which ethnicity has been constructed and applied as a category in research studies.[18] One example of this is a study that concluded that all members of minority ethnic groups are more likely to develop psychosis and that determinants of this increased risk are the personal and social pressures of belonging to a minority ethnic group in Britain.[19] Comparisons were made between a white group and all those who placed themselves in the Asian or black groups as defined by the Office of Population Censuses and Surveys (OPCS). However, 22 of the 39 people with psychotic disorders in the white group were also from ethnic minority groups, including Irish, Turks, Cypriots and Greek Cypriots, or were from other European countries. The study therefore did not examine what it set out to do. In order to test whether being a member of an ethnic group is implicated in the onset of psychosis the researchers should have made comparisons between all the minority ethnic groups and the white British sub-group.

One criticism of ethnic health research centres on the point that much of it focuses solely on ethnicity, thereby inferring that it is ethnicity itself that causes poor health. This 'victim blaming' is pervasive in studies on ethnic populations.[20] By contrast, critics argue that people's health experience is structured by factors associated with their ethnic background as opposed to ethnicity itself.

A further issue that current usage of the term ethnicity often fails to address is the heterogeneity of the ethnic populations studied. The terms Asian, Chinese and Afro-Caribbean for example, disguise important differences in diet, religion and language that are relevant to health and disease management. These categories also ignore the important differences that may exist according to social class, gender, age and generation. Research studies must acknowledge these factors and use methods that can deal with these intra-group differences, otherwise the data produced will be flawed. Another problematic way in which ethnicity has been operationalized has been in the way that it has been used to develop categories that people impose on others. The 1991 census for example, has been criticized for using categories that conflate race, ethnicity and nationality. Some observers argue that the difficulties with external categorization are that it is falsely non-political and that the people so categorized may not necessarily identify with these groupings.[21]

Certainly my own experience of doing research among Caribbean people has highlighted problems inherent in the ways people belonging to a distinctive group are labelled or defined. Caribbean people, for example, are often grouped together with Africans; this grouping is apparently organized on skin colour. This 'racializes' the groups and by so doing ignores the cultural heterogeneity between and among them. By default this implies that all black people are the same. The ambiguous categories 'African Caribbean' and 'Afro-Caribbean' are the popular constructs emerging from this misinformed view of black people among the ethnic majority. These terms are not widely accepted among Caribbean people. As one of my interviewees said quite sarcastically: 'What is Afro-Caribbean supposed to mean? Afro . . . Afro is a hair-do from the 1970s!'

The ambiguity of these terms creates practical problems for the researcher relying on the classification of ethnicity used for example, on hospital records. This confusion over the meaning of terms also leads to a suspicion of the integrity of the data produced and of statistics compiled by administrative bodies relying on these categorizations in the monitoring of health service use and provision.

Of course, taking issue with the current categories introduces the more complex conceptual question of what constitutes 'Caribbean' ethnic identity in the UK. This undoubtedly would be different to Caribbean identity in the Caribbean, if it does, in fact, exist, which some observers dispute.[22] An answer to this question is complicated and highly politicized. It raises further questions, such as who decides? And whose interests are represented in the construction of this identity? What mechanisms and forums exist at local and national level to facilitate a debate on this? If indeed a

UK Caribbean ethnic identity has been forged, how can it challenge and replace the dominant view of Caribbean people by the majority group? Does the political infrastructure exist to do so?

The research process

The nature and content of the data collection process and the factors influencing this are important but neglected issues in researching minority ethnic health. The qualitative interview is a socially constructed encounter, and the data produced are as much a product of the social relations characterizing the process as the research method used. Unfortunately many studies on ethnic minority health, particularly where interviewers have been members of the ethnic majority, have failed to adequately take this on board. Among the previously cited studies looking at the experiences of Caribbean people, Donovan is the only author who engaged with this issue.[23] She concludes that her racial identity as a white woman researching black people's health did have an impact on the process, although she does not elaborate on how. On the other hand, Thorogood's work very appropriately locates her research subjects in the context of power inequalities but she does not address the probability of inequalities that her membership from the ethnic majority may bring to bear on the research process.[24]

From my own experience in researching White British and Caribbean people with diabetes, I would certainly argue that there is evidence suggesting that my own Caribbean background was a distinct advantage in facilitating the interview process with the Caribbean interviewees. Rapport with the Caribbeans developed fairly spontaneously. Although I had decided beforehand to start by inviting interviewees to ask any question they had about the research or myself, it seldom proved necessary to issue this invitation to the Caribbean sample. We traded stories about how we ended up in England, what part of Jamaica or the Caribbean we are from and generally how we coped with the cold weather and lack of sunshine. The interviews developed out of these conversations and the ensuing discussions were punctuated with heartrending stories of loneliness and isolation as well as details of the trials of family demands and interpersonal conflicts, encounters with racism and love triangles. One woman shared quite explicit details of her husband's extra-marital affair, describing how she discovered them 'in flagrante' on the living room sofa. From her account it was clear she had come to accept this relationship. When she realized that I was having trouble locating Caribbeans with diabetes in the area because, for one reason, the hospital did not record ethnicity, she insisted on giving me this woman's phone number, and urged me to contact her because she had diabetes too. In another instance a male respondent admitted during the course of the interview that before coming to England he had been a 'gunman' and had served a custodial sentence for shooting a man.

These accounts may not have dealt directly with the issues being examined but they are significant in two ways. Firstly, they are an important signal of the trust and rapport characterizing the interview process and secondly, they facilitate an understanding and interpretation of the issues of the research as the data are contextualized by rich personal histories. In retrospect, most of these interviews, particularly those with women, more closely resembled social encounters as part of an ongoing relationship. Hospitality and invitations to return were extended, other members of the family were introduced and in situations where the interviewee lived alone family photographs and even decades-old wedding albums were brought out and displayed. In one instance, at the end of the interview, an old Jamaican lady asked me to accompany her upstairs to her bedroom and continue talking to her as she got ready for a chiropody appointment. As I sat on the edge of her bed watching her comb her hair, she resumed talking about some of the issues of the interview, digressing at times to talk about a daughter who was going to move back home because she had separated from her husband. This particular incident perhaps best represents the character and tone of interviews with the Caribbean sub-sample.

The interviews with the White British sub-sample differed significantly. Initial conversations were polite and were confined to matters relating to the interview and the invitation to ask the researcher questions was not taken up. Generally, there was no sharing of personal details and the interviewees did not elaborate on the issues of the research in the way that the Caribbean sample had. This meant that the interviews were shorter. There was however, one outstanding exception. A 54-year-old woman I spoke with was suffering from depression. Although she addressed the issues of the research, often in an oblique way, she spoke at length about her depression and her domestic and financial difficulties. She stressed repeatedly that her family did not give her any moral support at all and expected her to 'get on with things' at home. Her life was evidently extremely difficult and her physical appearance and surroundings spoke of neglect and deprivation. This woman clearly had a desperate need to be heard and her extreme distress acknowledged. As the interview progressed she appeared to get some therapeutic benefit from being allowed to speak. This experience served as a salutary reminder that a researcher must be ready and prepared to deal with a variety of scenarios, issues and other agendas while collecting data in this way. Apart from this interview there were two instances where men spoke about the very personal matter of impotence – a complication of diabetes. In one of these instances, the 55-year-old interviewee commented, 'You're the first person that's known about it because I feel at ease with you'. It is difficult to know with any certainty why this interviewee felt at ease to disclose this information.

Whatever the reason(s), the comment provides an insight into the complexity of factors affecting the interviewing process and the quality of data collected.

These comparisons bring several points into focus. The first concerns the argument that my own ethnic identity probably worked to my advantage while interviewing the Caribbean sample. This is not to suggest that researching black people's health should be the preserve of black researchers or that the research data on black people produced by white researchers are automatically biased. Certainly, there would be a case for inverting the argument and suggesting that my own intuitive understanding and knowledge of Caribbean culture could lead me to unwittingly over-interpret data or overlook data that an outside observer would probably view as significant. However, the potential tensions this introduces are not dissimilar to the usual tensions qualitative researchers face in deciding, for example, to place weight on an event because it took place or using their judgement to ascribe significance to some infrequent quotations or occurrences. What I am suggesting is that, consistent with the philosophical positions of relativism, which propose that there is no single, unbiased truth, the accounts of black interviewees elicited by both white and black researchers may differ in content and focus but are equally valid. However, it is incumbent on the researcher to expose to the wider research audience all characteristics of the interview process that may have influenced the responses given.

A further point that these comparisons underscore is the flexibility of qualitative research in accounting for differences between groups. The standard way of collecting data by interview is that the same questions are asked to different people or groups, a method that to some extent implies a homogeneity in the way people respond. However, the examples presented demonstrate that different ethnic groups respond differently to the experience of being interviewed by the same interviewer. The fact that one group of interviewees consistently replied and elaborated spontaneously on the topics raised whereas many of the other group required some measure of prompting to elicit information raises issues on how to interpret the data. In this particular study, however, the differences in beliefs, practices and experiences of the health service were so profoundly different that this modified the difficulties in interpreting the data. A virtue of using qualitative research methods to study health beliefs across ethnic groups is that it is able to deal with these differences.

The fieldwork experiences previously outlined also serve to expose possible ethnocentric biases in existing models of qualitative research. Cornwell's distinction between 'public' and 'private' accounts in qualitative research interviews for example, does not appear to be appropriate in describing the interviewees' responses.[25] One component of Cornwell's argument in support of this model is that private accounts that more faithfully reflected respondents' views and opinions were more likely to be elicited over time when they had developed trust in the researcher. This viewpoint does not, however, easily 'fit' with the profile of my interviews with the Caribbeans. These interviews were generally characterized by open discussion about the research topics as well as intimate details about their lives. This does not necessarily mean that the Caribbean sample did not have their own ways of what Cornwell terms 'managing their appearance' in the interview. It is yet to be proven though whether this dichotomous model of the public and private is elastic enough to cope with the idiosyncratic or culturally specific ways that people from minority ethnic groups respond to the experience of being interviewed.

Feminist models of research, which argue that a non-hierarchical relationship in the qualitative interview is ethically desirable, do address the question of unequal power relations in research. However, how appropriate is this model to address and describe situations where the researcher and researched are bonded at some level by an assumed shared experience of exclusion and racism and as a result could arguably be considered as equally 'powerless' in that sense? The relative ease with which Caribbean interviewees engaged with me apparently on the basis of our shared ethnicity seemed to diminish or at least mask any need on my part to redress any power imbalances that could be viewed to exist based on our differing class or educational backgrounds.[26]

In fact the 'power relations' characterizing the interviews were fluid and constantly shifting. Quite often I was asked fairly personal questions, particularly by some of the male respondents who saw the interview as a 'man–woman' encounter at some level and so sexualized the experience. In these instances I sometimes became aware of my own vulnerability and 'powerlessness' as a woman. Where the general personal probing by interviewees left me feeling exposed, the 'power' inherent in the relative anonymity of the traditional interviewer role was stripped away. This reversal of the 'researcher' and the 'researched' roles clearly altered the dynamic of the interview and disrupted the research agenda in several ways. It was only in situations where I felt to some degree uncomfortable or threatened by unwanted male attention that this disruption convinced me to alter or abort the interview or research plans. No research data are worth risking one's personal safety for. On a more general level these experiences argue for the development of a code of practice for researchers that would offer guidelines for dealing with potentially threatening situations.

Doing research among any social group raises the difficult question of how far the researcher has a responsibility to feed back the results of the research. The further question of whether or not study participants actually want to know the research outcomes must also be considered. None of the Caribbean people interviewed in the studies referred to here requested information on the research results. This could well be rooted in a view of research as remote and 'powerless' to effect change in their lives. It is ethically important though for the social researcher to attempt to alter this perception. This can be partly achieved by explaining to prospective participants how the research, particularly if it is health-related, can make a difference to their daily lives and enable their voice to be heard in forums where change can be effected. There are also channels at local levels – community newspapers, radio stations and organizations – that can be used to disseminate findings that may facilitate, for example, the management of chronic diseases such as diabetes.

Conclusion

Most current research on minority ethnic health is 'scientific' and therefore primarily serves the interests of health planners or the scientific community itself. There is a gap in the available research, which is critical or social constructionist in its methods and interpretations. When studying health conditions such as diabetes, which ascribe a responsible role to the individual in its management, only these approaches can generate the types of knowledge that facilitate a greater understanding of the disease's impact and that are ultimately of direct relevance to the Caribbean community.

This chapter has chronicled my attempts to secure funding and my experiences in researching Caribbean people's health. These experiences are instructive in illustrating the ways in which the researcher's power and agenda are constantly renegotiated within the various contexts of the process and in relation to the various actors who participate in it. The various compromises, trade-offs and experiences in any project constitute important information, which should both inform and frame the analysis of the data. A failure to do so can result in data that appear 'sanitized' or 'vacuum packed', as the important dimensions of 'power' and 'process' do not feature in the analysis.

Notes

1 Department of Health (1992) *The Health of the Nation*. London: HMSO.
2 Ibid., p. 41.
3 A. Giddens (1993) *Sociology*, 2nd edn. Cambridge: Polity Press, p. 54.
4 K. Amin and C. Oppenheim (1992) *Poverty in Black and White*. London: Child Action Group/Runnymead Trust; T. Jones (1993) *Britain's Ethnic Minorities*. London: Policy Studies Institute; D. Owen and A. Green (1992) Labour market experience and occupational change amongst ethnic groups in Great Britain, *New Community*, 19 (6): 845–60.
5 D. Gillborn (1996) Exclusions from school. *Viewpoint*, 5: 1–8.
6 R. Cope (1989) The compulsory detention of Afro-Caribbeans under the Mental Health Act, *New Community*, 15 (3): 343–56; Commission for Racial Equality

(1997) *Criminal Justice in England and Wales*. London: Commission for Racial Equality; R. Carr-Hill and D. Drew (1988) Blacks, Police and Crime, in A. Bhat, R. Carr-Hill and S. Ohri (eds) *Britain's Black Population*. Aldershot: Gower.

7 P. Scott (1995) *Ethnicity, Lay Beliefs and the Management of Disease Among Diabetics*. Report to the Economic and Social Research Council. London: Social Science Research Unit.

8 N. Chaturvedi, P. Mckeigue and M. Marmot (1994) Relationship of glucose tolerance to coronary risk in Afro-Caribbeans compared with Europeans, *Diabetologia*, 37: 65–72.

9 Chaturvedi *et al*. op. cit.; J. Cruickshank and S. Alleyne (1987) Black West Indian and matched white diabetics in Britain compared with diabetics in Jamaica, *Diabetes Care*, 10: 170–9; J. Cruickshank (1989) Diabetes: contrasts between peoples of black (West Indian), Indian and white European origin, in J. Cruickshank and D. Beevers (eds) *Ethnic Factors in Health and Disease*. Guildford: Butterworth-Heinemann.

10 K. Nikolaides, A. Barnett, H. Spilipoulos *et al*. (1981) West Indian diabetic population of a large inner city diabetic clinic, *British Medical Journal*, 283: 1374–5; O. Odughesan, B. Rone, J. Fletcher *et al*. (1989) Diabetes in the UK West Indian Community: The Wolverhampton Study, *Diabetic Medicine*, 6: 48–52; J. Cruickshank, D. Beevers, V. Osbourne *et al*. (1980) Heart attack, stroke, diabetes and hypertension in West Indians, Asians and whites in Birmingham, England: Hospital admission analysis, *British Medical Journal*, 281: 1108–9.

11 R. Bhopal (1986) Asians' knowledge and behaviour on preventive health issues: Smoking, alcohol, heart disease, pregnancy, rickets, malaria prophylaxis and surma, *Community Medicine*, 8 (2): 315–21; A. Bowes and T. Domokos (1993) South Asian women and health services: A study in Glasgow, *New Community*, 19 (4): 611–26; C. Currer (1986) Concepts of mental well- and ill-being: The case of Pathan mothers in Britain, in C. Currer and M. Stacey (eds) *Concepts of Health, Illness and Disease: A Comparative Reader*. Oxford: Berg.

12 N. Thorogood (1990) Caribbean home remedies and their importance for Black women's health care in Britain, in P. Abbot and G. Payne (eds) *New Directions in the Sociology of Health*. London: Falmer Press; N. Thorogood (1989) Afro-Caribbean women's experiences of the health service, *New Community*, 15 (3): 319–34; J. Gabe and N. Thorogood (1986) Prescribed drug use and the management of everyday life: Experiences of black and white working-class women, *Sociological Review*, 34 (4): 737–72; M. Morgan and C. Watkins (1988) Managing hypertension: beliefs and responses to medication among cultural groups, *Sociology of Health and Illness*, 10 (4): 561–78; J. Donovan (1986) *We Don't Buy Sickness, It Just Comes*. Aldershot: Gower; B. Howlett, W. Ahmad and R. Murray (1992) An exploration of white, Asian and Afro-Caribbean peoples' concepts of health and illness causation, *New Community*, 18 (2): 281–92.

13 C. Pope and N. Mays (1995) Researching the parts other methods cannot reach: An introduction to qualitative methods in health and health services research, *British Medical Journal*, 311: 42–5.

14 C. Smaje (1995) *Health, 'Race' and Ethnicity*. London: Kings Fund Institute.

15 A. Hill (1989) Molecular markers of ethnic groups, in J. Cruickshank and D. Beevers (eds) *Ethnic Factors in Health and Disease*. Guildford: Butterworth-Heinemann.

16 C. Smaje op. cit.

17 S. Wallman (1986) Ethnicity and the boundary process in context, in J. Rex and D. Mason (eds) *The Ghetto and the Underclass: Essays on Race and Social Policy.* Aldershot: Gower.

18 P. Senior and R. Bhopal (1994) Ethnicity as a variable in epidemiological research, *British Medical Journal*, 309: 327–30; C. Smaje op. cit.

19 M. King, E. Coker, G. Leavey *et al.* (1994) Incidence of psychotic illnesses in London: Comparisons of ethnic groups, *British Medical Journal*, 309: 115–19.

20 J. Donovan op. cit.

21 W. Ahmad (1993) Making black people sick: 'race', ideology and health research, in W. Ahmad (ed.) *'Race' and Health in Contemporary Britain.* Buckingham: Open University Press; D. Mason (1990) 'A rose by any other name . . . ?: Categorisation, identity and social science', *New Community*, 17 (1): 123–33.

22 W. James (1993) Migration, racism and identity formation: the Caribbean experience in Britain, in W. James and C. Harris (eds) *Inside Babylon: The Caribbean Diaspora in Britain.* London: Verso.

23 J. Donovan op. cit.

24 N. Thorogood (1989) op. cit.

25 J. Cornwell (1984) *Hard-earned Lives.* London: Tavistock Publications.

26 K. Bhopal (1995) Women and feminism as subjects of Black study: The difficulties and dilemmas of carrying out research, *Journal of Gender Studies*, 4 (2): 153–68; J. Stacey (1988) Can there be a feminist ethnography? *Women's Studies International Forum*, 11 (1): 21–7; R. Edwards (1990) Connecting method and epistemology: A white woman interviewing black women, *Women's Studies International Forum*, 13 (5): 477–90; J. Ribbens (1989) Interviewing – an 'unnatural' situation?, *Women's Studies International Forum*, 12 (6): 579–92.

▶ 7

▷ Frail elderly people: difficult questions and awkward answers

▷ **Valerie Hey**

Defining the focus of the research

This chapter reflects on my experience of conducting a small qualitative study of community care, decision making and the frail elderly. It tries to capture how some frail elderly people live out their lives in the context of social divisions and their associated forms of social exclusion. The authorial voice assumes the impossibility of doing value-free social science investigation.[1] The chapter focuses on specific methodological issues in order to raise wider theoretical and sociopolitical questions common to all social policy investigations. The main intention is to trace how different 'stakeholders' come to define how people (in this case, the frail elderly) are positioned in terms of policy, practice and research accounts. A major concern is to promote an understanding of the impacts of policy, practice and representation on the frail elderly, who are so often made subject to the intentions of others.

The context of social policy: the 'new' community care, rights and the position of elderly people

During the 1980s and early 1990s, major policy changes in the field of the care of the frail elderly brought an enormous expansion in private sector care. During the 1980s, capacity in the private sector more than trebled and public sector investment virtually ceased. Current community care policies in the UK emphasize the importance of 'consumer' choice, and of professionals consulting fully with their clients. A great deal has been written about the intentions of community care under the Griffiths reforms.[2] A main aim of the NHS and Community Care Act 1990 was the encouragement of the private sector as provider of 'customized' social services. Greater emphasis was placed on clients having a 'choice' within this newly invigorated private sector. Social Service departments (SSDs) were divested of much of their role as providers of services and seen instead as 'enabling authorities'. The main platform of the then Conservative government's reforms was a series of claims to:

- enable people to live as normal a life as possible in their own homes or in a 'homely' environment in the local community;
- provide the amount of care and support needed to achieve maximum independence;
- give people greater choice and independence

As Julian Le Grand has argued, the shift to marketization has meant the growth of a new managerialism within a culture of what can be termed 'quasi-markets'.[3] The development of marketization raises fundamental issues to do with the exercise of choice.[4] Since different consumers and 'stakeholders' hold different 'collaterals' as well as different interests, there is concern about the way in which these 'social markets' may intensify existing inequities and/or produce new ones.

Defining the 'frail' elderly in the literature

Age is an important defining characteristic in all human societies, but the statuses, rights and responsibilities associated with being both 'young' and 'old' differ considerably between different societies.[5] One of the features of a culture that considers biological age important is 'age determinism' – the tendency to attribute to age itself a whole range of individual characteristics and personal problems. A popular cartoon in pensioners' publications is the one that shows a doctor bent over an elderly woman's leg and saying, 'It's your age'. Her reply is, 'But the other one is just as old, and it's alright!'[6]

This problem of definition extends to social research. In choosing to research the 'frail elderly', the researcher may be accused of ageism and thus of defining elderly people out of the 'normal' population of adults. Many of the difficulties older people experience are problems of the body and of dependency, and are assumed at the opposite end of the age scale. None the less, older people do commonly experience many different social circumstances, perceptions and experiences, which together provide a framework for research, professional practice and policy domains. Funders and social policy makers are properly interested in what will, after all, come to be an increasingly larger group of the population.[7]

Research traditions

There is an overwhelming tendency within academic and social policy literature to pathologize, stigmatize and marginalize the elderly. Old people are generally defined negatively as lacking physical, financial and mental resources, and as a 'liminal' group.[8] The negative stereotype arises through the domination of gerontology in the literature, with its emphasis on normative psychological and medical models.[9] This confluence of disciplines has worked to suppress the perspectives of older people themselves.[10] However, there is a developing analytic literature, which studies elderly people's talk, in the context of intergenerational exchanges.[11] But there are significant gaps in what is known about the situation of elderly people with respect to their involvement in care decisions. The existing accounts tend to take the form of superficial 'customer satisfaction' surveys and hence lack the 'thick descriptions' that can offer important insights into the social processes of ageing. One irony is that although the literature includes many studies about the elderly body, they construct elderly bodies in disembodied ways separated from social accounts. In contrast, the fictional/semi-fictional literature with extreme old age as its theme – especially work by Margaret Forster and Michael Ignatieff[12] – provides this missing account of the social, psychological and material processes involved in becoming frail or elderly.

In locating my self against the medical and social gerontological literature I also took a decision to break away from the practice of qualitative studies, which allow proxy respondents, frequently the 'carers' of older people, to speak on their behalf. I wanted to disrupt the 'Does s/he take sugar?' syndrome so resented and remarked upon by the elderly people I spoke with. As reported below, the challenges prompted in the process of face-to-face participant observation make up an important group of the research 'findings'; moreover they draw attention to what is at stake in the delicate (far from transparent) networks of meaning-making that underlie social research. More pragmatically, what I discovered about process powerfully reminded me of the need for generation-sensitive approaches and for theoretical attention to how the elderly are 'spoken' in our society.

The goals of the research

The Headley Trust, commissioners of the research reported on here, were rare in specifically wanting to discover the views of the frail elderly themselves. There has been an increasing emphasis on collecting recipients'/clients' views but overall it is still a minority position within social policy research and social work practice. On the basis of medicine and psychology and their associated professional ideologies and practices, those purchasing services and providing them for elderly people continue to view clients in traditional ways as passive recipients of care. The study formed part of the move to new policy developments that welcomed people's engagement in community care decision making. But as I report below, even well intentioned initiatives and individual actors are themselves caught within configurations of power that they might simultaneously wish to change and challenge.

Certainly the group of people I interviewed and got to know included some of the most disadvantaged in our society. Several of the study participants had been diagnosed as having dementia, many were incontinent, most were physically disabled and the majority were extremely poor, including two who, prior to social services intervention, were defined as in a state of extreme self-neglect. This is a depressing and familiar but also a problematic representation of the frail elderly. They are neither a homogeneous nor a powerless group of victims.[13] I specifically set my study in a more interactive tradition, one that recognizes respondents as more than the casualties of circumstance, however disadvantaged.[14] My interpretation shows how respondents' tenacity, humour and occasional resistance worked to complicate and at times almost unravel my research agenda. I believe there are lessons here to be drawn about other information gathering practices, notably 'needs assessments'.

But I do not want to overstate the extent of individual agency. As I gathered stories from the people I interviewed, I became acutely aware of how our ageist and 'healthist' society structures the social experience of the frail elderly. Most frail elderly people have little 'physical capital',[15] and one major effect is marked by their virtual social elimination from public view, designed-out of communities, homes and facilities that presume able-bodiedness. The frail elderly are one version of 'the disappeared'.

The research process

The study

The main aims of the study were to explore the social contexts of community care, and to understand how decisions about the care of elderly people were actually made, with a focus on the place of 'consumer choice' in community care outcomes. More specific objectives were:

- to explore the views and experiences of frail elderly people and those caring for them when making choices about their care;
- to look at relationships between mental competence and physical dependence, health, social support, and the social circumstances of frail elderly people;
- to make practical and policy recommendations about the involvement of frail elderly people in choices about their living circumstances.

The study was undertaken in two sites in London (Inner City and River-side). These pseudonyms offer raw clues about their different socio-demographic profiles. However, getting access to the frail elderly was equally difficult in both sites. Indeed this difficulty is a marker of their lack of social and political power. For reasons of pragmatism, I relied upon sponsorship from their 'gatekeepers': care managers/social workers, since they were the first point of contact for this specific group of clients and their carers/families. The sample was recruited through the snowballing technique. As I wanted to learn about the social processes of decision making, I used a participant observation approach, seeking out occasions when profes-sionals, family members and clients were involved in critical care decisions. In particular, I focused upon recording discussions between elderly people and their social workers/care managers. These sometimes took the form of a formal *community living assessment* – effectively risk assessments – when the care managers were appraising their clients' social, health and personal circumstances in order to obtain a picture of their care needs. I also attended *review* meetings; where care managers/social workers obtained feedback from elderly people and their carers about the current status of their pattern of care. In addition, I accompanied health and social work profes-sionals on ward rounds in geriatric hospitals. I also visited several day centres.

In total, I interviewed 17 elderly people, (many of them several times) five social workers involved in their care; and key people who were in the elderly person's social network. This group included two neighbours, four family carers, one unpaid non-family carer and two family members not involved in the practical care of the elderly person. I additionally inter-viewed one home care organizer and two senior nurses; one at a geriatric hospital and the other at a voluntary sector nursing home.

On the whole, the elderly people I spoke with were accustomed to being 'interviewed'; to people coming to do something 'to' them or 'for' them. They were not generally experienced at making 'choices' in the newly privatized marketplace of personal social services. Thus it was difficult to frame an ostensible research task designed to encourage reflexivity – that is to discover frail elderly people's views about their role in consultations concerning their care – since they seldom identified themselves as 'con-sumers', let alone 'consultees'. These contradictions emerged at their most intense within initial exchanges. This is because first meetings involve the negotiation of levels of trust, which orchestrate, often at an unconscious level, what is said in the immediate moment as well as set up the viability of longer term and repeat visits. At these times they confused me *with* a social worker. The use of the term 'social researcher' seemed to stimulate this innocent mistake and they then assumed that I could offer advice about services. Conversely, at other times, I was told that because I was unable to do anything about someone's situation there would be no point in talking with me. Clearly these and other issues of power organize the negotiation of degrees of disclosure and continue to impact at all stages in the research process, none more so than in the production, interpretation and representation of others' voices. I turn to these concerns next.

Interpreting dissident discourses – means and ends

One major imperative for the funders and the researcher was to discover the prior, as well as current, circumstances of the elderly person in terms of housing, social relationships and health. It was evident that only those with sufficient amounts of 'capital' had managed to benefit from 'care in the community'.[16] My requests for information were overlaid by the complexities of some elderly subjects' mental confusion, social isolation and relative powerlessness. But although power might appear to lie with me and my well intentioned quest to know, I was 'read' by interviewees and frequently resisted in terms of this power as the following two extracts show:

VH: Can you tell me how long you've lived here?
FB: Mmm.
VH: How long have you been here?
FB: Not really very long, about three weeks.
VH: About three weeks, and where were you living before?
FB: In my own home.
VH: Yes, was that a flat or . . .
FB: Yes, it was.
VH: Were you managing to live there on your own?
FB: Yes, I was, I don't want to be . . . about my business all the time.
VH: Don't you?
FB: [unclear]
VH: No, I remember you said last time, well the time I called in for the last visit you said . . . if you're a social worker I won't fill any forms in. Yeah, what else do you like doing?
FB: I like that! There you go again you must ask questions . . .

Or again, in another example I am trying in this opening exchange to establish an acceptable territory of talk:

VH: I'm a social researcher from the University of London and I'm involved in some work on community care.
GR: Community what?
VH: Community care and what happens to older people in the community and . . .
GR: Well, I'll do my best.

VH: Yes.

GR: I don't suppose we're all the same.

VH: No . . . I've got some very different stories, from some . . . I'm interested in the sort of patterns of care and whether older people themselves feel they've been consulted about what happens to them.

GR: Well I think that's a mistake you know in the beginning.

VH: What . . . to consult with them?

GR: To ask them too many questions, and then to . . . you know with what they [unclear] and I've had to do so much in my life by myself . . . I don't know what I can do about that . . . go on, carry on and see what you can do.

These responses are not examples of elderly 'eccentricity' – although I think 'common-sense' often constructs this group as the originators of the bizarre. Instead I want to suggest that the 'failures' to comply shown by Miss Beech or the equally interesting reinterpretation proposed by Miss Rowan, offer opportunities to think aloud about the (taken for granted) social processes in play when researchers attempt to locate themselves in someone else's world. Inevitably, the work of location is easier to see when things *do not* go smoothly!

Although it is important to acknowledge the specific challenges of gathering data within the context of elderly frailty, these should not be conflated in (paternalistic) notions that inevitably presume elderly people's bodily and mental *in*capacities. Respect for the integrity of elderly people was the basis of my approach – indeed it was this assumption that was most often undermined by staff in the social settings in which the research discussions took place. These occurrences put me, like the people interviewed, under pressure to comply – whereas I was a guest, they were residents (see later). However, and paradoxically, some of the most 'vulnerable' people in the study proved to be the most resourceful in resisting my attempts to consult them. Why do my opening questions lead Miss Beech and Miss Rowan in their opposing ways to variously sabotage or reposition my agenda? They had, after all, both agreed to 'be interviewed' but then both question my questioning. Each woman has different concerns but both review my intentions. Miss Beech is more worried about 'ends'; where is her information going? ('I don't want to be . . . about my business all the time.'). Miss Rowan is also dubious about 'ask(ing) them too many questions' and declares her independence from notions of 'community' by insisting 'well I don't suppose we're all the same' and declaring 'I've had to do so much . . . by myself'. These small phrases are telling, even in their incompleteness. They are not 'answers' to my questions and yet they signal a set of values and social histories that are neither accidental nor random but are best seen as traces of alternative discourses that I needed to explore in order to throw light upon the substantive topic of my study.

The provisional power of refusal and re/wording

All elderly people in my study had to make sense of why I wanted to talk with them. They constructed me in terms of previous experiences of interviews (real, televisual and fictional). In the first case it is clear that Miss Beech constructs me as part of the problem rather than as a solution. I presented both women with a particular form of social power; my urgent professional need to know. It was *my* work that was at stake and *my* need to satisfy funders and superiors.[17] They had every right to be circumspect about this educated 'stranger' parachuting into their lives, especially since I had the luxury of escape. Very few of them could remove themselves from their circumstances. Indeed the ideology of 'choice' was so far removed from the realities of their lives, their being literally and metaphorically 'pushed around', that at times this dissonance threatened to stall the research itself. This power imbalance was frequently dramatized in the research encounter for example, when Miss Beech was summarily wheeled out from watching television when I arrived at the appointed time. And yet the extracts show respondents 'answering back' in far from straightforward ways.

Both of the above fragments show two elderly women intent on exercising (in however unstable a mode) a form of provisional personal power – the power of refusal or reinterpretation. In the first extract, Miss Beech is very clear that I pose something of a threat: 'I like that! There you go again you must ask questions'. It is possibly the first time ever for me that having agreed to an interview an interviewee tells me that I can't ask questions. I discovered later, that there were sound reasons for this response. Miss Beech was suspicious of all 'officials', that is social workers and other 'related' 'nosey parkers' because 'these people' were intent on getting her to make a practical decision about giving up her tenancy on a housing association flat.[18] However, to do this would have made her financially liable for contributing to the cost of her place at the nursing home. Ironically, she talks later in the interview of 'never having a crust of bread off the council'. Miss Beech was not the only subject who used the power of *not* making a decision to sustain what she took to be her best interests.[19]

My initial attempt to interview Miss Rowan similarly faltered until we agreed a way to talk. My opening remarks strike me as clumsy. In print it reads like a somewhat instrumental bid for a subject's attention that arises perhaps from doing too many research projects in too short a time. Yet Miss Rowan persevered in talking to me for two hours. It is clearly impossible to display all of this – the transcript runs to 35 pages. In short, she interpreted the research interview as an opportunity to do a life-history review, in the course of which she rehearsed her most troubling and pleasurable stories. The impact of these and other stories will be discussed in the next section.

Miss Rowan had little narrative 'grip' on the sequential history of her life because of impaired memory, yet her reconstructions of specific childhood scenarios was cinematic. She was completely uninterested in the present, and appeared to prefer her past, even though it contained difficult, unresolved experiences. Other researchers have suggested that institutional life is invariably accomplished by routinization and subsequent depersonalization.[20] It seemed to me that conversations about the past were seen by some elderly people as a rare opportunity to reclaim the 'self'. This same impulse may have inspired Miss Rowan's complex attempt to produce a life story that she was often compelled to replay to herself in silence. My questions about 'how she ended up' in the home, which I intended as an invitation to explain her recent circumstances, stimulated a series of flashbacks to childhood, young adulthood and middle age although not necessarily in that order. 'Interviewing' Miss Rowan was a very postmodern experience. In response, I felt driven to cling even more desperately to the 'here and now' of the social policy agenda:

VH: Were you a housekeeper?
GR: No, nothing like . . . oh, I wouldn't be in charge of anybody not even now . . . no it wasn't that sort of service but ahem . . . oh, hell, what can I do? . . . I was 14 . . . I was . . . I left school there's a lot to remember you know.
VH: There is a lot to remember – you needn't remember it all for me at once. [giggles]
GR: [unclear] well I often think about it 'cos they were happy times really.
VH: When you were . . . [puzzled]?
GR: 14 . . . till I left the potteries in '37 that's what you want me to get at don't you?
VH: Well partly that, but I'm also interested in how you lived . . .
GR: . . . before.
VH: If you're not too tired, tell me how you lived in London before you came into this home.
GR: Oh, this home ah . . . I mean this is . . . I've only been here a few months give me a chance.
VH: I know . . . well you have a view about it do you [slight exasperation]?
GR: Well its not me . . . I . . . like freedom.
VH: I know most people would prefer . . .
GR: They're not bad to me but . . . then I'm not as strong as I was at 60. How old am I?
VH: 90.
GR: 90 and I can't do the things I used to do.
VH: Well you can tell me what . . . you can tell me why you ended up here?
GR: You want me to come to London?

VH: Yes [increasing exasperation]. Tell me why you ended up in Hanover [the old peoples residential home].

Although I eventually 'got Miss Rowan to London' and I hoped somewhere nearer to the research agenda, she suddenly shifted both topic and 'discursive register':[21]

GR: Oh this doesn't count at all.
VH: This doesn't count?
GR: No this doesn't count at all. I'm ready to die, I really am.

In the context of a first and only interview such disclosures secured closure. Whatever else our exchange produced it was *not* a neutral consumer review about current social arrangements. Yet it said everything about people coming to their own conclusions above and beyond a concern with 'better social services'. Paradoxically, it would seem that one unpalatable consequence of surviving self-starvation through 'community care' was, for some elderly people, an extenuation rather than an elimination of their difficulties.

Theorizing discourses of elderly frailty: the unspoken, spoken and different

Even fragments of personal narratives can suggest what is involved in the processes of 'ideological becoming'.[22] In this study, frail elderly talk was framed by a moral discourse that seeks to establish the superiority of health and physical robustness. The discourse of 'healthism' works to contain, constrain and filter out frailer voices. At the same time, it carries forward forms of thought associated with possessive individualism – a mindset endorsed by the move to import 'marketization' into ever increasing aspects of civil society.[23] We therefore need to read elderly people's responses carefully as much for what they *do not say* as for what they do.

In this light we can note how the moral discourse of 'healthism' resonates and can be said to articulate with powerful values already offered within the social biographies of some frail elderly people. (Indeed these same Victorian values were actively invoked by the Thatcher government in opposition to the 'nanny' state.) As we have found, two frail elderly women insisted on the values of self-sufficiency to the point that their misplaced independence resulted in their self-starvation. Their removal to institutions – effectively a form of protective custody – meant a loss of personal autonomy that chimed not only against their personal values but also against the philosophy of 'choice' and self-determination. How else did the elderly people in the study respond to being positioned as frail, elderly and marginal?

It was possible to identify several general discursive features in elderly people's accounts. These precepts were co-constructed and can be summed up as follows:

- minimal expectations of the local community and the state;
- maximal aspirations of 'coping' – 'The Life of Brian Syndrome' – accompanied by a compliant tendency to non-complaint about services they were in receipt of

Occasionally elderly people resisted in the form of a refusal or a deferment of decisions. It was extremely rare for them to adopt the 'consumer' role of demanding their 'rights'. Recall that I was actually trying to elicit their *demands*, in the context of a project about their *'needs'*. These 'conservative' responses are inextricably bound in with each other and taken together they determined how elderly people responded to questions about their care. Their answers carried assumptions that in competing and contradictory ways constituted reactions both to their immediate circumstances and to the wider forces of ageism/healthism. I have shown how I was also caught up within these power relays – forced to negotiate different forms of minimal expectations. A different (but equally inhibiting) response was that of relentless cheerfulness – what I have termed colloquially as 'The Life of Brian Syndrome'. This position implied a refusal to acknowledge a stigmatizing definition, in this case the degree of physical frailty, a process that has been called 'dis/identification'.[24] In my study dis/identification was frequently constructed through a willingness to convert impossible situations into 'opportunities'. This was a feature that was far more prevalent in elderly women than in men. Miss Andrews in Riverside noted that there were other people much worse off then herself. She reinterpreted her being 'put to bed' at 5 o'clock in the evening (to conform with the scheduled 'home care') as an opportunity to read. She also refused to wear her mobile alarm because it reminded her of another fall(!), eventually compromising on this by attaching it to her Zimmer frame.

Complaints about care were especially noteworthy because they were so rare. Critical comments about services and their delivery were more in evidence when I talked with the elderly people's advocates – family, neighbours or friends. Those without these forms of social support seldom voiced reservations about their care regimes or the decisions affecting their care.

As noted, some people held out against making decisions as they were influenced by fears about people who asked questions. One source of this reluctance to talk to 'officials' related to personal pride; many subjects stressed that they had managed previously without help. My data clearly provided evidence of a specific ethic that equated help from others with 'charity' and thus saw it as a sign of personal failure. Indeed one way to read the cases of self-neglect (Miss Rowan and Miss Beech) is to reinterpret their withdrawal as a fear of loss of control, which calling in the 'social' might mean.

As an earlier much larger study also found, few elderly people were familiar with the vocabulary of 'consumer choice'.[25] Few took up the decisive role of an active 'consumer'.[26] Since most were either poor or destitute and unused to manipulating 'choices', few had ideas about what 'community care' might mean, and only one of them saw himself as a consumer of 'services'.[27]

Emotional hard labour

Dealing in the above processes was emotionally demanding for both researcher and participants.[28] But as so little is written about the difficulties and demands of researching the frail elderly,[29] it is important to stimulate further discussion about some of the ramifications of interviewing frail elderly people in particular and the elderly in general. The ensuing commentary arises not from any claim to inherent social sensitivity, but because I was not prepared for talking with this group. I suggest that some of these difficulties are practical (about how best to communicate) and some are emotional and social and involve the challenges of listening to harrowing stories and yet being able to 'detach' and 'walk away'. Despite working to a research brief designed to evaluate the workings of social policy, the actual research process meant I must negotiate an entry into people's lives and their prevailing concerns. These tended to be about highly charged events: stories of the tragic deaths of children, of illnesses and deaths of family members. I heard also of family betrayals and neglect.

Feminist researchers have paid detailed attention to the interpersonal nature of research.[30] However, even this literature offers little about researching within the context of extreme old age: it reflects daughters' rather than mothers' stories. Nor is there much about the practical problems of communicating with and understanding people who may have lost the powers of full speech or memory and who are also unable to control their bodily or emotional states. But 'misunderstandings' were also essential clues about why their talk was (as I have shown) frequently wildly dissonant from my fixation with getting them to focus upon 'community care' or to comment upon what they wanted. Moreover, the accumulated effects of listening to highly charged, and apparently off-task topics meant that I created my own coping tactics. These, ironically, mimicked survival strategies used by the people I studied. My interview approach at times consisted of my own resistance to their answers as well as embracing a counselling or caring rather than a 'pure' interviewer role.

My first response to reinterpret stories emerged out of listening to difficult retributive narratives. Part of me wished for more optimistic accounts and in this way I could be said to have incited the 'Life of Brian Syndrome'. For example, I found one elderly woman's insistence that her daughter-in-law 'hated her' so upsetting that I began to gloss her daughter-in-law's actions in positive ways. More generally, I found myself pulled into a counselling role, advising elderly subjects to give people more chances, and even more crassly to keep their proverbial spirits up. More urgently, I found myself chivvying elderly people to eat, or to attend their home's social events, especially in the case of one elderly woman who was so depressed that I was concerned she might just 'give up'.

Intriguingly in view of the above, several of the social workers I interviewed felt that the counselling and mediating aspects of their work were being squeezed out by the demands for practical action stressed in the mechanics of community care.[31]

Conclusion

In conclusion I want to draw out some of the implications of researching questions about decision making in the context of the social divisions of age. All of these bear upon the struggle to understand and represent the complex social realities of any 'minority' or marginalized group. I want to arrange these implications at different levels – the practical, personal, theoretical, political and professional – even if in reality these levels are lived each within the other.

Practical

Interviewing and negotiating meaning-making in the context of extreme old age calls for methodological adaptability. This can start with recognizing and accommodating people's physical disabilities – speaking louder, sitting within very close proximity, sometimes using improvised sign language, seeking out validation about timings and sequencing from others because of memory loss. Old people are frequently ill and can reasonably change their minds about obliging interviewers. Sometimes they forget that they had agreed earlier. Close contact with them via wardens, neighbours and friends is advisable. Indeed I felt it necessary to meet with such 'gatekeepers' as existed, especially neighbours, in case they thought that the elderly person was 'at risk'.

Personal

This concerns the emotional impact of eliciting life histories. We need to bear in mind our own responsibilities here and the effects on the interviewee as well as on the interviewer. This is because such intensity of disclosure is frequently unwarranted in terms of the elderly person's familiarity with the researcher. Loneliness may well propel the elderly to disclose information in order to retain the company of the researcher. Subsequently, they may regret engaging in too much personal talk. We need to be aware of the power we hold as interested strangers who, having established trust and encouraged disclosure, can then move on. Leaving 'the field' may well mean consigning elderly people back to a heightened awareness of their social isolation.

Theoretical

There is a broader, interrelated and more theoretical question that relates to how we think through social divisions and their consequences. As a social policy researcher I am sometimes compelled to act as if the 'client group' under consideration is subjected to one dimension of social disadvantage, and this is particularly true of the 'frail elderly'. I certainly do not want to add to this age essentialism here. Yet it would be specious to discount either the materiality of bodily frailty, or the power of the discourse of 'frailty' and its associated material practices. At the same time I am aware that not all people identified with the category of 'frailty'; frailty was gendered. As I have argued elsewhere, the identification was performed by some elderly men as a tactic of power, in order to extract 'community care' resources from women professionals.[32] In contrast, most women *dis*-identified with the term, precisely because it was in contradiction with the feminine subject position of care-*giving*.[33] This suggests that 'frailty' is not a transparent term.

This chapter has also sought to show how the force of hegemonic discourses about 'proper' bodies has influenced what the frail elderly feel entitled to and thus entitled to say. As I have discussed elsewhere, access to different discourses is not equally available to all.[34] Importantly, whereas traditionally social analysis has always paid attention to the said, the 'notsaid' is also crucial.[35] Moreover, identifying 'structured absences', in this case why so few frail elderly identify themselves as 'consumers' (at least in this research), indicates the conditions of knowledge production: who or what is made into the subject and object of knowledge. Here resonates the full force of elderly people's minimal expectations and 'refusal' to complain.

Political

By investigating 'community care' and its derivative professional health and social welfare actions, I too became inextricably part of an apparatus of power that bears down even within that apparently 'private' encounter known as an interview. In concentrating upon methodological complications I do not wish to claim that these are unique to studying the frail elderly. Physical frailty intensifies the inherent difficulties of understanding the 'other' in research (as in life) and the delicate interpretive manoeuvres involved in meaning-making (and thus of sustaining an interaction) are common to *all* interview exchanges.[36]

Professional

Finally, since 'needs assessment' is the principal means for making claims on 'community care' resources, care in its design and administration is essential. Social workers, like social researchers, stand in an (unwanted) structural relationship to frail elderly subjects. This has a number of consequences, some of which I have outlined above. Care management within family contexts requires the sort of attention to detail and the sort of time and investment of professional labour that are simply not being made available; the cost in terms of the dilution of care for elderly people has yet to be properly recognized. Paradoxically, elderly people are frequently interviewed (by medical staff, by social services staff and occasionally by social researchers).[37] Self-evidently, asking questions is not the same as listening to often uncomfortable answers. Autobiographical talk constitutes a potentially rich source of material and ought to form the groundwork for understanding how the elderly person is coping with their current situation, but it makes numerous demands on the listener – to listen to the spoken and for the silenced. The implications of my own engagement with elderly frail people are clear: practitioners too need to recognize that complex social forces configure elderly people's responses. We will be in a stronger position to understand elderly people's needs if we recognize the social complexities of asking as well as answering questions.

Notes

1 C. Ramazanoglu (1992) 'On feminist methodology: Male reason versus feminist empowerment', *Sociology*, 28 (2): 46–57.
2 R. Griffiths (1988) *The Griffiths Report: Agenda for Action*. London: HMSO.
3 J. Le Grand (1991) Quasi-markets and social policy. *The Economic Journal*, 101: 1256–67.
4 V. Hey (1996) A game of two halves: A critique of some complicities between hegemonic and counter hegemonic discourses concerning marketisation and education, *Discourse*, Special Issue 7 (3): 351–62.
5 A. van Gennep (1960) *The Rites of Passage*. London: Routledge and Kegan Paul.
6 J. Cornwell (1989) *The Consumer's View: Elderly People and Community Health Services*. London: Kings Fund Centre, p. 12.
7 A. Walker (1983) Care for elderly people: A conflict between women and the state, in J. Finch and D. Groves (eds) *A Labour of Love: Women Work and Caring*. London: Routledge.

8 J. Hockey and A. James (1993) *Growing Up and Growing Old: Ageing and Dependency in the Life Course*. London: Sage; B. Macdonald and C. Rich (1984) *Look Me in the Eye: Old Women, Aging and Ageism*. London: The Women's Press.

9 V. Hey (1994a) *Putting the Old in their Place: Age, Ageing and Community Care: A Critical Review of the Literature*. London: Social Science Research Unit.

10 Cornwell op. cit.; M. Henwood (1992) *Through a Glass Darkly: Community Care and Elderly People*. Research Report 14. London: Kings Fund Centre; Hey (1994a) op. cit.; V. Hey (1994b) *Elderly People, Choice and Community Care: A Report of a Research Project*. London: Headley Trust/Social Science Research Unit.

11 N. Coupland, J. Coupland, H. Giles (eds) (1991) *Language, Society and the Elderly: Discourse, Identity and Ageing*. Oxford: Blackwell.

12 M. Forster (1989) *Have the Men Had Enough?* Harmondsworth: Penguin; M. Ignatieff (1994) *Scar Tissue*. London: Vintage.

13 See Hey (1994a) op. cit.; see Hey (1994b) op. cit.

14 V. Hey (1997a) *The Company She Keeps: An Ethnography of Girls' Friendship*. Buckingham: Open University Press.

15 C. Shilling (1991) Educating the body: physical capital and the production of social inequalities, *Sociology*, 25 (4): 653–72.

16 V. Hey (1994b) op. cit.

17 A. Oakley (1997) Women and the gendering of research methods: A case of mistaken identity? Paper presented at the SSRU series Research: For what? For whom?, 25 June. London: Social Science Research Unit.

18 It was impossible for Miss Beech to return to her flat – it could not be adapted for wheelchair use.

19 Hey (1994b) op. cit.

20 T. Kitwood (1992) Towards a theory of dementia care: personhood and well-being, *Ageing and Society*, 12: 269–87.

21 E. Frazer and D. Cameron (1989) Knowing what to say: The construction of gender in linguistic practice, in R. Grillo (ed.) *Social Anthropology and the Politics of Language*. London: Routledge.

22 J. Maybin (1994) Childrens' voices: Talk, knowledge and identity, in D. Graddol, J. Maybin and B. Stierer (eds) *Researching Language and Literacy in Social Context*. Clevedon: Multilingual Matters, in association with the Open University.

23 A. Oakley and A.S. Williams (eds) (1994) *The Politics of the Welfare State*. London: UCL Press; J. Kenway and D. Epstein (eds) (1996) Introduction: the marketisation of school education, feminist studies and perspectives, *Discourse*, 17 (3): 351–62.

24 See B. Skeggs (1997) *Formations of Class and Gender: Becoming Respectable*. London: Sage, p. 13.

25 I. Allen, D. Hogg and S. Peace (1992) *Elderly People, Choice, Participation and Satisfaction*. London: Policy Studies Institute.

26 See Hey (1996) op. cit.

27 V. Hey (1994c) Surrogate mothers and good wives: gendered interactions between community care workers and elderly frail men. Paper presented at the British Sociological Association, Medical Sociology Conference, University of York 23–25 September.

28 A. Beattie (1995) *Identifying Actionable Frameworks for Health Promotion: An Interim Note on the Likely Practice Implications of the Family and Housing Research Project.* London: Health Education Authority.

29 A notable exception is E. Fairhurst (1990) Doing ethnography in a geriatric unit, in S.M. Peace (ed.) *Researching Social Gerontology: Concepts, Methods and Issues.* London: Sage.

30 H. Roberts (1981) (ed.) *Doing Feminist Research.* London: Routledge and Kegan Paul; A. Opie (1992) Qualitative research, appropriation of the 'other' and empowerment *Feminist Review*, 40, Spring: 52–69.

31 See S. Hood (1997) The purchaser/provider separation in child and family social work: Implications for service delivery and for the role of the social worker, *Child and Family Social Work*, 2 (1): 25–35.

32 See Hey (1994c) op. cit.

33 See Hey (1994b) op. cit.

34 See V. Hey (1997b) Northern accents: southern comforts: subjectivity and social class, in P. Mahony and C. Zmroczek (eds) *'Class Matters: "Working Class" Women's Perspectives on Social Class'.* London: Taylor and Francis.

35 J. Scheurich (1995) A postmodernist critique of research interviewing, *International Journal of Qualitative Studies in Education*, 6 (3): 239–52.

36 Hey (1997a) op. cit.

37 Elderly people are frequently and necessarily engaged in struggling to decode interviewers' motives and intentions, especially when so many elderly subjects are endlessly 'interviewed' to so little benefit and have been said to suffer from 'consultation fatigue' and 'consultation cynicism', as cited by a respondent in P. Alderson (1995) *Sharing Health and Welfare Choices with Old People.* Report of a Consent Conference. London: Social Science Research Unit, p. 57.

▶ 8

▷ Gay men: drowning (and swimming) by numbers

▷ **Chris Bonell**

Defining the focus of the research: gay men as a disadvantaged group

Gay men continue to be discriminated against by institutions, including the British National Health Service (NHS). In 1992 King *et al.* reported that the balance of provision in the UK of human immunodeficiency virus (HIV) prevention services (such as safer sex education and free condom provision) targeted to gay men in comparison to that targeted to other groups did not reflect the greater risks of infection amongst gay men, as indicated by the incidence of HIV.[1] HIV infection is not restricted to discrete 'risk groups' since behaviour rather than identity determines risk, but infections do tend to be concentrated amongst what Parker has termed 'socially vulnerable groups'.[2] While globally 70 per cent of HIV infections are transmitted via sexual intercourse between men and women, in the UK men infected via sexual contact with men continue to constitute the group with the highest rate of new HIV infection.[3]

Arguably, because of lessons learnt during the recent history of civil rights campaigning, gay men in the UK have been relatively successful in organizing both in order to educate themselves about HIV prevention, and in order to lobby for government funded HIV prevention.[4] However, the neglect of HIV prevention services targeted towards gay men still remains;[5] despite the existence since 1992 of a 're-gaying' movement, which has sought to highlight inequity of provision and bring about more provision for gay men.[6]

Since 1991 the NHS has been run as an internal market, with health authorities and General Practice (GP) fund holders acting as commissioners, and NHS Trusts and other organizations from the statutory, voluntary and private sectors acting as providers. Some form of commissioner–provider split is likely to remain despite the election of a Labour government in

1997. Most HIV prevention services are commissioned by NHS managers working within health authorities.[7] Commissioners are charged with assessing health needs and issuing specifications for services. Providers then tender for these services, tendering being competitive and judged by commissioners on criteria of cost and quality. A significant amount of HIV prevention research is commissioned locally in this way. NHS managers, based in health authorities, are reported as frequently commissioning HIV prevention research with little or no specialist advice available as to how they use and commission research.[8]

Quantitative research is often equated with positivism,[9] an epistemology that is considered by many to deprioritize and delegitimate the views of research participants. Kitzinger argues that quantitative social research has often been oppressive to gay men, both in how it is undertaken and in its impact upon social policy.[10] MacDonald argues that it is not necessary to reject quantitative methods in order to escape this legacy of oppression.[11] In this chapter, I survey various examples of quantitative HIV prevention research and explore the development of the concept of 'relapse'. I will argue that both qualitative and quantitative social research have valuable parts to play in developing targeted and effective HIV prevention, but poor research, whether quantitative or qualitative can misrepresent gay men's experience; provide an unsound basis for service development; and pathologize gay men. I will suggest that quantitative research does not have to rely on a positivist framework and is most sound, and least oppressive, when it does not. I will question the accuracy of the binary distinction between positivist and interpretivist methods, and suggest that a cloudier picture is more accurate.

I treat gay men's research as a case study for one particular argument, rather than presenting an overview of the field as a whole. This chapter is not an exploration of disadvantage nor a survey of all types of research in the fields of sexuality or HIV prevention. No claim is made that the views set out represent a methodological innovation. Frequent reference is made to the work of Sigma Research and to Project Sigma. This reflects Sigma's considerable input into critiques of poor quality HIV prevention research. I merely attempt to pinpoint what good quantitative HIV prevention research already involves, and to link this with certain arguments presented in the methodological and social theory literature. In doing so, I hope that the lessons learnt in particular research projects might be generalized more effectively, both within the field of HIV prevention research as well as more generally.

Research traditions: disciplines involved in HIV prevention research

Empirical social research has an important role to play in HIV prevention. For example, research can collect evidence about sexual risk taking that is vital in informing both the targeting and the content of HIV prevention projects. Research is needed to describe and to explain the behaviours that promote or limit the spread of HIV infection. In theory, research on gay men, sexual activity and HIV prevention could be the domain of natural, rather than social, science. Sexual acts could be observed and HIV sero-statuses of partners could be tested. Of course, in reality this approach is impossible for practical and ethical reasons. Instead, social research is employed, and gay men's accounts are the major focus of research.

Social and behavioural researchers from a range of disciplines, including psychology, sociology and epidemiology, are involved in HIV prevention research.[12] It is frequently suggested that psychology and sociology employ distinct frameworks within which data are viewed: psychology aiming to explain individual actions; and sociology aiming to explain social practices and institutions.[13] It is also frequently claimed that psychology is mainly positivist in orientation, whereas sociology increasingly is not. While there may be some patterns of distinction between sociology and psychology, differences in how research is pursued are not reducible to disciplinary boundaries. Within HIV prevention research, there is a definite blurring of borders between disciplines. Indeed authors such as Burrows *et al.* suggest that in the current era, frequently labelled 'late-modernity', most social science disciplines are riven with internal disagreements about ontology (theory concerned with the nature of the world under study) and epistemology (theory concerned with the basis of knowledge).[14]

In addition, many of the teams working in HIV prevention research – and health services research in general – include members from a range of disciplines. These so-called 'trans-disciplinary' teams[15] usually work on projects, the terms of which are set by health service commissioners and other funders rather than by academic disciplinary imperatives. In contexts such as HIV prevention research, where funders with limited research advice have a significant influence over the terms of research, it is in social researchers' interests, and in the interests of the disadvantaged groups themselves, for researchers to consider how to retain a certain critical and reflective distance from funders' agendas. Developing a consensus amongst social scientists regarding the framework that underlies quantitative and qualitative research would help in achieving this aim. In this chapter, I hope to make a small contribution to the development of such a consensus.

Positivism versus interpretivism

Hickson *et al.* highlight the intense debate that is raging between positivism and interpretivism amongst HIV prevention researchers.[16] Positivism is generally characterized as an approach that can be applied both to natural and to social scientific research. Blaikie identifies a number of central tenets of positivism.[17] One of these is the priority that is given to observational data; the researcher develops concepts and collects data according to these concepts. A second tenet is positivism's aim of producing general, law-like statements to explain observations. Other tenets include a focus on exploring cause and effect; a striving for objectivity, measurability and repeatability; and a use of reductionist explanatory logic.

Giddens suggests that the roots of interpretivism lie in the belief that different approaches are required in the social sciences compared with the natural sciences:

> The difference between the social and the natural world is that the latter does not constitute itself as 'meaningful': the meanings it has are produced by men [sic] in the course of their practical life, and as a consequence of their endeavours to understand or explain it for themselves. Social life – of which these endeavours are a part – on the other hand, is *produced* by its component actors precisely in terms of their active constitution and reconstitution of frames of meaning whereby they organise their experiences.[18]

Giddens also notes that two points make positivism, as set out in the terms above, an inappropriate framework for social research. Firstly, the social world is one that has been given meaning by its constituent actors. Therefore, in order to explore this world, it is necessary to draw on the concepts that actors themselves use. Consider the difference between a virologist and a social scientist. A virologist can develop the concept of 'viral load' without referring to how viruses constitute themselves. Viruses do not speak and do not characterize their own behaviour. However, a social scientist who wishes to explore why gay men have unsafe sex must explore what gay men, or where relevant a particular sub-group of gay men, themselves understand by terms like unsafe, protection and sex. A positivist approach, whereby the concepts used are developed by the researcher without a dialogue with the researched, is not therefore appropriate.

Secondly, human activity involves a volitional component (since humans possess 'agency') in a manner that the behaviour of atoms or viruses does not. Therefore, positivist science's aim of producing law-like statements is not appropriate to social science. Social science will inevitably and rightly aim to generalize from the context within which research is conducted to other contexts, but this must be on the basis of careful consideration of contextual contingencies, as well as being limited by an acknowledgement that human activity is ultimately beyond mechanical prediction. Both of these points follow from Giddens' assertion in the quotation above that examination of the social world differs from that of the natural world. Admittedly however, in drawing this analytic distinction, adequate consideration is not given to recent developments in the philosophy of natural science, which suggest that positivism is equally inappropriate as a basis for exploration of the natural world.

Quantitative research can be undertaken without signing up to the positivist tenets listed above. Such work can concern itself with: describing associations; identifying locally applicable theories and considering how they might apply to other locales; acknowledging that measures are approximate and partial; and acknowledging the contextual nature of any analysis generated. Indeed, Hammersley has argued that the distinction between positivism and interpretivism is questionable.[19] He argues that social research is characterized, not by distinct paradigms, as the positivism versus interpretivism split suggests, but instead by constellations of ideas that different social researchers adopt to lesser or greater extents. Hammersley argues that the notion that all the features of positivism listed earlier belong together as a united whole is neither logically nor empirically necessary. A researcher might, for example, strive for measurability without seeking to develop general law-like statements.

Hammersley's point is an important one. Examples of quantitative research focused on HIV prevention are set out in the next section. These are not easily divided into positivist and interpretivist. It is clear however that some researchers sign up to *some* of the positivist tenets listed above more than do others. One key area of difference concerns researchers' development of key research measures. Some researchers fall into the trap of not considering sufficiently the views of research participants during the process of developing measures. It is useful to draw a distinction between what could be called 'positivist-leaning' research, which falls into this trap, and 'interpretivist-informed' quantitative research, which does not. I must stress that my use of these terms does not reflect any acceptance of a binary distinction between positivism and interpretivism.

Goals of research: quantitative research under scrutiny

The failing that often afflicts 'positivist-leaning' descriptive research is one of 'premature quantification'. For example, Stall *et al.* attempt to assess sexual risk taking amongst gay men via two measures: anal sex with casual partners regardless of condom use; and unprotected anal sex within a relationship.[20] The researchers' conceptions of risk taking are likely to have differed from the gay men's own notions. Anal sex between casual partners is likely to be relatively safe provided condoms are used. Anal sex between partners in a relationship can be unprotected yet safe provided both partners are HIV negative and do not have unsafe sex with others. The research of Stall *et al.* develops measures of safety and risk without adequately considering how real gay men approach the complex question of avoiding infection with HIV. The implications of this kind of research will be considered later in this chapter.

In social research, especially on such a personal and often private subject as sex between men, it cannot be assumed that there is a sharing of concepts between researcher and researched, or even amongst those being researched. In other words 'mutual knowledge' cannot be assumed, even when both researchers and participants are gay men. Terms such as 'risk' and 'safer sex' may have very different meanings for the researchers and the researched. As a result, the information gained from such surveys is likely to give a very misleading impression of the reality of gay men's sexual activity.

I will now discuss an example of descriptive research that does not suffer from premature quantification. Project Sigma, based at the University of Essex, explored the sexual activity of cohorts of gay men between 1986 and 1992.[21] The main method employed was asking the gay men involved in the research to complete diaries. Rather than using concepts that were developed by the researchers and that could not in reality be assumed to have the same meanings for the gay men involved in the research, the diaries used basic descriptive concepts that could reasonably be assumed to have the same meanings for researchers and researched. The solidity of this assumption was explored in the course of the study: before taking the diaries away for one month, participants recalled, with researchers, the sexual activity that they had been involved in during the past week. This was done in order to explore the meanings of the key concepts, so that researcher and researched understood the terms used in the same way. Sigma asked men to record in the diaries the sex they had in terms of:

> Time, place and antecedents: Day, hour; location (for example, in whose accommodation or external sites, such as parks, toilets, the activity took place), together with antecedents such as the use of alcohol, drugs and nitrites; the participants: (if any); description of the sexual partner/s involved in the session; the sexual activity: for each constituent sexual act in a session – the behaviour; the modality (who did it to whom) and the outcome (whether and how ejaculation occurred); accompaniments: especially use of condoms, lubricants, 'toys', etc.[22]

The Sigma diaries did not attempt to explore issues such as the reasons behind safer or unsafe sex. The researchers concluded that any such analysis of reasons would require qualitative research exploring gay men's own accounts.

Let us now consider the genesis of the concept of 'relapse'. Hart *et al.* suggest that 'relapse' was developed by some researchers, to explain the rising trend in unsafe sex amongst gay men after the initial phase of the HIV epidemic.[23] 'Relapse' portrays gay men as giving up on safer sex, having previously adopted it at the onset of the epidemic. While some gay men may have given up on safer sex, the concept of 'relapse' has in many cases misrepresented gay men's activity.[24] Development of the concept was largely based on poor descriptive research. This resulted in unprotected sex often being wrongly equated with unsafe sex. Rather than simply reverting to unsafe sex, many gay men have developed sophisticated approaches to safer sex; for example, pursuing unprotected sex when they and their partner or partners have satisfied themselves of their convergent HIV status. This has been described as a 'reasoned risk minimization' approach to safer sex or 'negotiated safety'.[25] While the means by which men conclude that their partners are sero-concordant may not always be beyond question,[26] it is crucial to appreciate that a reasoned strategy rather than mere 'relapse' underlies many cases of *apparent* 'relapse'. Furthermore, 'relapse' has pathologized gay men because it portrays intrinsically 'risky' gay men reverting to type.

In summary, the frequently held conceptual distinction between quantitative and qualitative research whereby the former is seen as necessitating a purely positivist approach while the latter necessitates a purely interpretivist approach can be rejected. Instead, all social research – qualitative or quantitative – should flow from actors' own accounts rather than from researchers' prior categories. The distinction between quantitative and qualitative is, according to Anthony Giddens, a practical rather than a philosophical one:

> Quantitative techniques are usually likely to be demanded when a large number of cases of a phenomenon are to be investigated, in respect of a restricted variety of designated characteristics . . . [but] [a]ll so-called 'quantitative' data, when scrutinised, turn out to be composites of 'qualitative' – i.e. contextually located and indexical – interpretations produced by situated researchers . . . and others.[27]

An 'ethnographic moment' whereby research concepts are built on the concepts that actors themselves use, is just as necessary in large-scale quantitative surveys as it is in qualitative exploratory research. It is only permissible to skip the qualitative concept building stage in the design of a questionnaire, or other tool, if the concepts in question can be reasonably assumed to be shared by the researchers and those researched. It is, for example, more reasonable to assume that the question 'Have you ever bought a condom?' can be included in a questionnaire without prior qualitative work, than it is to assume that the question, 'Do you have safer sex?' can be included. Care must also be taken with pre-validated questions: a question may be validated with one group, say UK born, white gay men, but contain concepts that have little meaning for, say, men of other nationalities who have sex with men, but who do not identify as gay.

The research process: dialogue within the research process

I will not systematically consider the research process here. However, I will highlight two particular points within the process in order to illustrate the place of dialogue within it: the value of an ongoing dialogue between HIV prevention researchers and funders; and the importance of feedback to research participants and others from the community in question.

The first point was discussed at a recent HIV prevention conference entitled 'Building Bridges'.[28] In workshops, researchers stressed that they often wished to question some of the concepts present in research specifications issued by funders, on ethical or methodological grounds, while endeavouring to offer constructive alternatives. A researcher might, for example, wish to challenge a research specification if this asked for tenders for research aiming to explain why gay men 'relapse' into unsafe sex.

In order to do this, researchers need to be able to ground their arguments in a coherent methodological and theoretical position. A researcher, for example, with a sociological grounding is likely to find it easier to dispute a funder's request for research on 'relapse' than a researcher with no such grounding. The researcher could, for example, support arguments about the inappropriateness of 'relapse' with theories regarding the social negotiation of sexual activity as well as with data about the extent of the negotiation of unprotected safer sex. The importance of a theoretical underpinning for HIV prevention research cannot be underestimated, given the tendency for research to be commissioned by NHS managers with little or no access to research advice, and for research to be conducted in transdisciplinary teams. Without a firm basis of their own, researchers may find it difficult to question powerful interests within the NHS or to protect the interests of disadvantaged groups. I hope that the approach discussed here contributes to the development of a shared framework for both qualitative and quantitative research.

Secondly, social research should ideally involve ongoing feedback to research participants and, where appropriate, others from the community being researched. This is necessary for ethical reasons, so that the research is not mindlessly parasitic on the views of the researched, without giving them some potentially useful information and analysis in return. It is also useful in order to explore the validity of the analysis presented. Although difficulties may arise if participants reject the conclusions presented by the researcher, researchers should strive for a productive discussion with participants and be open to any criticisms that arise. However they should, at the same time, be prepared to defend their conclusions when they feel that their analyses continue to have validity in the face of criticism.

This position assumes that a researcher has an opportunity to develop a distinct, although by no means a superior explanation of social action. This distinction comes about for two related reasons. Firstly, the researcher should ideally have more time and resources to explore the context of action from a number of examples. Secondly, the researcher is likely to have different aims from the actor: the researcher aims to develop descriptions of sets of actions and explanations for typical episodes of action, whereas actors generally aim to comprehend or justify a particular episode, and may therefore have no desire or need to consider broader factors. Latour suggests that scientific accounts, whether deriving from social scientists or natural scientists, differ from everyday accounts not in their objectivity or rationality, but in their goals.[29] When a researcher's analysis deviates from participants' own analyses and the researcher decides to maintain his or her position, research reports could perhaps indicate where feedback to participants or to others resulted in criticism, without necessarily having to overhaul the analysis so that it can meet with participant approval.

In conclusion: whose interests are served by research?

HIV prevention presents urgent problems that, to be addressed, require evidence. A complex picture of HIV transmission and a complex set of needs require sophisticated research. Quantitative and qualitative research are not incompatible and are both required in order to understand risk taking and to develop effective HIV prevention services. There is an increasing need to understand risk taking resulting from factors other than lack of knowledge about HIV transmission and about safer sex approaches.[30]

While it is undoubtedly the case that structural factors need to be addressed in order to tackle health inequality,[31] it does not follow from this that all short-term responses, which focus on community norms and behaviour, are pointless or even sinister. Similarly, the use of quantitative research to plan HIV prevention strategies cannot automatically be dismissed as surveillance of gay men by the state (although in some cases this may be so). The key question to consider is whose interests are being served by the research and by the provision which is informed by it? In order to consider whose interests are served by research, it is useful to consider how power operates in the research process. Power relations are complex, multi-dimensional and multi-levelled, and vary between contexts. Giddens argues that power is fundamental to all action and equates with the possibility of actors being able to act otherwise. Control is a related but distinct concept. He defines control as 'the capability that some actors, groups or types of actor have of influencing the circumstances of the actions of others'.[32]

Control, in other words, comes down to one actor or group exercising power in order to limit the possibility of one or others acting otherwise. Power cannot simply be seen as equating with the oppression of one group by another, although this undoubtedly is one important example of the exercise of power. The collection of information by state agencies about the behaviour of gay men, for example, may well add to the *power* of these agencies to act. This does not necessarily mean however that the collection of the information leads to increased *control* of gay men by the state. The collection of the information may, in some cases, even add to the power of gay men to organize the provision of community based initiatives or to avoid HIV infection. Oppression is not inevitable. Quantitative research can even be undertaken by gay men's community organizations with the intention of highlighting the inadequacies of state action.[33] The operation of power is, in other words, not a zero sum game.

Furthermore, power and control are causally complex; power play is often difficult to view since the consequences of actions, as Giddens has indicated, are so hard to unravel. Consider, for example, the following question. Is a researcher who uses a structured interview schedule that focuses on relapse controlling the participant seated opposite? The answer depends, in part, on whether the participant feels that he can leave the interview, make points that deviate from the researcher's agenda, or criticize the researcher's ideas. Although in many cases participants clearly are oppressed by the encounter itself, many participants will actually feel bored or irritated rather than oppressed when being asked lots of questions that appear to have little relevance to their own life.

Power-play within the interview is only part of the picture however. Often, a more important implication of research in terms of power is what is done with research once it is completed. Lukes has suggested that the operation of power may be considered in terms of whether the actions in which people are involved work for or against their own interests.[34] It was suggested earlier that the research on 'relapse' caused gay men's sex to be further pathologized and probably caused some HIV prevention for gay men to be misconceived. This connection is, however, a difficult one to establish.

What has been argued here is that non-positivist quantitative research, although clearly prioritizing the analysis of the researcher in research reports, enables the concepts used by participants to be put at the centre of analysis in a way that 'positivist-leaning' research does not allow. This point has been illustrated with reference to 'positivist-leaning' research on 'relapse'. Furthermore, quantitative research does not necessarily deny 'voice' to participants any more than does qualitative research, as the latter puts participants' accounts into the researchers' own framework of meaning. Giddens argues that 'The descriptive language used by sociological observers is always more or less different from that used by lay actors. The introduction of social scientific terminology may . . . call into question discursively formulated beliefs . . . which actors hold'.[35]

As a hypothetical example of this distance between observer and actor, Giddens gives the description that an anthropologist might give regarding a tribal grouping X: the anthropologist will say that 'the X *believe* their ceremonial dance will bring rain' but is quite happy to say of another of their activities that 'the X *grow* their crops by planting seeds every winter [emphasis added].'[36] In similar vein, van Maanen and Kolb have written:

The field worker's understanding of the social world under investigation must always be distinguished from the informant's understanding of this same world . . . To argue that we have become part of the worlds we studied, or that we understand them in precisely the same way as those who live within them do, would be a grave error.[37]

In other words, even research that aims to explore participants' accounts can never simply give voice to participants; voice is always to some extent appropriated. I conclude by arguing therefore that, while quantitative social research is sometimes implicated in the oppression of gay men and other disadvantaged groups, there is nothing inherent in quantification *per se* that brings about this oppression. Social research, whether it is quantitative or qualitative, has the potential to serve or act against the interests of the disadvantaged. Social researchers engaged in quantitative projects have an ethical duty to ensure that the measures that they develop and use represent adequately the conceptual worlds of those being researched.

Acknowledgements

I would like to thank Ann Oakley, Ford Hickson and the editors of this collection for their comments on an earlier version of this chapter.

Notes

1 E. King, M. Rooney and P. Scott (1992) *HIV Prevention for Gay Men: A Survey of Initiatives for Gay Men in the UK*. London: North West Thames Regional Health Authority.
2 R.G. Parker (1996) Empowerment, community mobilization and social change in the face of HIV/AIDS. Paper presented at XI International Conference on AIDS, June 1996, Vancouver. Abstract No. Tu.06.
3 *AIDS/HIV Quarterly Surveillance Tables No. 33: Data to end September 1996*; (1996) London: Public Health Laboratory Service AIDS Centre & Scottish Centre for Infection and Environmental Health.
4 E. King (1993) *Safety in Numbers*. London: Cassell.
5 A. Ridley and S. Jones (1995) *Criteria for Prioritising HIV Prevention Services*. London: HIV Project. Seminar Notes No. 5.
6 King op. cit.
7 C. Bennett and E. Ferlie (1994) *Managing Crisis and Change in Health Care*. Buckingham: Open University Press.
8 C. Bonell (1996) *Outcomes in HIV Prevention*. London: HIV Project.
9 J. Clark (1995) Nursing research, in M.E. Baly (ed.) *Nursing and Social Change*. London: Routledge.
10 J. Kitzinger (1992) Sexual violence and compulsory heterosexuality, in S. Wilkinson and C. Kitzinger (eds) *Heterosexuality*. London: Sage.

11 G. MacDonald (1997) Social work: beyond control, in A. Maynard and I. Chalmers (eds) *Non-random Reflections on Health Services Research*. London: BMJ Publishing Group.

12 M. Boulton (ed.) (1994) *Challenge and Innovation: Methodological Advances in Social Research on HIV/AIDS*. London: Taylor & Francis.

13 R. Bunton and R. MacDonald (eds) (1992) *Health Promotion: Disciplines and Diversity*. London: Routledge.

14 R. Burrows, R. Bunton, S. Muncer *et al.* (1995) The efficacy of health promotion: health economics and late modernism. *Health Education Research*, 10 (2): 241–9.

15 M. Gibbons, C. Limoges, H. Nowotny *et al.* (1994) *The New Production of Knowledge: The Dynamics of Science and Research in Contemporary Societies*. London: Sage.

16 F.C.I. Hickson, P.M. Davies and P. Weatherburn (1997) *Community HIV/AIDS Prevention Strategy Research & Development Review* (unpublished). London: Sigma Research.

17 N. Blaikie (1993) *Approaches to Social Enquiry*. Cambridge: Polity Press.

18 A. Giddens (1974) *Positivism and Sociology*. London: Heinemann, p. 79.

19 M. Hammersley (1995) *The Politics of Social Research*. London: Sage.

20 R. Stall, L. McKusick, J. Wiley *et al.* (1986) Alcohol and drug use during sexual activity and compliance with safe sex guidelines for AIDS: the AIDS behavioural research project, *Health Education Quarterly*, 13 (4): 359–71.

21 A.P.M. Coxon (1994) Diaries and sexual behaviour: the use of sexual diaries as method and substance in researching gay men's response to HIV/AIDS, in M. Boulton, op. cit.

22 Ibid., p. 130.

23 G. Hart, M. Boulton, R. Fitzpatrick *et al.* (1992) Relapse to unsafe sexual behaviour among gay men: a critique of recent behavioural HIV/AIDS research. *Sociology of Health and Illness*, 14 (2): 216–32. The research cited by Hart *et al.* as being responsible for developing the concept of relapse included the following. M.L. Ekstrand and T.J. Coates (1990) Maintenance of safer sexual practices behaviours and predictors of risky sex: the San Francisco Men's Health Study. *American Journal of Public Health*, 80 (8): 973–7; L. Sherr and C. Strong (1990) *Can safe sex be maintained? A study of relapse*. Paper presented at the British Psychological Society Conference, June, London; Stall *et al.* op. cit.

24 Hart *et al.* op. cit.

25 P.M. Davies, F.C.I. Hickson and P. Weatherburn (1996) Contextual and strategic approaches to safer sex among gay men in the UK. Poster presented at XI International Conference on AIDS, Abstract No. Tu.C.2401; S. Kippax, J. Crawford, M. Davis *et al.* (1993) Sustaining safer sex: a longitudinal study of a sample of homosexual men, *AIDS*, 7 (2): 257–63.

26 Davies *et al.* op. cit.

27 A. Giddens (1984) *The Constitution of Society*. Cambridge: Polity Press, p. 33.

28 K.E. Deverell (1996) *Building Bridges Conference Report*. London: National AIDS Manual.

29 B. Latour (1987) *Science in Action*. Cambridge MA: Harvard University Press.

30 Hickson *et al.* op. cit.

31 R. Crawford (1977) You are dangerous to your health: the ideology and politics of victim-blaming, *Journal of Health Services*, 7 (4): 663–80.

32 Giddens op. cit. p. 283.

33 Such as P. Kelley, R. Peabody and P. Scott (1996) *How Far Will You Go? A Survey of London Gay Men's Migration and Mobility*. London: Gay Men Fighting AIDS.

34 S. Lukes (1974) *Power: A Radical View*. London: Macmillan.

35 Giddens (1984) op. cit.

36 A. Giddens (1993) *The New Rules of Sociological Method* 2nd edn. Cambridge: Polity Press.

37 J. van Maanen and D. Kolb (1985) The professional apprentice: observations on fieldwork roles in two organizational settings, in S.B. Bacharach and S.M. Mitchell (eds) *Research in the Sociology of Organizations*, volume 4. Greenwich CT: JAI Press.

▶ **9**

▷ # The 'targets' of health promotion

▷ ## Greet Peersman

This chapter explores the dilemmas of health promotion in its struggle to establish itself as distinct from disease prevention focused on changing individual behaviour. Although the language of health promotion has changed, unbalanced power relations between 'professionals' and 'targets' are nevertheless sustained. The concept of empowerment as 'the process of enabling people to take control over and to enhance their own health', often masks a top-down approach. Consequently, health promotion efforts still tend to focus on the individual only; fail to address the social, economic or ecological determinants of health; and very rarely start from ordinary people's own agendas. For health promotion to survive within an era of cost containment, whatever its approach, it will have to prove what it currently, in most cases, only claims: its impact on health. However, a debate is raging on what constitutes health promotion and how to evaluate it, distracting attention away from the fundamental admonition of 'first do no harm'. I argue that current health promotion practice analysed within a framework of 'distributive justice' and 'intervention ethics' is failing on both accounts, and that it is mainly 'professional' attitudes that are obstructing improvement.

The scope of health promotion: old or new?

Health promotion is often thought of as a 'new' concept, a development of the 'new public health' of the 1970s and 1980s. However, some authors argue that it is merely a 'renaissance' of a broad and encompassing concept of public health.[1] Others claim it is the increased government interest that is 'new', driven by an ageing population, rising healthcare costs, a widening social class gradient in health and pressure from health lobby groups.[2] We have to look at the changing directions of public health over time to be able to understand health promotion as it stands today.

From the seventeenth to the nineteenth century public health was preoccupied with eliminating diseases such as the plague, cholera and smallpox, which posed a threat to a large number of people. With industrialization and rapid urbanization in the nineteenth century, public health gained a broader vision, dealing with all aspects of environmental sanitation including living conditions, mainly with the aim of securing a functioning working population.[3] The bacteriological revolution and further scientific advances in the late nineteenth and early twentieth century shifted attention away from the social and structural causes of ill health towards personal hygiene and an increased interest in the 'healthy body'.[4] Subsequently, three post-war eras then led to the development of a health promotion policy in the USA: 'the era of resource development', which produced a disease-focused medical infrastructure; 'the era of redistribution', which introduced laws to give consumers medical purchasing power and used health education to increase health service utilization; and 'the cost containment era', which aimed to control costs by decreasing the need for medical care and used health education to target appropriate use of health services and to advocate self-care.[5] Rising health care costs and the increase in chronic diseases, most of them preventable, put disease prevention and health promotion on the political agenda.

The term 'health promotion' emerged in US health policy in 1975, it is said, as a last minute substitute for the term health education, merely to avoid having the bills referred to the education committees where they would have died for lack of interest or priority.[6] The publication of 'the Lalonde Report' in Canada and the 'Healthy People Report' in the USA institutionalized a vision of health promotion that, although not exclusively, stressed disease as being associated with controllable risk factors rooted in individual behaviour.[7] The 'Objectives for the Nation' in the USA provided both clear performance indicators and listings of activities for achieving each objective. Although strategies at the levels of institutional change, legislation and policy were included, they proved difficult to implement, especially in an era of fiscal conservatism.[8] As citizen participation and self-care had taken the shape of a significant social movement and represented a welcome relief for programme budgets, it was a short step for public health to shift its emphasis from institution building and centrally planned programmes to self-reliance, person-centred initiatives, and individual participation in health.[9]

The notion of health promotion in Europe had its origins in 1980 when the World Health Organization (WHO) regional office, recognizing that health education in isolation from other measures would not necessarily result in radical changes in health, introduced a range of non-educational approaches, designated 'health promotion'.[10] These centred around health as 'a complete state of physical, mental and social well-being and not merely the absence of disease' and focused on the social, political and economic determinants of health not amenable to improvement by medical care.[11]

Because the discourse of health is so powerful, and because much of our economy is health based, various groups and institutions have varying interests in how health and health promotion are conceptualized. While there is no unanimity, the dominant vision among health promoters today is that too much emphasis has been placed on the healthcare system – relabelled by some a 'sickness care' system – and that priorities need to be re-examined.[12] To this extent, health promotion is a 'reform movement' with its own ideas, language and concepts.[13] The 'new' health promotion aims to go beyond individual lifestyle strategies and embraces empowerment – enabling people to increase control over and to improve their health – as a key strategy. Empowerment implies community participation in identifying both health problems and strategies for addressing those problems.[14]

'Targets' of the 'new' health promotion

While the separation between people and their health status may provide a refreshing alternative to the medicalized notion of health, the notion of positive health cut loose from a disease basis assumes that the desire for health is a moral imperative.[15] Indeed, the Alma Ata Declaration by the WHO and UNICEF proclaimed health as a fundamental human right and the main social aim.[16] Yet, good health does not have a unique value, but is compared with and sometimes exchanged for other desirable goals.[17] Concern for *future* health is in any case a luxury item: all efforts of the poor and unemployed are needed to cope with more pressing and immediate problems.[18] The Ottawa Charter for Health Promotion, which emerged out of the first International Conference on Health Promotion, does acknowledge that the basic prerequisites for any improvement in health are peace, shelter, education, food, income, a stable eco-system, sustainable resources, social justice and equity.[19] Consequently, there seems to be a fundamental ideological conflict about the goal of health promotion: should it target health as an end, or should it aim at social justice using health as a means?[20] According to Michael Yeo, health promotion ethics essentially needs to address two main issues: 'distributive justice' and 'intervention ethics'.[21]

'Distributive justice' is aimed at clarifying principles and values for allocating resources to health, one of which is reducing inequity in health status across populations.[22] A large body of evidence has demonstrated that having a low socio-economic status is one of the major risk factors for disease.[23] Consequently, targeting disadvantaged population groups and putting the emphasis on changing their social and economic context, which often constrains choice in health related matters, should be inherent in ethical health promotion.

'Intervention ethics' deals with assessing various health promotion interventions for their impact on cherished values such as privacy, freedom, responsibility and the common good. 'The individual-versus-the-system-debate' polarizes, on the one hand, the power of free will and a focus on individual behaviour (individual approach) and on the other hand a focus on external circumstances as a determinant of health (systems approach). The individual approach tends to be aligned with interventions towards the voluntary end, whereas the systems approach tends to employ interventions toward the coercive end of the continuum. The difference is essentially a moral debate. Advocates of the individual approach argue the right to choose one's lifestyle free from coercive state intervention: advocates of the systems approach assert the interests, rights and obligations of the community against the individual, and they justify this approach by reference to a need to protect the way of life that holds a community together.[24]

The 'new' health promotion claims to transcend these opposing debates by introducing as a centrepiece of its paradigm the concept of empowerment; for empowerment claims to attribute responsibility to people not for the existence of the problem, but for finding a solution to it. The goal is then 'full and organised community participation and ultimate self-reliance',[25] and the role of the health promotion professional is to facilitate the strengthening or building of such communities. These approaches imply that the 'new' health promotion should start from ordinary people's own priorities and that professionals should be involved only *if* required and *when invited in*. However, no guidance is provided on how to deal with potential conflicts over perceived needs and resources between different communities and stakeholders, or between the agenda of the community and the larger agenda of equity and social justice.[26]

Intervention ethics should also, and perhaps as a priority, address the fundamental admonition of 'first do no harm'.

> Health practitioners who advocate the new health promotion cannot continue to implement these strategies simply because they sound good. Rather, practitioners must be able to demonstrate that the approaches advocated indeed do achieve more health and social benefits for more people than previous approaches. Otherwise, how will we know if anything has changed with respect to health promotion other than the language we use to talk and write about it?[27]

The 'new' health promotion: has anything changed?

Has anything changed in health promotion other than the language? Apparently not. Many health promotion efforts have been criticized for their continued individualized focus, inadequate social and environmental support and failure to 'empower'.

In the UK, for example, the Health of the Nation strategy, launched in 1992, set national objectives and targets commited to the pursuit of 'health' in its widest sense both within the government and beyond. But surely setting targets is diametrically opposed to the essence of the 'new' health promotion in letting communities decide what their priorities are. Moreover, any approach to health promotion that concentrates on telling people not to smoke rather than placing constraints on the tobacco industry, must be serving the interests of capital rather than authentically pursuing good health.[28] Health promotion has also been used as a mechanism for deviance amplification and reinforcement of the stigma associated with illness or disability, thereby justifying intervention in the lives of subordinated populations.[29]

Empowerment has been a much abused term. Policy makers have used it as a rationale for cutting back needed health and social services.[30] Some have argued that its use in the discourse of health promotion professionals effectively masks the existence of a priori concepts that actually direct their actions, with the result that the dynamism of health movements to transform health related social processes is dissipated.[31] Health promotion campaigns have widened the information gap between the better educated and less well educated groups,[32] and those in structurally advantaged positions have benefited most from the changes in lifestyle advocated.[33] Feminist critiques have pointed to the negative effects that campaigns have had on women's feelings of guilt for seemingly not responding to health education messages.[34] The emphasis has been on people's failure and poor attitudes rather than on what they have achieved in often difficult circumstances. A study of child safety care, for example, revealed that parents in poor housing were severely constrained in their ability to safeguard their children because the housing had unalterable dangerous features. However, mothers had a keen sense of when, where and why their children were in danger, and were already taking many practical and imaginative steps to try and keep their children safe.[35] Similarly, approaches aimed at promoting the health of minority ethnic communities have often stressed cultural and linguistic differences and how these inhibit good health related behaviour but have obscured or played down more fundamental issues that inhibit equality of opportunity to achieve good health: socio-economic differences and gender inequalities.[36]

Perhaps the most harmful side of health promotion has been the creation of an 'epidemic of apprehension' converting 'persons at risk' into 'anxious persons at risk' who do not manage to achieve much change in their health related behaviour. In addition, the mass media, well aware that we are now a society obsessed with health matters, has often attributed an unjustified degree of certainty to new health related findings and exaggerated the risks posed by putative health hazards.[37] The creation of the 'health promoting self', the structuring of choice, and the commodification of health products are commonly the topics of critiques.[38] As Meredith Minkler points out: 'health promotion is rapidly becoming a $10 billion industry in its own right . . . the centrepiece of the information industry with some 5,000 lay health texts and numerous popular health promotion magazines doing a brisk business.'[39]

Researching health promotion: looking for evidence of the 'new' direction

But are things really that bad? In analysing the health promotion literature, it certainly looks as if the 'new' health promotion has not yet established itself. Over the past three years, a research team at the SSRU has addressed the questions: what health promotion interventions have been carried out and what evidence is there for their impact on health? This research took place as part of the work of the Centre for the Evaluation of Health Promotion and Social Interventions (EPI-Centre), an information, resource and training centre established in 1995 with the aim of promoting evidence based health promotion.[40]

We have systematically searched for health promotion studies through personal contacts, electronic database searching (including Medline, EMBASE, Social Science Citation Index, PsycLIT and ERIC), hand searching of key journals and scanning of reference lists. All relevant references were compiled in a bibliographic register and coded for the type of study, the health focus, the country where the study was carried out and the population involved. Intervention studies were further coded for the setting, the intervention provider and the type of intervention. With the purpose of conducting effectiveness reviews, we focused specifically on some topics: reports on evaluations of workplace health promotion, and of sexual health interventions targeting young people and men who have sex with men.[41] We described these studies in terms of the development, content, implementation and acceptability of the intervention, the methodological quality of the evaluation, and the impact on health related outcomes.

The bibliographic register contains 6,790 references to health promotion related studies to date. Most (74 per cent) are descriptive studies (including surveys, case control studies, cohort studies and reviews) rather than studies reporting on the evaluation of interventions (26 per cent). This indicates that answering the question 'what works in health promotion?' is complicated by the fact that relatively few relevant studies have been carried out. In addition, the impact of many interventions has been assessed on intermediate outcomes, such as knowledge, attitudes, intentions, and clinical risk factors, rather than on health outcomes *per se*.

Of the 1,141 studies describing and/or evaluating interventions (Table 9.1), only 2 per cent were carried out in developing countries; and very few (2 per cent) focused on reducing health inequalities by specifically targeting disadvantaged populations in resource-rich countries. The vast majority (80 per cent) of studies involved populations in institutionalized settings (formal education, health care system, workplace); few (14 per cent) took place in a community setting and even fewer (3 per cent) by means of outreach. Only 17 per cent tackled particular health problems in different settings concurrently. These figures are problematic in the sense that although socially disadvantaged groups and countries should be specifically targeted to tackle health inequalities, most health promotion work has been carried out in well resourced countries with easy-to-reach populations. For example, with more than 90 per cent of people with HIV living in developing countries, but with most of the research capacity going on in the established market economies, there is an urgent need to bridge the gap through the development of prevention programmes and the access to treatment. Although the boundaries between different settings are artificial as far as people's health and its determinants are concerned, few interventions have tackled health issues across settings. In addition, it is well known that the majority of disadvantaged people worldwide live in circumstances that offer little intersection with formal education, health services or the workplace setting. Hence, more effort and resources need to be expended on community based and outreach activities.

In terms of the types of interventions provided: 25 per cent included education only; 22 per cent aimed at increasing access to resources and/or services; 9 per cent involved an environmental modification; and regulation (such as a smoking ban) or legislation (such as a cycle helmet law) was the subject of only 5 per cent of studies (Table 9.1). The majority (65 per cent) of interventions were individualized approaches; only 26 per cent provided an individualized approach complemented by at least one change in the environment. Although there is no inevitable link between knowledge and behaviour change or the ability to increase control over one's health,[42] a quarter of interventions still consisted of education only. Interventions addressing the wider social context were limited both in frequency and scope.

Of the 139 evaluation studies of workplace health promotion that we identified, very few (9 per cent) were based on 'felt' need – what people say they want or what they think are the problems that need addressing; only 17 per cent involved employees in the development of the intervention; and just 19 per cent included a measure of acceptability as part of the evaluation.[43] These results imply that few opportunities have been created for the 'target' group to be involved in the planning, development and evaluation of health promotion interventions, and hence that a lot of health promotion is driven by 'professionals'. The picture we have currently obtained from evaluations is incomplete; this is because few studies

Table 9.1 *Health promotion intervention studies (N = 1,141)*

	N	%
*Health focus**		
Accidents/injury	110	10
Mental health	61	5
Nutrition	133	12
Physical activity	100	9
Sexual health	363	32
Substance abuse	472	41
Inequalities in health	23	2
Other	143	13
*Country**		
North America	819	72
Europe	218	19
Developing countries	19	2
Other	97	9
*Intervention setting**		
Educational institution	416	36
Workplace setting	301	26
Community setting	159	14
Health care setting	158	14
Mass media	77	7
Home	56	5
Residential care	46	4
Outreach	36	3
Unspecified setting	41	4
More than one setting	192	17
*Intervention type**		
Education	830	73
Skill development	335	29
Education only	280	25
Personalized advice	268	23
Resource access/service		
Access/social support	246	22
Screening	165	15
Physical activity	130	11
Environmental modification	100	9
Legislation/regulation	55	5
Other	97	9

*not adding up to 1,141 or 100% due to overlap

have included the range of measures necessary to answer questions about whether or not an intervention works, and how it works or why it does not.

The effectiveness reviews of sexual health promotion targeted at young people or at men who have sex with men included 123 studies overall. Although 86 per cent of these studies claimed success in changing at least one of the targeted outcomes, most (78 per cent) of the evaluations had methodological flaws that invalidated the authors' conclusions. This clearly indicates the need to improve the standard of evaluation research in health promotion and to be critical in the use of evidence to inform decisions in planning and implementing services.

Discussion: beyond the good intentions

Where does it go wrong? Some have claimed it is the political will that is lacking:

> The individualistic approach will persist . . . because however misguided, [it] is less costly politically as well as for programme budgets, and for economies – at least in the short term.[44]

For instance:

> An inquiry . . . into the cost-effectiveness of the Health of the Nation strategy [in the UK] showed that spending on health promotion in 1996 . . . represents less than 1 per cent of the National Health System (NHS) annual budget and less than the expenditure on staff cars and travelling and subsistence in 1994–95. Yet anecdotal evidence suggests that costs pressures, coupled with the inability to present conclusive evidence of effectiveness, are conspiring to make health promotion contracts a soft option for budget cuts.[45]

Given the reality of cost containment, competition and positioning for resources and markets are well known phenomena within the present health care culture:

> In Canada . . . a greater share of resources will be allocated to health promotion, and probably a lesser share to the health care system . . . Thus we see various agencies and institutions redescribing their mandate in terms of health promotion. The document A Guideline for Health Promotion by Health Facilities (1990), which to the chagrin of health promotion purists comprehends even transplant programmes under the heading of health promotion, is a telling case in point.[46]

Marshall Becker ironically argues that:

> It is not surprising that all this attention and allocation of resources has led the research community on a relentless search for new 'risk factors'. Could wearing a wrist watch cause cancer? Possibly. After all, there is often skin irritation; the luminous dial might be trouble; perhaps watching the time fly by leads to stress, depression, heart disease, or suicide. Handled properly, this idea contains three grants, five papers, and a movie (although for the experiment, we will have to devise a method for attaching a watch to a mouse's foot).[47]

Clearly, professionals are having a hard time vying for limited resources, and a commitment to start from people's own agendas seldom provides a competitive advantage.

But are only the policy makers and the market economy to blame? As Hunt indicates:

> A neglected issue in . . . community participation is the need for education and enlightenment of professionals and officials, planners and politicians who may exhibit more rigidity of attitude and behaviour than will be found among lay people.[48]

This point is endorsed and amplified by Meredith Minkler, with emphasis on the realities of power relations:

> Behind the euphemisms of empowerment and community participation lay the realities of power, control and ownership. The very real structural distinctions that exist between professionals and communities, and our very location as professionals in health agencies and bureaucracies, confer a certain power that includes the power to set the health agenda.[49]

She goes on to describe how elderly residents in a neighbourhood with daunting health problems, organized efforts toward crime prevention. These efforts were given much of the credit for the 18 per cent drop in the crime rate twelve months into the project:

> When asked what their major health concerns were, they responded 'crime', and the students politely said, 'you misunderstood, we were asking about health problems'. The residents held their ground, pointing out that they couldn't safely go outdoors without being mugged, and therefore couldn't get to the doctor's office, go for a walk, or get an evening meal. Crime, they argued was their biggest health problem . . . Then [they] helped the residents organise a community-wide meeting on the subject of crime and enlist the support of the mass media . . . The students and staff also helped, but always in the

background, as residents began the Safehouse Project . . . Had the students and staff [of the project] failed to pay attention to and support the community's definition of need, they might still be running support groups in hotel lobbies one morning a week – if indeed they were still welcome at all.[50]

Professionals are finding it very difficult, consciously or not, to let go of their own ideas and judgements, whether in determining which problems to address or what should be done. And this also extends to the domain of establishing whether one is doing more good than harm:

> Many health promoters are nervous of the terms 'success' or 'failure' in relation to programmes, as if in some way programme performance is tied directly to their own professional self-esteem. To avoid failure, they avoid evaluation.[51]

Good practice in health promotion is not self-evident: some programmes have failed to achieve their goals; others have made problems worse. The need to improve both the quantity and quality of evaluation research has been stressed by many authors.[52] Evaluation of health promotion, however, is a hotly debated issue. In a presentation on 'how to move towards evidence-based health promotion interventions', Erio Ziglio argues that the definition of a health promotion intervention is one of the most salient issues to be addressed:

> there is a wide range of programmes which, although labeled health promotion, do not fit the theoretical and operational principles which define health promotion . . . health promotion interventions tend to be complex, use multiple strategies and operate at different levels . . . To mention just one implication, there are some significant practical difficulties in employing a randomised control group approach to evaluate health promotion programmes/policies.[53]

His suggestion not only excludes the vast majority of ongoing programmes, it effectively contracts health promotion out of rigorous evaluation. According to his argument, and that of other commentators, the appropriate quest seems to focus on finding methods that will inevitably show the effectiveness of health promotion:

> The current search for evidence of effective health promotion is unlikely to succeed and may result in drawing false conclusions . . . health promotion may be designated 'not effective' because it is being assessed with inappropriate tools . . . Action needs to be taken urgently to redress the negative consequences on health promotion of a misdirected search which is veering off course.[54]

The 'new' health promotion has certainly helped to move the field beyond the victim blaming rhetoric that often accompanied the lifestyle approach,[55] and in concept at least, has become synonymous with 'empowerment' and 'community participation'. However, it has tended to cast the notion of empowerment as meaning essentially collective political action. In doing so, the 'new' health promotion disregards the multi-dimensionality of power and ignores the point that empowerment can in fact occur at many different levels. For example:

> for an individual to join a smoking cessation programme and succeed in quitting smoking may be as empowering as a community taking action to prohibit cigarette advertising on its local billboards ... Direct services of health and social service professionals can be empowering ... The important criterion is how the direct services are delivered.[56]

In other words, there is a wide choice of interventions involving a range of professionals, from health care workers targeting individual behaviour to politicians making policies on employment, housing conditions, transport and so on, that potentially contribute to improving health, preventing disease and reducing social inequalities. Rather than continuing the debate about what constitutes 'true' health promotion, 'professionals' need to reflect on how they interact with their 'clients' and how they justify why they do what they do. As Ann Oakley requests: 'join me in finding ways of spending less time in paradigm disputes and boundary-marking and more time trying to systematise our knowledge in such a way that it can be used to reduce the damage unsystematic professional beliefs do to people's lives, and even to change the world for the better.'[57] What are we waiting for?

Notes

1 L. Green and M. Kreuter (1991) *Health Promotion Planning: An Educational and Environmental Approach*. Mountain View, California: Mayfield Publishing Company.
2 P. Hawe, D. Degeling and J. Hall (1995) *Evaluating Health Promotion: A Health Worker's Guide*. Sydney: MacLennan and Petty.
3 J. Lewis (1986) *What Price Community Medicine? The Philosophy, Practice and Politics of Public Health since 1919*. Brighton: Harvester.
4 Lewis op. cit.
5 Green and Kreuter op. cit.
6 Ibid.
7 M. Lalonde (1974) *A New Perspective on the Health of Canadians*. Ottawa: Government of Canada; US Surgeon General (1979) *Healthy People: The Surgeon General's Report on Health Promotion and Disease Prevention*. Washington DC: Department of Health and Human Services.
8 M. Minkler (1989) Health education, health promotion and the open society: an historical perspective, *Health Education Quarterly*, 16 (1): 17–30.
9 Green and Kreuter op. cit.

10 R. Parish (1996) Health promotion. Rhetoric and reality, in R. Bunton, S. Nettleton and R. Burrows (eds) *The Sociology of Health Promotion. Critical Analyses of Consumption, Lifestyle and Risk*. London: Routledge.

11 A. Robertson and M. Minkler (1994) New health promotion movement: a critical examination, *Health Education Quarterly*, 21 (3): 295–312.

12 M. Yeo (1993) Toward an ethic of empowerment for health promotion, *Health Promotion International*, 8 (3): 225–35; D. Seedhouse (1997) *Health promotion: Philosophy, Prejudice and Practice*. Chichester: John Wiley.

13 Minkler (1989) op. cit., p. 225.

14 Robertson and Minkler op. cit.

15 M. Kelly and B. Charlton (1996) The modern and postmodern in health promotion, in R. Bunton *et al.* op. cit.

16 G. Macdonald and R. Bunton (1992) Health promotion: discipline or disciplines?, in R. Bunton and G. Macdonald (eds) *Health Promotion: Disciplines and Diversity*. London: Routledge; World Health Organization (1978) *Alma Ata 1978: Primary Health Care*. Geneva: World Health Organization, Health for All Series, no. 1.

17 C. Davidson and G. Davey Smith (1996) The baby and the bath water. Examining socio-cultural and free-market critiques of health promotion, in R. Bunton *et al.* op. cit.

18 G. Rose (1995) *The Strategy of Preventive Medicine*. Oxford: Oxford University Press.

19 *Health Promotion*. Ottawa: Ottawa Charter for Health Promotion (1986), 1 (4): i–v.

20 Robertson and Minkler op. cit.

21 Yeo op. cit., p. 226.

22 Minkler (1989) op. cit.

23 P. Townsend, N. Davidson and M. Whitehead (1992) *Inequalities in Health*. Harmondsworth: Penguin; S. Feinstein (1993) The relationship between socio-economic status and health: a review of the literature, *Milbank Quarterly*, 71 (2): 279–322; N. Kreiger, D.L. Rowley and A.A. Herman (1993) Racism, sexism, and social class: implications for studies of health disease, and well-being, *American Journal of Public Health*, 83 (1): 82–122; G. Davey Smith, D. Blane and M. Bartley (1994) Explanations for socio-economic differentials in mortality. Evidence from Britain and elsewhere, *European Journal of Public Health*, 4 (2): 131–44.

24 Yeo op. cit.

25 Ibid., p. 223.

26 Robertson and Minkler op. cit.

27 Ibid., pp. 308–9.

28 S. Nettleton and R. Bunton (1996) Sociological critiques of health promotion, in R. Bunton *et al.* op. cit.

29 N. Schiller (1992) What's wrong with this picture? The hegemonic construction of culture in AIDS research in the United States, *Medical Anthropology Quarterly*, 6 (3): 237–54.

30 M. Minkler (1994) Challenges for health promotion in the 1990s: social inequities, empowerment, negative consequences, and the common good, *American Journal of Health Promotion*, 8 (6): 403–13.

31 V.M. Grace (1991) The marketing of empowerment and the construction of the health consumer: a critique of health promotion, *International Journal of Health Services*, 21 (2): 329–43.

32 Hawe *et al.* op. cit.

33 Nettleton and Bunton op. cit.

34 N. Daykin and J. Naidoo (1996) Feminist critiques of health promotion, in R. Bunton *et al.* op. cit.

35 B. Mayall (1986) *Keeping Children Healthy*. London: Allen & Unwin.

36 J. Douglas (1996) Developing anti-racist health promotion strategies, in R. Bunton *et al.* op. cit.

37 M.H. Becker (1993) A medical sociologist looks at health promotion, *Journal of Health and Social Behaviour*, 34: 1–6.

38 For discussion see Robertson and Minkler op. cit., Grace op. cit., and Becker op. cit.

39 Minkler (1989) op. cit., p. 21.

40 G. Peersman, S. Oliver, A. Oakley *et al.* (1996) Establishing an information resource and training centre on evidence-based health promotion. Paper presented at the 3rd European Conference on Effectiveness, Turin: 12–14 September, p. 17; G. Peersman and J. Levy (1998) Focus and effectiveness of HIV prevention efforts for young people, *AIDS* 12 (Suppl. A): S191–S196.

41 A. Oakley, S. Oliver, G. Peersman *et al.* (1996b) *Review of Effectiveness of Health Promotion Interventions for Men Who Have Sex with Men*. London: EPI-Centre; G. Peersman, A. Oakley, S. Oliver *et al.* (1996b) *Review of Effectiveness of Health Promotion Interventions for Young People*. London: EPI-Centre; G. Peersman, A. Harden and S. Oliver (1998) *Review of Effectiveness of Health Promotion Interventions in the Workplace*. London: EPI-Centre.

42 Peersman *et al.* (1996b) op. cit.

43 Peersman *et al.* (1998) op. cit.

44 Yeo op. cit., p. 339.

45 V. Speller, A. Learmonth and D. Harrison (1997) The search for evidence of effective health promotion, *British Medical Journal*, 315: 316–63.

46 Yeo op. cit., p. 227; Health and Welfare Canada (1990) *A Guide for Health Promotion by Health Care Facilities*. Ottawa: Minister of Supply and Services.

47 Becker op. cit., p. 3.

48 S. Hunt (1990) Building alliances: professional and political issues in community participation. Examples from a health and community development project, *Health Promotion International*, 5 (3): 179–85.

49 Minkler (1994) op. cit., p. 406.

50 Minkler (1994) op. cit., p. 406.

51 Hawe *et al.* op. cit., p. 14.

52 Peersman *et al.* (1996b) op. cit., N. Clark and K. McLeroy (1995) Creating capacity through health education: what we know and what we don't know, *Health Education Quarterly*, 22 (3): 273–89; D. Kirby and R.J. DiClemente (1994) School-based interventions to prevent unprotected sex and HIV among adolescents, in R.J. DiClemente and J.L. Peterson (eds) *Preventing AIDS: Theories and Methods of Behavioural Interventions*. New York: Plenum Press; D. Kirby, L. Short, J. Collins *et al.* (1994) School-based programs to reduce sexual risk behaviours: a review of effectiveness, *Public Health Reports*, 109 (3):

339–60; B. Israel, K. Cummings, M. Mignan *et al.* (1995) Evaluation of health education programs: current assessment and future directions, *Health Education Quarterly*, 22 (3): 364–89; A. Oakley, D. Fullerton and J. Holland (1995) Behavioural interventions for HIV/AIDS prevention, *AIDS*, 9: 479–86; A. Oakley, D. Fullerton, J. Holland *et al.* (1995) Sexual health education interventions for young people: a methodological review, *British Medical Journal*, 310: 158–62.

53 E. Ziglio (1996) How to move towards evidence-based health promotion interventions, Paper presented at the 3rd European Conference on Effectiveness, Turin. 12–14 September, p. 4.

54 Speller *et al.* op. cit.

55 Robertson and Minkler op. cit., p. 363.

56 Robertson and Minkler op. cit., p. 302.

57 A. Oakley (1998) Personal views. Living in two worlds. *British Medical Journal*, 316: 482–3; (p. 483).

10

Users of health services: following their agenda

Sandy Oliver

'Celia,' said Dorothea, with emphatic gravity, 'pray don't make any more observations of that kind.'

'Why not? They are quite true,' returned Celia, who had her own reasons for persevering, though she was beginning to be a little afraid.

'Many things are true which only the commonest minds observe.'

'Then I think the commonest minds must be rather useful.'[1]

Defining the focus of the research: who or what?

The focus of health services research depends fundamentally on our understanding of its goal. Is the focus the work of clinicians, how they apply their skills and resources and organize health services, with the goal of how best to attain sufficient physical health for discharge? Or is it the health of people needing or requesting services for themselves and their families, and their experiences of these services and the impact on their lives?

Before the launch of the NHS Research and Development (R&D) Programme in Britain in 1991 there had been no systematic attempt to relate important health issues to the national effort in research. 'Innovation in *medical* research [had] been driven largely by the intrinsic interests of disease processes to clinicians and scientists [emphasis added]'.[2] An additional impetus came from the commercial interests of industry. Thus the focus was primarily set within the vision and interests of the medical profession and industry, although those with the greatest vested interest in the quality of the health service and the research that guides its development are people who might benefit from its services for their own health. The NHS R&D programme aims to direct research towards questions of practical importance to a wide range of health professionals and those in their care. Increasing importance is now attached to seeking out and acting upon the views of NHS service users and the wider public on the coverage and delivery of those services,[3] although progress has been limited.[4]

Views may be drawn from a broad range of lay people to inform health services and focus related research on the interests of service users. These lay people include current users of services; contingent or potential users (i.e. the general public); potential users of specific services (e.g. disease-specific groups, older people, pregnant women); carers of those with specific needs (e.g. families of people who are ill or handicapped); and organizations speaking for users and potential users, especially those least able to speak for themselves, such as Community Health Councils and disability-specific organizations.[5]

Defining 'service users', 'lay people' and 'consumers' presents practical difficulties for identifying and attracting appropriate individuals with ideas and skills to shape research agendas. This difficulty is heightened when token lay involvement is more common than equal partnerships so that lay organizations and their members may compete for the few positions of potential influence. Consequently it is not unusual for meetings of lay people to be dominated by discussion of alternative definitions. Such differences of opinion have sometimes been exploited to further undermine token involvement. One example of a 'real' consumer who would be attractive to a service committee obliged rather than committed to work in partnership would be a new mother with fresh personal experience of the service, who has also barely come to terms with her newly acquired life role and is unable or unwilling to rock the boat at her local maternity unit where she hopes to return to give birth a second time in the near future. Meanwhile, an experienced lay spokesperson supported by an organized group with the potential to express a range of views is dismissed as 'unrepresentative'. Similarly lay groups committed to fund raising for the service may be more welcome than those seeking partnership and shared decision making.

Some people with personal experience of ill health mistrust what they call 'professional consumers'; staff employed within the voluntary sector who may be invited to speak on their behalf. Similar doubts have been expressed by paid staff themselves about their ability to consult sufficiently widely to represent a wide range of views accurately when resources and time are limited. However, lay groups are expected to behave in a professional manner, maintaining a proper standard, and be businesslike rather than amateurish. Given adequate time, paid staff supported by office resources may be better placed to gather views and prepare briefing materials for spokespeople, whether these be volunteers or staff.

Describing these people as 'lay' is sometimes misleading. Many of them draw on professional experience and skills from other spheres. For instance HIV/AIDS health services attract activists who are typically white, well educated gay men, rather than intravenous drug users or prostitutes who are also at high risk of HIV. In the field of cancer too, many activists are well educated, well organized, professional women who can draw on legal and scientific skills. Their efforts have focused on breast cancer, a disease associated with early onset of menstruation, late childbearing and hormone replacement therapy,[6] all of which are more common amongst this social group. There is no similar groundswell of lay people proactively participating in research focused on cervical cancer, a disease more frequent amongst lower socio-economic groups, although lay involvement in developing and evaluating services is ongoing where professionals have taken the initiative. Similarly in maternity care research, the British National Childbirth Trust, with its middle-class membership, has a long history of involvement in research. However, there are exceptions to this trend, such as the accident prevention project in Corkerhill,[7] led by residents of a deprived area (see below). It is also likely that ethnic minority groups are less well represented, and research into this issue has recently been commissioned within the NHS R&D programme.

In addition lay people with an intimate knowledge of their health, ill health and social circumstances may be better informed than their professional carers because to their experiential knowledge they have added research based knowledge, which they have been highly motivated to seek out.

The common feature shared by all these disparate groups is who they are not. They are not agents of the NHS with responsibilities for developing, delivering, monitoring or evaluating health services. So I exclude general practitioners and other professional groups (such as social workers, community nurses) who are sometimes called upon to represent lay views by acting as spokespeople and agents for their patients or as customers of other services, in the same capacities, and internal customer departments within the health and social services.[8] I also exclude professional researchers commissioned to evaluate health services, who have to respond to their commissioners while undertaking research that serves the needs and accommodates the values of lay people, as well as those of professionals asking how best to develop or deliver a service.

Given these boundaries, I can claim first-hand lay experience of health services research as a member of the National Childbirth Trust's Research and Information Group (1989–94). The lay/professional divide is illustrated by my reports of this experience, which appeared only in lay publications at that time, and in professional and academic literature only after I had joined the academic community in 1995.

Research traditions: within professional boundaries

Health services research includes a broad range of methodologies to determine what services are needed; how they may be delivered and at what cost; how they may be received; and what impact they may have on the health of individuals and populations. Which interventions to develop and how to evaluate them are choices conventionally made by professionals in light of their experience and interest, and differences are thus reflected in the conduct and use of research by different professions. For instance, although trials of smoking cessation programmes have been judged effective in terms that satisfy obstetricians and paediatricians, whose interests are primarily the birth weight and health of the baby,[9] they do not convince health promotion specialists, who criticize the narrow focus of such trials, which ignore possible feelings of guilt or the strain on family relationships that may ensue when women refrain from smoking.[10] A wider vision of what constitutes good health is reflected in trials of social support for disadvantaged mothers (whom we know from epidemiological data are often smokers)[11], which address a broad range of outcome measures embracing their children's health as well as how the women feel physically and emotionally and how they cope socially.[12]

A comparable variation in definitions of health arises from studies concerned with helping women in labour. Evaluations of epidural anaesthesia have focused attention on immediate physical health, such as pain, length of labour, complications and interventions during labour, foetal distress and neonatal well-being,[13] and interpretations of laboratory measures, to inform the practice of anaesthetists. Meanwhile, studies of social support for labour that have ignored laboratory measures, but included measures of social and emotional well-being (including postnatal depression), have justified changes in midwifery practice.[14] However, neither approach reveals whether additional benefit can be gained from social support alongside epidurals or whether epidurals negate the benefits of social support, and trials of epidurals have ignored detrimental outcomes, which, it is hypothesized, may arise from diverting midwives' attention away from the labouring woman to the instrumentation that accompanies epidurals.

Recognizing the natural bias of research led by single professions, commissioners encourage multidisciplinary teamwork to tackle health services research questions, but if such teams do not include lay people they lack a critical dimension.

Goals of research: to meet the needs of service users

Lay critiques

The shortcomings of a report on a drug treatment for people with Alzheimer's disease[15] have been highlighted by people who provide an information service to the public outside a clinical setting. Consumer health information staff recognized that carers' questions had been ignored, so we cannot know whether their distress was prolonged rather than relieved.

Evidence of effectiveness may be distorted by the choice of outcomes, as in the examples above, or in the choice of interventions to be compared. Given that, in the NHS, medical and technological care is more likely to be assessed in trials that influence key decision makers in NHS management, there is a risk that social aspects of health and care will be overlooked even if these are appreciated particularly highly by service users. If social care requires investment or change of practice, evidence of its effectiveness may be required to justify the costs or, indeed, provide evidence of cost-effective alternatives if low technology care has to compete in a culture of evidence-based healthcare.[16] Examples of social aspects of care being overlooked are in a systematic review of trials comparing the effectiveness of Caesarean section and vaginal deliveries for breech-presenting babies.[17] We do not know whether planned Caesarean section was compared with supine labour or upright and mobile labour, because social and behavioural aspects of labour were not reported. Biasing knowledge by focusing research on narrow technical questions that ignore social context and outcomes is unjustifiable when there is relevant experience to draw on elsewhere. For instance, there are rigorous evaluations of support for childbearing women by familiar carers, extra support if the women are socially disadvantaged, a cosy place to give birth, encouragement for mothers to cuddle or breastfeed their new-born babies, and help for them to teach their babies socially acceptable sleeping patterns.[18]

Lay influence?

Varying perspectives may be apparent when planning research, as well as after it is reported. A survey of home births and lay responses to planning meetings highlight markedly divergent views.[19] The researchers wanted to 'assess this problem' of 8000 home births a year and saw a need to compare *planned home confinements* with *planned hospital confinements*. But among lay groups, as well as their preference for different use of language, there was concern that the focus of the research question on comparing *planned* home births with *planned* hospital births would systematically exclude the collection of information from women who keep an open mind about the place of birth until they are in labour, and women who have 'unplanned' home births because they were prevented by service providers from formally arranging a home birth. The researchers took into account many lay comments such as replacing 'place of confinement' with 'place of birth', and giving more attention to collecting information about details of social support and non-medical pain relief in labour. However, although the scope of the research question was broadened to include unplanned home births, the survey instruments continued to bias systematically against providing data from women who were discouraged from giving birth at home. The limited influence lay people have on research in its planning phases, despite timely discussion, emphasizes the power held by the researchers, who may have their own goals for advancing knowledge.

When reviewing the findings of trials testing professional support for families of people with schizophrenia, lay people recognized some short-comings: the trials failed to address emotional well-being or the stress experienced by the family or carers. Views of both patients and carers are relevant because their interests may not always concur: rehospitalization is a relapse for the patient but may be a relief for their families. In this instance the researchers allowed the lay views to be incorporated in a report of a systematic review,[20] which may not be such a radical measure as there is no immediate consequent need to redirect research effort. Indeed, the science of systematically reviewing evidence of the effects of health care lends itself to lay involvement because it allows criticism of the primary research without challenging the reviews' authors. Already reviewers are seeing opportunities to recruit lay people to their cause when they wish to challenge professional colleagues with whom they disagree. So who really has the power of influence? And over whom?

Lay-instigated research

Lay people not only identify missing social and emotional aspects of professionally led research, they also try to redress this imbalance with their own research, by focusing primarily on social and emotional issues. For instance, to explore in greater depth the findings of an earlier piece of work, which had asked parents of children who were blind and partially sighted how they thought the services and care they received could be improved, the Royal National Institute for the Blind (RNIB) investigated parents' experiences of the help and support they received when learning that their child was visually impaired.[21] Arthritis Care, working with the Social Services Inspectorate of the Department of Health, identified key issues essential to the provision of responsible community services for isolated disabled people and highlighted examples of local good practice to help social services departments, voluntary organizations and others develop services.[22]

The National Childbirth Trust, working with North Essex Health Authority, Mid Essex Community Health Council and the University of North London, explored women's expectations and experience of choice during pregnancy, childbirth and early parenthood.[23] Maternity Alliance and NCH Action for Sick Children studied poverty and undernourishment in pregnancy.[24] Maternity Alliance also studied the effectiveness of three linkworker and advocacy schemes in empowering minority ethnic community users of maternity services.[25]

Paying attention in research to social aspects of care may have important influence on people's lives. Accident prevention as a focus for potential intervention and research often attracts more interest in changing the behaviour of individuals to keep themselves and their families safer, than addressing the risks that may be imposed by the environment. A notable exception to this was research in Corkerhill, an economically and socially deprived area of Glasgow, where residents took the initiative and approached researchers for help. The subsequent research showed that:

> parents were acutely aware of the risks, and that they take many practical and imaginative steps to keep their children safe. Safety behaviours are more common and valued than risky behaviours, and to a large extent the limits on child safety have more to do with design and adaptability than with knowledge and motivation.[26]

A number of health gains followed this research. Three times a week up to 50 children join the local 'Dangerwatch' scheme where, rather than being 'talked at' about safety, children are given the much more interesting job of identifying potential dangers in their homes, backcourts and streets. Also, Glasgow City Council invested £970,000 in a central heating system for Corkerhill. This was probably the result of a number of initiatives: the Corkerhill Damphouse inquiry; representations made by Corkerhill Community Council to the Scottish Office; and evidence from the accident prevention research on the risks people perceived as being related to their damp housing. 'While in traditional accident prevention terms, the installation of central heating might seem a long way from getting children to cross roads safely, from the tenants' perspective, a warm house is more likely to be a safer house for their children.'

Lay people may adduce, from their own experience, potential explanations for health or disease, or propose innovative ways of improving health, which provoke new research questions. For instance, biochemical investigation of essential fatty acid metabolism in boys with attention-deficit hyperactivity disorder[27] was inspired by a survey of a large population of children with hyperactivity conducted by a self-help group in West Sussex.[28] Another example is a study of HIV/AIDS and suicide,[29] which followed the decision of a lay group that 'something had to be done: the mental health burden of this problem was becoming unbearable for many individuals and voluntary organizations were signalling that staff were now finding it difficult to cope'.[30]

Advanced innovative service development and evaluation arising from lay people's perceptions of health can be found in the work of Changing Faces, a charity that aims to create a better future for people of all ages who have a facial disfigurement, whatever its cause or severity. Rather than campaigning or fund raising to improve clinical services, Changing Faces aspires to make the process of learning to live with facial disfigurement easier for all concerned and intends that all its work be underpinned, monitored and informed by objective research.[31] In partnership with the

Faculty of Community Studies at the University of West of England, Changing Faces evaluated the impact of its own programme of social interaction skills workshops to help adults tackle the problems associated with facial disfigurement.[32]

Lay priorities

An interest in the social and emotional aspects of well-being also emerges when lay people consider what research questions should be prioritized and these have featured in lay responses to written consultations from the NHS R&D programme.[33] When formally requested to identify important research questions the National Childbirth Trust discussed the issue with their members in their quarterly journal, *New Generation*, at their Members' Conference and in a mailing to the 350 local branches. Twenty-four responses were received from individual members, branch committees, working mothers' groups and members attending social gatherings and a study day. Topics recommended for further research included a wide range of issues: some high-technology practices, some established practices, some new ideas and many variations on the theme of patient information and support.

When this wide ranging list was restricted to five 'burning issues' for a national study to establish priorities for research in midwifery,[34] suggestions were scored by a panel of ten NCT members, half of whom had a particular interest in research. Their final choices were all issues that call for preventive measures, excellent communication skills and an appreciation of the social context and long term consequences of care.

Methods for service user centred research

In addition to the influence of lay perspectives on the choice of interventions to be developed and evaluated, and the terms and outcomes with which they are evaluated, lay perspectives may demand new methodologies. In some areas of health care, for instance skin care, lay people are sceptical of the value of large randomized controlled trials because they know that not everyone sharing a condition responds equally well to the same treatments, and they fear that treatments that are seen as effective for only a minority of people may be withdrawn from the health service. Their priority for research may not be trials evaluating different preparations, but a search for the best design of 'n of 1' trials, which identify effective treatments for individuals. 'N of 1' trials include only one individual who is seeking the best treatment for their particular chronic problem. Different treatments are employed at randomly allocated time intervals to determine the most effective care for the individual patient. Changing the time periods,

including gaps between treatments and developing personally relevant outcome measures are all methodological challenges that are highly relevant
to people with chronic disease. Recurrent diseases or diseases that alter-
nate relapse with remission pose additional methodological problems, which
may also be faced within the context of an '*n* of 1' trial. Multiple sclerosis
is such a disease where conventional measures of effectiveness do not take
into account the unpredictability and devastating impact of relapse, which
patients and their families recognize as such an important problem.[35]
Indeed, unpredictable ill health can be more stressful to families than
predictable but more serious illness or disability. There is a need for better
measures of relapse, recurrence or remission as part of a comprehensive
array of outcomes for assessing health and effectiveness of care for chronic
conditions.

The research process: balancing the power

Actively engaging the communities in a study of their needs, their aspirations and their services can be seen as a moral and strategic imperative.[36]
That professional and lay priorities may not coincide is both the reason for
involving lay people, and the reason for excluding them. Time and resources invested in lay involvement might otherwise be spent on pressing
clinical problems. But time and resources need to be invested in open
debate to determine which problems are most pressing: both clinical problems, and the social (communication and support) problems more frequently highlighted by lay people. Lay people with time for thought and
discussion will be more challenging than those struggling to keep up with
a pre-set agenda, so investment in time and resources in lay involvement
changes the balance of power.

Language and channels of communication, as well as time, can limit the
potential for research. Insights about the limitations and potential for
health and health services research can come to light through qualitative
research methods where the interviewee is encouraged to speak in their
own terms and not merely respond to other peoples' specific questions.
They also come to light through the efforts of journalists, through discussions amongst lay people, and through the research and campaigning activities of lay groups – keeping an ear to the ground in the voluntary sector
rather than the postgraduate medical centre. Lay concerns can inform the
research process through bridging lay language and technical language;
and through linking lay networks with professional networks.

When lay people's insights are not merely the fruits of the research
process, but also direct research, the boundaries between the researchers
and the researched are blurred and the research agenda changes. Thus the
research process must address not only the methodology for answering

research questions, but also the methodology for asking them. There is a need to focus on the methodology for identifying priorities, shaping research questions and developing socially applicable outcome measures: the methodology of involving lay people in guiding research. Such shifting interests can only increase the role of social science in health services research, and the tasks of social scientists in undertaking research. Lay involvement may be through community meetings, structured group discussions, drop-in centres, Delphi surveys or collaborative ventures, but the degree of participation may vary with the degree of lay interest and the quality of facilitation, making evaluation essential.

The impact of involving lay people in research could be revolutionary. But any revolutionary outcome will be missed if, as is often the case, the moral and strategic imperative recognized by health promotion specialists, of involving lay people is restricted to 'a self-study of their needs and aspirations'[37] and excludes their services: involving lay people in the evaluation of services is rarer and more challenging. In addition, a revolution may be more imagined than real, depending on the criteria for success. In health promotion, where enthusiasm for lay involvement has coined the phrase 'healthy alliances', it has been suggested that the success of such alliances may be evaluated by investigating the characteristics of the alliances themselves. Criteria for success are proposed to include clear and common goals at all organizational levels with appropriate contributions of resources from all the partners to indicate a shared commitment. Clear roles and responsibilities when working together, sharing information, decisions and accountability, are seen as integral components for following the principle of equal partnership.[38] But whose criteria for success are these, and who applies them, when they have been developed in a project where all those named as report authors, advisory group members and test site participants are health service, government or university employees? More objective measures of successful partnerships are also proposed as the outcomes they achieve such as changes in policy, services, environment, knowledge or behaviour. But objective measures can also be partial, and such changes may be interpreted differently by those initiating a project and those subsequently invited to respond. The inescapable conclusion is that initiatives must be partial and so must their evaluation. However, the degree of partiality may be open to scrutiny if reporting includes how the research question posed has been developed, as well as how it has been answered and reported, and by whom.

An exceptional example of a report including details of the research partnership, as well as the technical aspects of the research, combined the participatory principles of health promotion and the concepts of effectiveness research. It was a multi-site, randomized, controlled trial of a health education programme for coke oven workers in the American steel industry, which aimed to reduce the risk of occupational lung cancer.

The effective implementation of the program was dependent on the unique collaboration between the union and the university. This collaboration began eight years before the development of the coke oven intervention programme and provided a foundation for an integrated approach to its design, implementation and evaluation. Specifically, the collaboration affected the substance of the programme, the presentations, the development and operation of a publicity campaign, the design and content of the questionnaires and telephone interview schedules, and the hiring and training of laid-off coke oven workers who served as telephone interviewers. All levels of the union were involved in the programme, including the international office, district officials, and individual local unions . . . [the] programme was unique in combining the expertise of coke oven workers themselves and university personnel, and allowed [them] to meet fully the criteria for developing health education programmes espoused by the American Public Health Association.[39]

Even more unusual was a report reflecting on the research process where the first named author was a lay member of the community at the focus of the research.[40] Despite their disappointing experiences with previous research, residents of Corkerhill approached researchers for help:

> We in Corkerhill do of course recognise that the professional research body may be able to take information through doors which the community cannot open, but we have learned to be cautious, if not downright suspicious, of those who would 'assist' us in this way.
>
> Too often we have been subjected to the 'goldfish bowl' approach to research. We have been researched upon. The researcher selects the topic, studies his subject and returns to the lofty towers of academia leaving a bemused community who very soon realise that they have gained nothing from the experience. Despite this apparent cynicism, not only do we recognise the need for good research and the powerful potential it has, but we are confident enough to believe that we have a contribution to make to it . . . because living daily with problems of poverty, poor housing, unemployment and raising children in what can only be described as a hostile environment, we have our own 'expertise'.

Residents played an important role in helping to devise the survey, arranging interviews and forming a lynchpin between the researchers and the community for the research they instigated themselves. Meanwhile they denied access to other would-be researchers who arrived at their doors unannounced. Thus, vested interest appears to be a strong motivating factor for individuals to participate in research, and the goal of relevant sound research should also be a strong motivating factor for researchers to involve lay people in research.

In conclusion

The active involvement of lay people has been described as part of the evolutionary process of health services research.[41] An increasing role for lay people in health services research demands changes similar to those attributed to the entry of women into science.[42] The relatively new discipline of health services research can be expected to mature through:

1 lay people undertaking scientific roles, collecting data, refining instruments;
2 lay people and their research needs becoming the focus of the research, rather than professional interventions being the focus of the research;
3 inclusion of long-term, socially relevant health measures, rather than merely applying short-term health measures conveniently accessible in hospital settings;
4 using new methodologies to address the complexity and the variation of people's life situations, alongside those tools developed with conventional approaches;
5 questioning the values that have driven health services research, and setting priorities afresh by integrating lay perspectives.

Researching the social context of healthcare and social well-being will not only yield a better understanding of complex conditions and complex ways of caring, but it will also offer lessons for research on more conventional subjects of health and health services, such as drugs, which have spearheaded evidence-based healthcare, albeit within narrow frameworks.

Acknowledgements

The ideas in this chapter rest on discussions over many years, while I was a lay member of the National Childbirth Trust's Research and Information Group and the Cochrane Collaboration, and later as a member of the Social Science Research Unit. Examples of lay critiques of research are drawn from this experience and from work with the Critical Appraisal Skills Programme, Oxford Institute of Health Science (supported by the Kings Fund). I am particularly grateful to the many lay people who responded positively to a request from Phyll Buchanan and myself for examples of their own research (work funded by the Standing Advisory Group on Consumer Involvement in Research and Development).

Notes

1 G. Eliot (1871) *Middlemarch*. Harmondsworth: Penguin (1994), p. 72.
2 M. Peckham (1991) Research and development for the National Health Service, *Lancet*, 338 (8763): 367–71.

3 M. Peckham (1995) Consumers and research in the NHS: Forward, in *Consumers in the NHS: An R&D Contribution to Consumer Involvement in the NHS*. Leeds: Department of Health.

4 S. Oliver and P. Buchanan (1997) *Examples of Lay Involvement in Health Research*. Report to the Standing Advisory Group on Consumer Involvement in the R&D Programme. London: SSRU.

5 M. Blaxter (1995) Consumers and research in the NHS: consumer issues within the NHS, in *Consumers in the NHS* op. cit.

6 J.R. Harris, M.E. Lippman, U. Veronesi *et al.* (1992) Breast cancer, *New England Journal of Medicine*, 327 (5): 319–28.

7 C. Rice, H. Roberts, S. Smith *et al.* (1994) 'It's like teaching your child to swim in a pool of alligators': Lay voices and professional research on child accidents, in J. Popay and G. Williams (eds) *Researching the People's Health*. London: Routledge.

8 Blaxter op. cit.

9 J. Lumley (1995) Strategies for reducing smoking in pregnancy, in J.P. Neilson, C.A. Crowther, E.D. Hodnett *et al.* (eds) *Pregnancy and Childbirth Module of The Cochrane Database of Systematic Reviews*, [updated 27 September 1993]. Available in The Cochrane Pregnancy and Childbirth Database, 1995, Issue 1.

10 H. Graham and S. Hunt (1994) Women's smoking and measures of women's socio-economic status in the UK, *Health Promotion International*, 9 (2): 81–8; A. Oakley (1989) Smoking in pregnancy – smoke screen or risk factor? Towards a materialist analysis, *Sociology of Health and Illness*, 11 (4): 311–35.

11 H. Graham (1987) Women's smoking and family health, *Social Science and Medicine*, 25 (1): 47–56.

12 E.D. Hodnett (1996) Support from caregivers for socially disadvantaged mothers, in M.W. Enkin, M.J.N.C. Keirse, M.J. Renfrew *et al.* (eds) *Pregnancy and Childbirth Module of The Cochrane Database of Systematic Reviews, 1996* [updated 29 February 1996]. London: Cochrane Library, BMJ Publishing Group.

13 C. Howell (1995) Epidural versus non-epidural analgesia in labour, in J.P. Neilson, C.A. Crowther, E.D. Hodnett *et al.* (eds) *Pregnancy and Childbirth Module of The Cochrane Database of Systematic Reviews*, [updated 6 May 1994]. Available in The Cochrane Pregnancy and Childbirth Database, 1995, Issue 2.

14 E.D. Hodnett (1996) Support from caregivers during childbirth, in J.P. Neilson, C.A. Crowther, E.D. Hodnett *et al.* (eds) *Pregnancy and Childbirth Module of The Cochrane Database of Systematic Reviews*, [updated 6 June 1996]. Updated quarterly. London: Cochrane Library, BMJ Publishing Group.

15 D. R. McLachlan, A. J. Dalton, T. P. Kruck *et al.* (1991) Intramuscular desferrioxamine in patients with Alzheimer's disease, *Lancet*, 337 (8753): 1304–8.

16 L. Sherr (1995) Suicide and AIDS: lessons from a case note audit in London, *AIDS Care*, 7 (supplement 2): S109–S116.

17 G.J. Hofmeyr (1996) Planned elective Caesarean section for term breech presentation, in M.W. Enkin, M.J.N.C. Keirse, M.J. Renfrew *et al.* (eds) *Pregnancy and Childbirth Module of The Cochrane Database of Systematic Reviews, 1996* [updated 29 February 1996]. London: Cochrane Library, BMJ Publishing Group.

18 The Cochrane Library [database on disk and CD ROM]. The Cochrane Collaboration. Oxford: Update Software; 1996. Updated quarterly.

19 G. Chamberlain, A. Wraight and P. Crowley (1997) *Home Births: Report of the Confidential Enquiry by the National Birthday Trust Fund*. Carnforth: Parthenon Publishing Group.

20 J.J. Mari and D. Streiner (1996) Family intervention for those with schizophrenia, in C. Adams, J. Anderson and J. De Jesus Mari (eds) *Schizophrenia Module of The Cochrane Database of Systematic Reviews*, [updated 6 June 1996]. London: Cochrane Library, BMJ Publishing Group.

21 I. Cole-Hamilton and S. McBride (1996) *Taking the Time: Telling Parents their Child is Blind or Partially Sighted*. London: Royal National Institute for the Blind.

22 Social Services Inspectorate and Arthritis Care (1996) *Disability and Isolation; A Joint SSI/Arthritis Care Study of Isolated People with Arthritis*. London: Social Services Inspectorate and Arthritis Care.

23 M. Gready, M. Newburn, R. Dodds *et al.* (1995) *Birth Choices: Women's Expectations and Experiences*. London: National Childbirth Trust.

24 Maternity Alliance and NCH Action for Sick Children (1995) *Poor Expectations: Poverty and Undernourishment in Pregnancy: Summary*. London: Maternity Alliance and NCH Action for Sick Children.

25 The Maternity Alliance, London (1996) *Consumer Empowerment: A Qualitative Study of Linkworker and Advocacy Services for Non-English Speaking Users of Maternity Services*. London: Maternity Alliance.

26 Rice *et al.* op. cit.

27 L. Stevens, S.S. Zentall, J.L. Deck *et al.* (1995) Essential fatty acid metabolism in boys with attention-deficit hyperactivity disorder, *American Journal of Clinical Nutrition*, 62 (4): 751–8.

28 I. Colquhoun and S. Bunday (1981) A lack of essential fatty acids as a possible cause of hyperactivity in children, *Medical Hypotheses*, 7: 673–9.

29 Sherr op. cit.

30 J. Campbell (1995) HIV and suicide: is there a relationship? *AIDS Care*, 7 (supplement 2): S107–S108.

31 Changing Faces Annual Report. 1995–1996. London: Changing Faces.

32 E. Robinson, N. Rumsey and J. Partridge (1996) An evaluation of the impact of social interaction skills training for facially disfigured people, *British Journal of Plastic Surgery*, 49: 281–9.

33 S. Oliver (1995) How can health service users contribute to the NHS research and development programme? *British Medical Journal*, 310 (6990): 1318–20.

34 J. Sleep and E. Clark (1993) Major new survey to identify and prioritise research issues for midwifery practice, *Midwives' Chronicle*, 106 (1265): 217–18.

35 P. Cardy (1997) Multiple Sclerosis Society. Talk at the Anglia and Oxford Annual Conference of Community Health Councils, 15 October 1997, Northampton.

36 L.W. Green and M.W. Kreuter (1991) *Health Promotion Planning: An Educational and Environmental Approach*, 2nd edn. London: Mayfield.

37 R. Funnell, K. Oldfield and V. Speller (1995) *Towards Healthier Alliances: A Tool for Planning, Evaluating and Developing Health Alliances*. London: Health Education Authority.

38 Rice *et al.* op. cit.
39 D. Parkinson, E.J. Bromet, M.A. Dew *et al.* (1989) Effectiveness of the United Steel Workers of America Coke Oven Intervention Program, *Journal of Occupational Medicine*, 31 (5): 464–72.
40 Rice *et al.* op. cit.
41 A. Maynard and I. Chalmers (1997) *Non-Random Reflections on Health Services Research.* London: BMJ Publications.
42 L. Dumais (1992) Impact of the participation of women in science: on rethinking the place of women especially in occupational health, *Women and Health*, 18: 11–25.

11

▷ People's ways of knowing:
gender and methodology

▷ **Ann Oakley**

Antoine de Saint-Exupery's
classic work *The Little
Prince* begins with an
account of how the author,
as a child, drew a picture
of a boa constrictor

From *The Little Prince*, 1974, p. 7

digesting an elephant. When he showed this to 'the grown-ups' he thought
it might frighten them, but they interpreted the drawing as a representation of a hat, which they found not in the least frightening. This moment
of contested perception provoked permanent scepticism in him about the
ability of grown-ups to demonstrate understanding and imagination. So
when the child who drew the boa constrictor became a grown up himself,
and a pilot, and his plane broke down in the middle of the Sahara desert,
and a little prince from asteroid B-612 appeared and asked him to draw a
sheep, he was not at all surprised. Saint-Exupery goes on: 'If I have told
you these details about the asteroid, and made a note of its number for
you, it is on account of the grown-ups and their ways. Grown-ups love
figures. When you tell them that you have made a new friend, they never
ask you any questions about essential matters. They never say to you,
"What does his voice sound like? What games does he love best? Does he
collect butterflies?" Instead, they demand, "How old is he? How many
brothers has he? How much does he weigh? How much money does his
father make?" Only from these figures do they think they have learned
anything about him'.[1]

These observations and experiences are one way of representing the
conflict between different ways of achieving knowledge about the world
that amongst social researchers are known as 'qualitative' and 'quantitative'
methods.[2] As is demonstrated elsewhere in this book, a commonly accepted

alliance has developed between research method and research subject, according to which 'qualitative' methods are often used to privilege the experiences of oppressed social groups. What I argue is that this division of methodological labour is, firstly, socially and historically constructed, and, secondly, problematic in terms of the potential of 'qualitative' methods to produce an emancipatory social science with trustworthy knowledge claims.

The argument about methods

'Qualitative' methods are usually taken to mean unstructured or semi-structured interviewing, participant observation, ethnography, focus groups, life histories and other approaches that involve researchers in actively 'listening' to what the researched say. 'Quantitative' methods are equated with questionnaires, surveys, structured observations and experimental studies, including randomized controlled and other kinds.[3] There are many grey areas. For example, is 'action research' a 'qualitative' or 'quantitative' method? What about the narratives that are often written on self-administered questionnaires? How 'structured' does interviewing have to be to escape the label 'qualitative'? But these uncertainties do not prevent the contrast between the two sorts of methods being widely perceived as a mutual antagonism.[4] While contentions about their relative merits could be politely termed a dialogue,[5] it is, in many ways, more appropriate to call the dialogue a war. Table 11.1 is taken from Reichardt and Cook's discussion of 'qualitative' and 'quantitative' methods in evaluation research.[6] The collections of features shown in the two columns of Table 11.1 have led some to propose that what is really going on here is a *paradigm* clash. The popularity of the term 'paradigm' is traceable to Kuhn's work on *The Structure of Scientific Revolutions*;[7] it can be defined as a 'total matrix of beliefs' about theories, research questions and research data.[8]

The main point about paradigms is that they are *normative*; they are ways of breaking down the complexity of the real world that tell their adherents what to do. Paradigms are essentially intellectual *cultures*, and as such they are fundamentally embedded in the socialization of their adherents: a way of life rather than simply a set of technical and pro-cedural differences. One advantage of seeing 'quantitative' and 'qualitative' methods as paradigms with their own cultures is that we can then trace the shaping of each culture by a distinct set of traditions. Over the past 50 years, the quantitative 'paradigm' has been fed principally by the dis-ciplinary traditions of natural science and medicine, while those providing 'qualitative' research, with its distinctive commitment to viewing events and situations from the perspective of the researched, include phenomeno-logy and ethnomethodology, symbolic interactionism, naturalism, and Weber's notion of *verstehen*.

Table 11.1   *Attributes of the qualitative and quantitative paradigms*[9]

Qualitative paradigm	Quantitative paradigm
Advocates the use of qualitative methods	Advocates the use of quantitative methods
Phenomenologism: concerned with understanding behaviour from actors' own frames of reference	Logical positivism: seeks the facts/ causes of social phenomena
Naturalistic and uncontrolled observation	Obtrusive and controlled measurement
Subjective	Objective
Close to the data: the 'insider' perspective	Removed from the data: the 'outsider' perspective
Grounded, discovery oriented, exploratory, expansionist, descriptive, inductive	Ungrounded, verification oriented, reductionistic, hypothetico-deductive
Process-oriented	Outcome-oriented
Valid: real, rich, deep data	Reliable: hard and replicable data
Ungeneralizable: single case studies	Generalizable: multiple case studies
Holistic	Particularistic
Assumes a dynamic reality	Assumes a stable reality

This notion that the division between 'quantitative' and 'qualitative' methods amounts to a paradigm clash, is supported by a striking feature of much of the argument about 'quantitative' versus 'qualitative' methods: how little of it is concerned with *the appropriateness of the method to the research question*. The choice of method is dictated by the paradigm rather than by the question to be addressed in the research. Another puzzling feature of much of the discussion can also be referred to an understanding of the debate about 'quantitative' and 'qualitative' methods in terms of paradigms: why the label 'positivist' so often appears as a term of abuse.[10]

The problem of positivism

Anyone who believes that hypotheses need to be warranted, anyone who uses numerical data or statistics, anyone who is concerned about representativeness or generalizability or the credibility of research findings is liable to be deemed a 'positivist'. One problem with this is that the term 'positivism' ceased long ago to have any useful function as a literal designator. As Hammersley has put it, 'all one can reasonably infer from unexplicated usage of the word "positivism" in the social research literature is that the writer disapproves of whatever he or she is referring to'.[11] The philosophers to whom the term accurately applied are long since dead; and in the words of another critic, 'any living social scientists who either bandy the term around, or are the recipients of it as an abusive label, are so confused about what it means that, while the word is full of sound and fury, it signifies nothing'.[12]

Of course, it is not quite true that the term signifies nothing. There *are* differences between research carried out by social scientists and by other scientists. Where the primary purpose of the research is, for example, to map patterns of health and illness in a community, or to identify effective therapeutic interventions for treating disease, the principal method of choice will not be in-depth interviewing of a small sample, but, respectively, collecting data from a large, representative sample, and undertaking a prospective experimental study using random allocation and enough people to produce statistical 'power'. This means that researchers trained in medicine or psychology *are* less likely than those trained as sociologists or anthropologists to use research methods that prioritize a view of research participants as active agents constructing their own meanings. Only 2 per cent of papers in medical journals report 'qualitative' research.[13] This is one reason why the *British Medical Journal* recently sponsored a series introducing these perspectives to the medical research community.[14] Characteristic of these different approaches to research is a pronounced difference of opinion about experimental methods as the 'extreme' end of the 'quantitative' range. Disagreement about the ethics, power relations and usefulness of experimental research designs is particularly marked in health promotion, although it also features prominently in the discourses of anti-quantitative feminist researchers.[15]

Ideas about what science 'is' commonly figure in discussions of the merits and demerits of different research methods. But equating positivism with 'science' is also problematic. Commonly held notions about science are that it consists of a unitary set of methods and procedures, and that its purpose is to uncover causal laws through a linear, evolutionary process. However, much of what social scientists implicitly refer to as science is not recognizable within science itself.[16] For example, contrary to the image of science as a linear activity carried on outside the domain of the social, scientific knowledge is developed in non-linear and culture-dependent ways;[17] scientists often do not agree among themselves as to the essential nature of scientific activity; and they are involved in constructing the character of the natural world rather than merely in describing pre-existing facts about it.[18] Local circumstances and conditions, including the social relations of science itself, thus shape the science that is produced. The creative and contingent nature of much scientific endeavour is well represented in Evelyn Fox Keller's biography of geneticist Barbara McClintock, with its suggestive title *A Feeling for the Organism*.[19] As the American methodologist Campbell has observed, 'science depends upon qualitative, common-sense knowing even though at best it goes beyond it'.[20]

In many ways, protests against 'positivist science' in the sociological and social research communities have involved proponents of the qualitative paradigm in a false war. Taking a brief look at the origins of research methods helps us to understand this better. Methods (procedures for collecting research data) and methodology (the study of methods) are intimately related to questions of epistemology (theories of knowledge). Thus, asking questions about the history of research methods leads us back to the institutional histories of both natural and social science.[21]

A (very) brief history of research methods

Modern science was delivered from philosophy by the midwife of empiricism during the eighteenth century. Crucial to this separation was a rejection by Enlightenment thinking of the dominant tradition of natural theology, which formulated laws about the nature of the universe irrespective of empirical evidence. In the 1920s a group of scientists, philosophers and mathematicians known as the Vienna Circle established 'logical positivism'. Its two central tenets were that data should be analysed logically and that only knowledge based on experience should legitimately constitute science.[22] Again, one main function of the argument was to contest the prevailing vogue for metaphysical philosophy with its introspective pursuit of 'unsolvable riddles'.[23] The philosopher and social scientist Michael Scriven called the Vienna Circle 'a band of cut-throats that went after the fat burghers of Continental metaphysics who had become intolerably inbred and pompously verbose'.[24]

The conceptual framework of positivism came originally from social science. The term 'social science' was first used in France in the 1790s by the revolutionary political philosopher, Condorcet.[25] What Condorcet envisaged was a mathematically based social science, which would place more faith in objective measures than in subjective impressions. For a time the terminology of '*art social*' competed with '*science sociale*'; throughout its history social science, and especially sociology, has been seen by some as closer to fiction than to science.[26] Comte, one of the 'founding fathers' of sociology, coined the term 'positivist' in the 1830s. He took the view that all sciences passed through a series of states beginning with the theological or fictitious, moving through the metaphysical or abstract and ending with the scientific or positive.[27] Comte condemned theory without observation as mysticism and observation without theory as empiricism: for him, like the later logical positivists, there was only one thing called science, and only one scientific method.

Professionalization, however, inherently demands differentiation. The struggle of social science to distinguish itself from natural science involved, particularly in Europe, rejecting the experimental method and also what J.S. Mill called 'abstract geometrical procedure'.[28] In many places, social science did abandon experimental studies, although in the USA there was a strong tradition of 'experimental sociology' throughout the first decades of the nineteenth century.[29] In the UK, in the late nineteenth and early twentieth century, empirical social investigation was the mainstay of social science. Although many of the early social surveys had pronounced 'qualitative' dimensions (for example Booth's house-to-house interviewing in his *Life and Labour of the People of London*,[30] and Beatrice Webb's participant observation as a 'trouser hand' in the sweating industries[31]), 'quantitative' methods were accepted as the dominant paradigm by social scientists until the 1960s. Not unlike the rejection of metaphysics by the logical positivists, those, like Webb, who espoused the 'craft of social investigation', experienced a 'flight from service of God to service of man [*sic*]' on the aeroplane of 'the scientific method'.[32] Social surveys involving large numbers of subjects necessitated procedures of quantification. The term 'statistics' comes originally from eighteenth-century Germany, where it meant the science of the description of the state.[33] The development of modern statistics was associated with biological theories of society, and the increasing vogue for numbers and numerical calculations can be seen as a technology of communication and a strategy for imposing social distance in a society dominated by the growth of bureaucracy and masculine professions.[34]

In the Middle Ages and the Renaissance, the idea of nature as both organic and female prevailed; human and physical realms were regarded as continuous with one another.[35] This feminine gendering produced the modern lexicon of the knower as masculine: 'homo sapiens', man the knower, distinct from the unknowing apes. For Descartes, with his famous contentions about existence being proved by consciousness, the aim of science was domination of the feminine natural universe. Reason was the ultimate tool in triumphing over the chaos of personal experience. On a more global level, the food crises, wars, plagues and poverty of the mid-sixteenth to mid-seventeenth centuries suspended peoples' beliefs in an all-provident nature; and the birth of a masculine cultural and scientific world imposed a further break on this fundamental identification. Thus, by the end of the nineteenth century, feminine nature had come decisively to be seen as yielding its secrets to masculine science.[36]

In the social science field, and as Graham has demonstrated,[37] we can decipher precisely the same theme of methods as controlling, masculine probes of an exterior, puzzling world. The survey method within social science owes its origins to the need men felt around the turn of the century for an empirically based social research that would explain social transformation not just at the level of the local community but more broadly, and that would provide a basis for concrete social policies. Basic assumptions of the survey method are individualism, equivalence and rationality, and of people as exchangeable units; these are also the principles of capitalist labour relations. It is thus hardly surprising that they fit less well with the perspectives of socially disadvantaged groups, including women's privatized work in the home.

As Bryman acknowledges in his *Quantity and Quality in Social Research*,[38] it is difficult to say at what point, or exactly why, the debate about method enters social science discourse in its current form. Positivism as a philosophical position fell under attack in the 1950s,[39] when subordinated traditions such as Marxism and continental European ideas such as phenomenology resurfaced.[40] Glaser and Strauss's *The Discovery of Grounded Theory* was an important prompt to researchers to examine the potential mismatch between 'academic' theory and the lives of the researched.[41] Since then, poststructuralism and postmodernism have expanded the repertoire of arguments in favour of 'qualitative' methods, largely by pressing us to abandon altogether any notion of a real world out there waiting to be discovered. But the most sustained war on the quantitative paradigm was undoubtedly waged by feminist social scientists, who, from the early 1970s on, identified pervasive masculine biases across the different disciplinary traditions of social science.[42] In so doing, they highlighted many of the arguments 'qualitative' researchers have subsequently made about the usefulness of these methods in prioritizing the experiences of socially disadvantaged groups.[43]

Agendas of gender

The basis of the feminist argument was that 'positivist, quantitative research methodology' cannot be used uncritically to further the political goals of academic women's studies because within it the voices of women as an oppressed group are unlikely to be heard.[44] The alliance between 'positivism' and the idea of objective knowledge renders suspect the notions of 'truth' and 'objectivity'.[45] Socially shaped hierarchies of power inform questions of research method, and they are also inevitably present in the research process. Power inequalities between researcher and researched are politically unacceptable. 'Quantitative' research is the worst culprit here, because it treats the researched as enumerable units; an approach which has marked parallels with men's desire to dominate women in social life.[46] While there are some notable exceptions to this argument, making the point that 'quantitative' methods are an essential tool for establishing the social marginalization of women (and other groups),[47] in the main, the feminist critique considered 'quantitative' methods 'masculine', and to be abandoned on this ground, with 'qualitative' methods the approach of choice.

Feminist social researchers in the 1970s and 1980s were clearly responding to a methodological tradition in which a mechanistic and strangely
asocial view of the research process had obscured the social relations of
research. As they noted, in practice interviewers do not live up to their
image in the methods textbooks as simply data collectors; they are involved in meaningful social interactions with the researched.[48] The recurrent problem of all research, how to separate the position of the knower
from what is known, cannot simply be solved by ignoring it. The feminist
critique also importantly highlighted the ways in which the theoretical and
conceptual tools of social science had come from the top rather than the
bottom; they had been formed, not from the lived experiences of the
socially marginalized, but in the heads of (mainly male) academics. Since
the experience of everyday life is the origin of everything,[49] the result of
this process was inevitably a reflection of men's social positions in the
'science' of the social. But there is, none the less, an ignorance running
through the feminist critique about the ways in which the social processes
shaping the evolution of both natural and social science have themselves
been gendered, and have thus spawned a gendered discourse about 'qualitative' and 'quantitative' methods.

The contrast between the 'quantitative' and 'qualitative' in research
methods is paralleled by many other dualisms: not only 'masculine' and
'feminine', 'control' and 'understanding', and 'reason' and 'intuition', but
'voice' and 'silence', 'hard' and 'soft', 'objective' and 'subjective', 'autonomy'
and 'dependence', 'public' and 'private', 'intellect' and 'feeling', and
'scientific' and 'artistic'. The fundamental issue here is the habit of dualistic
thinking, which is endemic to Western culture.[50] When annexed to an economic and social system marked by inequalities between social groups, the
result is bound to be a privileging of one set of dualisms over the other.
This, of course, can be put the other way round, for it is equally plausible
to suggest that the dualisms are epiphenomena of the social system. It is
for this reason that rejecting dualistic or dichotomous thinking has also
been seen as a critical item in most feminist approaches to knowledge.[51]

But the hegemony of 'qualitative' methods as the dominant epistemological assumption among feminist and other researchers whose interest
lies in 'hearing the silent' has a number of important implications. For the
most part, those working in this tradition do not discuss their knowledge
claims in terms of validity and reliability. But the other persistent problem
about knowledge is its *trustworthiness*. Put at its most simple, why should
the results of 'qualitative' research be believed more than those of 'quantitative' research? What kinds of standards (if any) are there for assessing
trustworthiness? How might the role of the researcher in shaping research
based knowledge relate to any such criteria?

In the rest of this chapter I raise some aspects of these questions, using
as a case study the report of one particular 'qualitative' research project:

Women's Ways of Knowing by Mary Belenky and colleagues.[52] This has become a classic of feminist, qualitative literature; it is one of a group of texts that are taken as promoting the existence of an authentic female perspective on ways of seeing and feeling about the world.

Women's ways of knowing and other problems

Belenky and colleagues used an intensive interview/case study approach in a five-year project to talk to a sample of American women about their experiences and problems as learners and knowers. As a result of these interviews, they describe five epistemological perspectives from which women view and know the world: silence; received knowledge; subjective knowledge; procedural knowledge and constructed knowledge.

There were 135 women in the research sample. Ninety were enrolled in six different kinds of academic institutions; these were selected after discussion with staff as being 'representative' in terms of age, interests, commitment, and academic performance; 25 of the 90 had previously been interviewed by a member of the research team for another project. The remaining 45 women came from three different family agencies, although the basis of selection here is not stated: an organization working with teenage mothers; a network of self-help groups for parents with a history of child abuse and family violence; and a children's health programme. A sub-sample of 15 of these 45 women was interviewed for a second time a year after the first interview. Although individual women appear in case studies and narratives throughout the text, we are given no sociodemographic information about the sample as a whole.

The interviews varied from two to five hours long and resulted in 5000 pages of transcribed text. The interview transcripts were scored by coders working 'blind' in the best tradition of positivist science; that is, unaware of the status of the people who had provided the interview material. However, no systematic account is offered of the means by which the five ways of knowing were extracted from the data. There is no information about the distribution of types of knowing across the categories, although there were only two or three women (about 2 per cent of the sample) in the 'silent' and 'constructed knowledge' categories, whereas 'almost half' were deemed to be 'subjective' knowers.[53]

It is significant in a number of ways that Belenky and colleagues chose to listen only to women. Their rationale was that, 'The male experience has been so powerfully articulated that we believed we would hear the patterns in women's voices more clearly if we held at bay the powerful templates men have etched in the literature and in our minds'.[54] However, they did use as comparative material a study completed a number of years earlier by William Perry and his colleagues, which followed the development of thinking in a sample of mainly male students at Harvard.[55] Thus, the comparisons are between a male all-student sample and a female sample of students and non-students; and between a male single institution sample and female multi-institution sample. In practice, however, the scheme of the ways women know appears to have been constructed largely without reference to the way the earlier study suggested that men know.

The question 'how can we be sure that the approaches to knowing described by Belenky and colleagues are ways *women* know, rather than the ways *people* know?' is difficult to answer. This question brings to mind the feminist critique of another important study, this time conducted in England, Brown and Harris's *Social Origins of Depression*.[56] This study constructed a convincing explanation of the relationship between what is called 'depression', on the one hand, and life events and socio-economic circumstances, on the other. But the study was based on interviews with women only, for the politically incorrect reason that women are easier to interview because they are more often to be found at home during the day. No reference is made in the title, and very little in the knowledge claims made by the book, to the fact that here we have an account of a human process that is derived from a social group (women) known to have a particular set of experiences. This is the obverse of the case raised by *Women's Ways of Knowing*. In one, women are used to provide a general narrative about something it is said only women do; in the other, women are interviewed to construct a generalized account of something that happens to both men and women. In both cases the epistemological error is to conceptualize gender as 'a property of individuals' rather than as 'a set of interactive processes that form a system of subordination'.[57] 'Quantitative' research often suggests that when direct comparisons are made between samples of men and women and when occupational and educational background is controlled for, many gender differences disappear; this is so for differences in ethical orientation and moral reasoning.[58] Ways of knowing are affected by social position, and gender is only one aspect of social position. But if we are to run with the anti-quantitative purists, we would reject the lessons of the 'quantitative' research and return to the more politically appealing conclusions of the 'qualitative' study: that women really do 'know' in different ways from men.

Some problems of 'trustworthiness'

The methodologist Campbell uses the well known example of the Muller–Lyer diagram to illustrate the different conclusions that can be reached as a result of using different methods (Figure 11.1). Any 'normal resident of a "carpentered" culture'[59] will deem the horizontal line in (a) to be longer than that in (b). But a ruler will usually reverse this perception: (b) 'is' longer than (a). The situation in which personal perception gives one answer and measurement another is not infrequent in research including

(a)   (b)

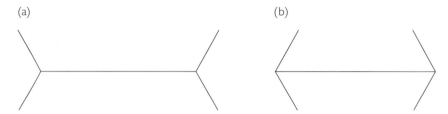

Figure 11.1   *The Muller–Lyer diagram*[60]

both 'quantitative' and 'qualitative' data. For example, ethnographic data collected as part of the evaluation of an experimental housing programme implemented in the USA in 1972 suggested that the programme was not working well, while quantitative outcome data produced the opposite conclusion.[61] It is quite commonly the case that participants in experimental studies may have different agendas and interpretations of effectiveness from researchers, for example in relation to such topics as social support in pregnancy[62] or treatments for asthma.[63] Clashes between different types of data may also occur when researchers try their hand at 'triangulation', as in a study of the health status of older women which employed different types of data (national statistics on mortality and morbidity, two large sample surveys and biographical interviews with 30 older women) and yielded 'a mass of paradox and downright contradictory evidence'.[64]

A classic example within the domain of 'qualitative' research of conflicting interpretations is anthropologist Margaret Mead's original and Derek Freeman's later conflicting accounts of growing up in Samoa.[65] Another example, discussed by LeCompte and Goetz in a paper on 'Problems of reliability and validity in ethnographic research' is two contrasting interpretations of life in a Mexican village.[66] Different perspectives, interests and informants produced highly discrepant descriptions of exactly the same culture.

Several problems are compounded here. One is that, precisely because of features of the qualitative paradigm, researchers who use these methods are in a position of more power over the researched and the research 'product' than is often acknowledged. Although the attractions of the qualitative paradigm include a more reflexive and potentially less exploitative attitude to the hierarchy of power between researcher and researched, experience has shown that the early optimism of feminist and other researchers about the democratizing potential of 'qualitative' methods may be less justified than was at first hoped. For example, after some years of experience trying to do 'feminist' ethnography, Stacey came to the conclusion that the appearance of respect and equality conveyed by ethnographic methods masked 'a deeper, more dangerous form of exploitation . . . than . . . much positivist research'. Precisely because of the importance of the relationship between the ethnographer and her/his subjects, there is the risk of manipulation and betrayal. Moreover, the researched have no control over the product of the research: an ethnography offers 'a researcher's interpretations, registered in a researcher's voice'.[67] In 'qualitative' research more generally, class and ethnicity interpose their own dimensions of inequality, complicating the notion of an equal social relationship between researcher and researched.[68] Partly because of this, there is a need for explicitness on the part of researchers about what is done to whom and how.[69] The vagueness in relation to the methods used, which is a feature of Belenky and colleagues' attempt to understand how women know, is by no means unique. In a discussion of survey methods, Catherine Marsh discusses a study of a chemical plant in the West of England which is characterized by 'a complete refusal to discuss methodology'. The influence of the researcher on the data is a significant black box; as Marsh says, 'Who knows what subtle pressures are at work when the researcher, obviously a committed "leftie", is buying the drinks?'[70]

Then there is the question of generalizability. Although 'qualitative' researchers using small (often homogenous) samples may stress they are after insights and hypotheses rather than full-scale hypothesis testing, many speak as though they have generated findings applicable to populations outside the range of the research. 'Systematic reviews' are increasingly fashionable in the 'quantitative', experimental research world as ways of collecting and synthesizing all the available evidence relating to a particular topic. The motive driving this effort is evidence that 'non-systematic' reviews produce conflicting and therefore unreliable findings. The 'narrative' reviews prevailing in the 'qualitative' research domain need equal scrutiny, because selecting studies for discussion in inexplicit and unsystematic ways increases the chances of researchers' own personal belief systems influencing the conclusions reached.[71] These considerations of trustworthiness apply to all forms of research. But, notwithstanding its ideological and other problems, 'quantitative' research is at least a strategy which in theory stresses explicitness in techniques of measurement, data and interpretative processes. As Sprague and Zimmerman observe in their discussion of 'quality and quantity' in relation to feminist methodology, such procedures effectively provide 'visible research standards, enabling critical discourse within a community of scholars'.[72]

Conclusion

Like everything else, the tools available to researchers have been subject to a long process of social construction. A key part of this social construction has been a 'gendering' of method and methodology whereby 'qualitative' approaches have been aligned with less powerful social groups. Understanding this process of social construction is important, because the goals of an emancipatory social science are not necessarily best served by espousing 'qualitative' and rejecting 'quantitative' methods.

The criticisms of 'qualitative' methods voiced in this chapter are not meant to suggest that these methods should be abandoned; nor is my argument meant to let 'quantitative' methods off the hook for tending to ignore those essential perspectives brought to the fore in much 'qualitative' research. It is important to disentangle criticisms of 'bad' practice from criticisms of methods *per se*, and to separate both of these from a generalized opposition to the culture of different paradigms: not to do so is to engage in a 'misleading and confusing form of debate'. While the logical positivists were proved wrong about the verifiability principle and about the possibilities of 'neutral' observation, the discourses of science (social and natural), and, most importantly, of everyday life, are informed by the assumption that an external world *does* exist, which human knowers can attempt to know.[73] It is time to move beyond the confines of the dialectical language about the advantages and disadvantages of 'qualitative' and 'quantitative' methods. We need to examine all methods from the viewpoint of the same questions about trustworthiness, to consider how best to match methods to research questions, and to find ways of integrating a range of methods in carrying out socially useful inquiries.

Notes

1 A. Saint-Exupery (1974) *The Little Prince*. London: Pan Books, pp. 17–18.
2 I put quotation marks round the terms 'quantitative' and 'qualitative' because of the argument, developed in the chapter, about the way in which these serve as ideological referents rather than procedural descriptions.
3 For a discussion see A. Bryman (1988) *Quantity and Quality in Social Research*. London: Unwin Hyman.
4 Ibid., p. 93 *et seq.*
5 E.G. Guba (ed.) (1990) *The Paradigm Dialog*. Newbury Park, CA: Sage.
6 C.S. Reichardt and T.D. Cook (1979) Beyond qualitative versus quantitative methods, in T.D. Cook and C.S. Reichardt (eds) *Qualitative and Quantitative Methods in Evaluation Research*. Beverly Hills, CA: Sage.
7 T.S. Kuhn (1962) *The Structure of Scientific Revolutions*. Chicago, IL: University of Chicago Press.
8 G. Gillett (1994) Beyond the orthodox: heresy in medicine and social science, *Social Science and Medicine*, 39 (9): 1125–31, p. 1125. See the discussion in Reichardt and Cook, op. cit.
9 Reichardt and Cook op. cit., Table 1, p. 10.
10 See A. Giddens (1978) Positivism and its critics, in T. Bottomore and R.A. Nisbet (eds) *A History of Sociological Analysis*. London: Heinemann; D.C. Phillips (1992) *The Social Scientist's Bestiary*. Oxford: Pergamon Press.
11 M. Hammersley (1995) *The Politics of Social Research*. London: Sage, p. 2.
12 Phillips, op. cit., p. 95.

13 M. Boulton, R. Fitzpatrick and C. Swinburn (1996) Qualitative research in health care: II. A structured review and evaluation of studies, *Journal of the Evaluation of Clinical Practice*, 2 (3): 171–9.

14 See C. Pope and N. Mays (1995) Reaching the parts other methods cannot reach: an introduction to qualitative methods in health and health services research, *British Medical Journal*, 311: 42–5; see also J.A. Chard, R.J. Lilford and B.V. Court (1997) Qualitative medical sociology: what are its crowning achievements? *Journal of the Royal Society of Medicine*, 90: 604–9.

15 See A. Oakley (1998a) Experimentation in social science: the case of health promotion, *Social Sciences in Health*, 4 (2): 73–89; A. Oakley (1998b) Science, gender and women's liberation, *Women's Studies International Forum*, 21 (2): 133–46.

16 P.T. Manicas (1987) *A History and Philosophy of the Social Sciences*. Oxford: Basil Blackwell.

17 Kuhn, op. cit.; S.J. Gould (1981) *The Mismeasure of Man*. Harmondsworth: Penguin.

18 S. Woolgar (1996) Psychology, qualitative methods and the ideas of science, in J.T.E. Richardson (ed.) *Handbook of Qualitative Research Methods for Psychology and the Social Sciences*. London: British Psychological Society.

19 E.F. Keller (1983) *A Feeling for the Organism: The Life and Works of Barbara McClintock*. New York: W.H. Freeman.

20 D.T. Campbell (1979) Assessing the impact of planned social change, *Evaluation and Program Planning*, 2: 67–90, p. 70.

21 See A. Oakley (forthcoming) Gender, methodology and people's ways of knowing. *Sociology*.

22 O. Neurath (1973) *Empiricism and Sociology*. Dordrecht, Holland: D. Reidel Publishing Company; L. Kolakowski (1972) *Positivist Philosophy: from Hume to the Vienna Circle*. Harmondsworth: Penguin.

23 C.G.A. Bryant (1985) *Positivism in Social Theory and Research*. London: Macmillan, p. 112.

24 M. Scriven (1969). In P. Achinstein and F. Barker (eds) *The Legacy of Logical Positivism*. Baltimore, MD: Johns Hopkins Press, p. 195.

25 L. McDonald (1993) *The Early Origins of the Social Sciences*. Montreal, Canada: McGill-Queen's University Press.

26 See, for example, R.H. Brown (1977) *A Poetic for Sociology*. Cambridge: Cambridge University Press; R. Nisbet (1976) *Sociology as an Art Form*. London: Heinemann.

27 A. Comte (1875) *The Positive Philosophy of August Comte*. London: Trubner and Co.

28 See W. Lepenies (1988) *Between Literature and Science: The Rise of Sociology*. Cambridge: Cambridge University Press, p. 105.

29 See, for example, W.A. McCall (1923) *How to Experiment in Education*. New York: Macmillan; E. Greenwood (1945) *Experimental Sociology*. New York: Octagon Books (1976); F.S. Chapin (1947) *Experimental Designs in Sociological Research*. New York: Harper and Row.

30 C. Booth (1889–1903) *Life and Labour of the People of London*. 17 vols. London: Routledge.

31 McDonald, op. cit., p. 277.

32 B. Webb, quoted in M.J. Lacey and M.O. Furner (1993) Social investiga-
tion, social knowledge, and the state: an introduction, in M.J. Lacey and
M.O. Furner (eds) *The State and Social Investigation in Britain and the United
States*. Cambridge: Cambridge University Press, pp. 12–13.

33 A. Desrosieres (1991) How to make things which hold together: social science,
statistics and the state, in P. Wagner, B. Wittrock and R. Whitley (eds) *Discourses on Society: The Shaping of the Social Science Disciplines*. London:
Kluwer Academic Publishers.

34 T.A. Porter (1995) *Trust in Numbers: The Pursuit of Objectivity in Science and
Public Life*. Princeton, NJ: Princeton University Press.

35 C. Merchant (1980) *The Death of Nature: Women, Ecology and the Scientific
Revolution*. San Francisco, CA: Harper and Row.

36 See L. Jordanova (1989) *Sexual Visions*. Hemel Hempstead: Harvester Wheatsheaf.

37 H. Graham (1983) Do her answers fit his questions? Women and the survey
method, in E. Gamarnikow, S. Morgan, J. Purvis *et al.* (eds) *The Public and the
Private*. London: Heinemann.

38 Bryman, op. cit., p. 3.

39 B.C. van Fraassen (1980) *The Scientific Image*. Oxford: Clarendon Press.

40 H. Rose and S. Rose (1976) The incorporation of science, in H. Rose and
S. Rose (eds) *The Political Economy of Science*. London: Macmillan.

41 B.G. Glaser and A.L. Strauss (1967) *The Discovery of Grounded Theory*. Chicago IL: Aldine.

42 See A. Oakley (1974) *The Sociology of Housework*. London: Martin Robertson,
Chapter 1; M. Millman and R.M. Kanter (eds) (1975) *Another Voice: Feminist
Perspectives on Social Life and Social Science*. Garden City, NY: Doubleday.

43 The feminist critique of 'quantitative' methods was prefigured and has been
followed by others making very similar points. See Bryman op. cit. and
Hammersley op. cit. for a discussion. The feminist critique provides the most
systematic focus on issues of power. I have some difficulty in speaking about
'the feminist critique' in this way, as I myself was part of it.

44 M. Mies (1983) Towards a methodology for feminist research, in G. Bowles and
R. Duelli Klein (eds) *Theories of Women's Studies*. London: Routledge, p. 120.

45 L. Stanley and S. Wise (1983) *Breaking Out: Feminist Consciousness and Feminist Research*. London: Routledge.

46 T. McCormack (1981) Good theory or just theory? Toward a feminist philosophy of social science, *Women's Studies International Quarterly*, 4 (1): 1–12.

47 See, for example, T.E. Jayaratne (1983) The value of quantitative methodology
for feminist research, in G. Bowles and R. Duelli Klein (eds) *Theories of Women's
Studies*. London: Routledge; T.E. Jayaratne and A.J. Stewart (1991) Quantitat-
ive and qualitative methods in the social sciences: Current feminist issues and
practical strategies, in M.M. Fonow and J.A. Cook (eds) *Beyond Methodology:
Feminist Scholarship as Lived Research*. Bloomington, IN: Indiana University
Press; C. Marsh (1984) Problems with surveys: methods or epistemology? in
M. Bulmer (ed.) *Sociological Research Methods: An Introduction*. London:
Macmillan; L. Kelly, L. Regan and S. Burton (1992) Defending the indefensible?
Quantitative methods and feminist research, in H. Hinds, A. Phoenix and
J. Stacey (eds) *Working Out: New Directions for Women's Studies*. London:
Falmer Press.

48 A. Oakley (1981) Interviewing women: a contradiction in terms? in H. Roberts (ed.) *Doing Feminist Research.* London: Routledge and Kegan Paul.

49 D.E. Smith (1988) *The Everyday World as Problematic.* Milton Keynes: Open University Press.

50 D. Bakan (1966) *The Duality of Human Existence.* Chicago, IL: Rand McNally; J. Curthoys (1997) *Feminist Amnesia: The Wake of Women's Liberation.* London: Routledge.

51 See, for example, B. Dubois (1983) Passionate scholarship: notes on values, knowing and method in feminist social science, in G. Bowles and R. Duelli Klein (eds) *Theories of Women's Studies.* London: Routledge.

52 M.F. Belenky, B.M. Clinchy, N.R. Goldberger *et al.* (1986) *Women's Ways of Knowing.* New York: Basic Books. Many other examples could have been chosen. See M. Crawford (1989) Agreeing to differ: feminist epistemologies and women's ways of knowing, in M. Crawford and M. Gentry (eds) *Gender and Thought.* New York: Springer Verlag, for a more sustained discussion of the Belenky *et al.* volume as a case study.

53 Belenky *et al.* op. cit., p. 55.

54 Ibid., p. 9.

55 W.G. Perry (1970) *Forms of Intellectual and Ethical Development in the College Years.* New York: Holt, Rinehart and Winston; W.G. Perry (1981) Cognitive and ethical growth: the making of meaning, in A. Chickering (ed.) *The Modern American College.* San Francisco, CA: Jossey-Bass.

56 G.W. Brown and T. Harris (1978) *Social Origins of Depression.* London: Tavistock.

57 Crawford op. cit., p. 142.

58 L. Walker (1984) Sex differences in the development of moral reasoning: a critical review, *Child Development,* 55: 667–91.

59 D.T. Campbell (1988) Qualitative knowing in action research, in E.S. Overman (ed.) *Methodology and Epistemology for Social Science.* Chicago: University of Chicago Press, p. 362.

60 Campbell op. cit., p. 362.

61 W.J. Filstead (1979) Qualitative methods: a needed perspective in evaluation research, in T.D. Cook and C.S. Reichardt (eds) *Qualitative and Quantitative Methods in Evaluation Research.* Beverly Hills, CA: Sage.

62 A. Oakley (1992) *Social Support and Motherhood.* Oxford: Blackwell.

63 A.J. Vickers and C. Smith (1997) Analysis of the evidence profile of the effectiveness of complementary therapies in asthma: a qualitative survey and systematic review, *Complementary Therapies in Medicine,* 5: 202–9.

64 M. Sidell (1993) Interpreting, in P. Shakespeare, D. Atkinson and S. French (eds) *Reflecting on Research Practice.* Buckingham: Open University Press, pp. 111–12.

65 M. Mead (1943) *Coming of Age in Samoa.* Harmondsworth: Penguin; D. Freeman (1983) *Margaret Mead and Samoa: The Making and Unmaking of an Anthropological Myth.* Cambridge, MA: Harvard University Press.

66 M.D. LeCompte and J.P. Goetz (1982) Problems of reliability and validity in ethnographic research, *Review of Educational Research,* 52 (1): 31–60; O. Lewis (1951) *Life in a Mexican Village: Tepoztlan Restudied.* Urbana, IL: University of Illinois Press; R. Redfield (1930) *Tepoztlan – a Mexican Village.* Chicago, IL: University of Chicago Press.

67 J. Stacey (1988) Can there be a feminist ethnography? *Women's Studies International Forum*, 11 (1): 21–7, pp. 21–3.
68 See, for example, J. Ribbens (1989) Interviewing – an 'unnatural' situation? *Women's Studies International Forum*, 12 (6): 579–92; J. Finch (1984) 'It's great to have someone to talk to': the ethics and politics of interviewing women, in C. Bell and H. Roberts (eds) *Doing Sociological Research*. London: Routledge; R. Edwards (1990) Connecting method and epistemology: A white woman interviewing black women, *Women's Studies International Forum*, 13 (5): 477–90.
69 J. Lofland (1974) Styles of reporting qualitative field research, *The American Sociologist*, 9: 101–11.
70 Marsh op. cit., p. 103.
71 R.J. Light and D.B. Pillemer (1983) Numbers and narrative: combining their strength in research reviews, in R.J. Light (ed.) *Evaluation Studies Review Annual* vol. 8. Beverly Hills, CA: Sage; G.V. Glass, B. McGaw and M.L. Smith (1981) *Meta-Analysis in Social Research*. Beverly Hills, CA: Sage.
72 J. Sprague and M.K. Zimmerman (1989) Quality and quantity: reconstructing feminist methodology, *The American Sociologist*, Spring: 71–86, p. 73.
73 See Woolgar op. cit.; Oakley (1998b) op. cit.

▷ Index

Page numbers in italics refer to tables.

REFLECTING ON RESEARCH PRACTICE
ISSUES IN HEALTH AND SOCIAL WELFARE

Pam Shakespeare, Dorothy Atkinson and Sally French

This book charts some of the hidden-from-view aspects of social research and explores many of the complex processes involved. Through a specially-written series of reflective accounts based on the personal experiences of ten researchers, it tells the 'real' story of what happens in research.

The writers are from a variety of social science and humanities disciplines. Individually and collectively, they reflect on the place of the 'self' in the various stages of the research process. Thus, the chapters range from developing ideas and negotiating with funders, to building research relationships and disseminating findings. All the book's authors are women with a particular interest in the exploration of the lives and experiences of marginalized and oppressed groups in society.

By addressing a wide readership, this book makes a major contribution not only to ongoing debates in social research but also to developing 'good research practices' in the health and social welfare field. It actively engages its readers in both processes.

Contents
Introduction – Thinking – Negotiating – Explaining – Observing – Relating – Sharing – Presenting – Performing – Interpreting – Telling – References – Index.

Contributors
Dorothy Atkinson, Joanna Bornat, Ann Brechin, Sally French, Sheila Peace, Alyson Peberdy, Pam Shakespeare, Moyra Sidell, Jan Walmsley, Fiona Williams.

160pp   0 335 19038 3 (Paperback)   0 335 19039 1 (Hardback)

SOCIAL RESEARCH (SECOND EDITION)
ISSUES, METHODS AND PROCESS

Tim May

Reviews of the first edition:
. . . a wide ranging text . . . provides a thorough coverage of official statistics, questionnaires, interviewing, documentary research and comparative research.

Journal of Social Policy

. . . stimulating and scholarly.

Social Science Teacher

This revised and expanded edition of a bestselling text incorporates the latest developments in social research. Additions to each chapter do further justice to ideas on the research process in general and aspects of its practice in particular. Chapter summaries, questions for reflection and signposts to further reading are incorporated into a new textbook format. The aim of the book, however, remains the same: to bridge the gap between theory and methods in social research, each of which is essential to understanding the dynamics of social relations. The style remains clear and accessible and the basic structure, similar.

Part 1 examines the issues in social research and Part 2 the methods available. The topics covered in Part 1 include an overview of perspectives and their relationship to research – such as realism, positivism, empiricism, feminisms, poststructuralism, postmodernism and idealism – and an examination of both the way theory relates to data and the place of values and ethics in social research. These issues are then linked into a discussion in Part 2 on the actual methods and process of social research with chapters on official statistics, survey research, interview techniques, participant observation, documentary research and comparative research. These chapters follow a common structure to enable a clear understanding of the place, process and analysis of each research method. This allows the reader to compare their strengths and weaknesses in the context of discussions in Part 1.

This book will have wide appeal as an introduction for undergraduates studying the methods and techniques of social science, as well as for postgraduate courses in research methods. In addition, it will enable those practising and teaching social research to stay abreast of key developments in the field.

Contents
Introduction – Part 1: Issues in social research – Perspectives on social research – Social theory and social research – Values and ethics in the research process – Part 2: Methods of social research – Official statistics: topic and resource – Social surveys: design to analysis – Interviewing: methods and process – Participant observation: perspectives and practice – Documentary research: excavations and evidence – Comparative research: potential and problems – Bibliography – Author index – Subject index.

240pp   0 335 20005 2 (Paperback)   0 335 20006 0 (Hardback)

RESEARCH METHODS IN HEALTH
INVESTIGATING HEALTH AND HEALTH SERVICES

Ann Bowling

- What research methods are used in the investigation of health and health services?
- What are the principles of the research method that should be followed?
- How do I design a research project to describe the topic of interest and to answer cause and effect questions?

This is the first comprehensive guide to research methods in health. It describes the range of methods that can be used to study and evaluate health and health care. Ann Bowling's impressive range and grasp of research methodology are manifest in the simplicity of her style and in the organization of the book. The text is aimed at students and researchers of health and health services, including those in: demography, economics, epidemiology, health management, health policy, health psychology, health sciences, history, medical sociology, medicine, nursing, pharmaceutics and other health care disciplines. It has also been designed for health professionals and policy makers who have responsibility for applying research findings in practice, and who need to know how to judge the value of that research.

Contents

Preface – Section 1: Investigating health services and health: the scope of research – Evaluating health services: multidisciplinary collaboration – Social research on health: sociological and psychological concepts and approaches – Health needs and their assessment: demography and epidemiology – Costing health services: health economics – Section 2: The philosophy, theory and practice of research – The philosophical framework of measurement – The principles of research – Section 3: Quantitative research: sampling and research methods – Sample size for quantitative research – Quantitative research: surveys – Quantitative research: experiments and other analytic methods of investigation – Sample selection and group assignment methods in experiments and other analytic methods – Section 4: The tools of quantitative research – Data collection methods in quantitative research: questionnaires, interviews and their response rates – Questionnaire design – Techniques of survey interviewing – Preparation of quantitative data for coding and analysis – Section 5: Qualitative and combined research methods, and their analysis – Unstructured and structured observational studies – Unstructured interviewing and focus groups – Other methods using both qualitative and quantitative approaches: case studies, consensus methods, action research and document research – Glossary – References – Index.

448pp   0 335 19885 6 (Paperback)   0 335 19886 4 (Hardback)